# CREATIVITY AND CONSTRAINT IN THE BRITISH FILM INDUSTRY

# Creativity and Constraint in the British Film Industry

Duncan J. Petrie

MACMILLAN

First published in 1991

ISBN 0–333–54546–X

Published by
MACMILLAN PRESS LTD
Houndmills, Basingstoke, Hampshire RG21 2XS
and London
Companies and representatives
throughout the world.

Printed in Hong Kong

For Nicole
with love

# Contents

# List of Illustrations

# Preface

This book is an edited version of a PhD thesis begun in October 1986 and completed in November 1989. Although intended to be a contemporary study of the British film industry, the bulk of the information in the text largely relates to the period 1987–88. The interviews which form a central source of information were also conducted during this period. Since then, certain developments have occurred which require acknowledgement. For instance, several individuals quoted in the text no longer hold the positions they did when I interviewed them. Hence the proliferation of descriptions such as 'former head of production', 'former director of marketing' and so on. In addition, my own evaluation of the object of study, the British cinema, has also been subject to change. These are inevitable problems associated with a contemporary study which is constantly being overtaken by events.

In 1986 the hype which had surrounded the British cinema in the early eighties had dissipated. The notion of 'renaissance' had been undermined, the flagship of the 'New British Cinema', Goldcrest, had been forced to curtail its interests in film production, Thorn EMI had also withdrawn from financing features and the National Film Finance Corporation had been disbanded by the government. But lessons had been learned and there was a hint of optimism in the air. Channel 4 continued to support low-budget film production on a formidable scale. Dynamic new companies who appeared to be able to combine enthusiasm for cinema with astute business acumen had emerged, including Zenith, Palace and Working Title. British Screen, the semi-privatised replacement for the NFFC, proved to be a more versatile and significant source of finance than its predecessor. In addition, low-budget films such as *My Beautiful Laundrette* and *A Room with a View* proved to be popular in the North American market, enabling British producers to secure crucial US distribution deals for their productions.

This was the prevailing state of affairs during the 1987–88 period when the bulk of the text was written. However, there have been subsequent developments which have made things rather less optimistic. I have attempted to signpost these developments throughout the text whenever possible and in the conclusion I have attempted to bring things more up to date.

Duncan J. Petrie
*University of Edinburgh*

# Acknowledgements

Many thanks to everyone who provided the help and encouragement to make this study possible, including all those who agreed to be interviewed, Gay Cox at Edinburgh Filmhouse, Marc Samuelson, Lisa Wills, and John Holmwood. (A comprehensive list of interviewees, dates and locations of interview is included in Appendix II.)

A special thanks to John Orr, my supervisor and co-editor of *Edinburgh Studies in Culture and Society*, and James Mackay.

# Introduction
# Creativity: The Theoretical Context

The purpose of this introduction is to define the idea of 'filmic creativity' in relation to its use in this study: as essentially an artistic/cultural process which is structured by material constraints. In this case these constraints are the institutional and aesthetic structures of the British cinema. The construction of such a definition necessarily entails an in-depth examination of the concept 'creativity' – how it has been conceptualised and used by various theorists – arriving at an understanding appropriate to the film-making process. Subsequently, we can proceed to examine the ways in which the concept 'creativity' has been used in film theory and criticism. Taken together, these separate but related discourses will form the theoretical basis for the substantive work in this study.

The idea of creativity is bound up with notions of change, development and process. It is therefore a central, though often unacknowledged, component of sociological explanations of culture. Social change occurs through the actions of individuals regardless of whether or not the critic holds 'creative activity' to be structurally compelled or the product of human volition. All critics and theorists – be they proponents of structure or voluntarism – acknowledge creativity in some form. Voluntarist critics understand creativity in terms of a force characterised by freedom and indeterminacy. This conception is informed by the popular notion that human beings have the ability to act spontaneously, to freely form ends and choose between means.

However, such a position does not necessarily tackle the question more adequately than structural or deterministic theories. There are problems with both types of approach but, following the example of Raymond Williams, this study will stress the importance of external factors, such as social and technological conditions and material resources, which constitute the necessary context within which creativity occurs, rather than endorse the idea of creativity as an innate human capacity. But first of all, we must examine variants of the

1

voluntarist perspective and identify its major flaws. This perspective can be generally referred to as the Romantic ideal, which came to fruition in the nineteenth century but whose roots stretch back to classical philosophy.


## THE ROMANTIC IDEAL

In *The Long Revolution*, Raymond Williams begins his elaboration of cultural theory with an interesting discussion of the development of ideas of creativity or the 'creative mind'.[1] At the outset he identifies the Renaissance as the period when explicit ideas of human creativity first emerged. However, he suggests that there are important links between Renaissance thought and the earlier tradition of Plato and Aristotle. Williams concentrates his discussion on the idea of artistic endeavour, the most popular locus of discussions of creativity, although the idea can and does extend to all forms of human activity. It is important therefore to make an explicit distinction between creativity on a general level as the dynamic of social change, and more specifically as the creation of particular art-objects. Aristotle saw art in primarily mimetic terms: art being the imitation (mimesis) of external reality rather than the transformation of reality through the creation of new art-objects.[2] This has formed the basis of a variety of different understandings of artistic activity, including the vulgar Marxist notion of cultural production as a reflection of developmental aspects of the capitalist mode of production, and also of commonsense notions, which evaluate art-works in terms of their correspondence to physical reality, and consequently have difficulties in analysing abstract or more conceptual art. The issue of realism and its relation to ideas of creativity is also very important with respect to film and I shall also explore this question in Chapter 1.

But within the melting-pot of Renaissance thought Williams identifies the germination of a new conception of artistic endeavour which shifts the stress away from the relation between art and reality and towards the idea of art as creative. This idea, which blossomed in nineteenth-century Romantic thought, represented an assertion of the human right to break out of the order of nature and to exercise creative will. It constituted human beings as autonomous self-determining entities. M. H. Abrams has identified two diverse currents within the early nineteenth-century Romantic aesthetic which he describes in terms of metaphors of 'the mirror' and 'the lamp'. The former conceptualises the mind in terms of 'a reflector of external objects' and is clearly consistent with the ideas of Plato and Aristotle. The latter, on the other hand, sees the mind in terms of 'a radiant projector which makes a contribution to the objects it perceives', typifying the prevailing Romantic conceptions of the mind and the autonomous subject which constituted the first shift in thought towards the idea of individual genius and the creative imagination.[3] Colin Campbell argues that nineteenth-century Romanticism shared the Enlightenment's emphasis on the individual but while the latter proposed a political philosophy of the right of individual self-determination within the community as a whole, the Romantics interpreted this as the right to self-expression and self-discovery, which are essentially creative processes:

> In comparison with earlier theodicies, what distinguished Romanticism was the fact that primary emphasis was placed upon the characteristic of creativity . . . whilst the divine itself was no longer represented as a named God, but as a supernatural force, which, whilst present throughout the natural world, also existed within each individual in the form of a unique and personalised spirit: that of his genius.[4]

As Williams remarks, art came to be seen as the creation of humankind in the same way that nature was the creation of God.

Concurrent with the divine conception of creativity within Romantic thought is the idea of the 'Romantic agony':[5] the notion of the isolated artist struggling with his or her demons in the act of creation. Frank Kermode identifies the widespread notion among the Romantics that in the joyful revelation of 'the truth of the image' (the act of creation), the artist must pay the price, which is suffering and isolation.[6] In some respects Romanticism can be seen in terms of a quest for organic wholeness with regard to the individual. The inability to achieve this state of grace gives rise to the demonic double or 'other' which is prevalent in much romantic fiction including Hoffman, Hogg, Stevenson and Wilde.[7] Campbell points out that many Romantics alienated themselves from a society they regarded as utilitarian and philistine. This isolation served to fuel ideas of split personality and opposing selves, an allusion to popular notions of artistic creativity as intrinsically linked to pain, suffering and madness. Williams, among other commentators,[8] sees the idea of pain as intrinsic to the creative process. He talks about 'the excitement and pain of the effort' being 'followed by the delight and rest of completion'[9] in his description of the dynamics of the creative act.

The central flaw of the Romantic ideal is that in enshrining creative ability as a naturally-given attribute, an exercise of will on the part of autonomous 'free' subjects, it disguises its own specific and historical nature by making its central concept transcendent. This postulates creativity as an aspect of mind or 'spirit' and consequently aligns the Romantic ideal with the idealist philosophy of Kant and Hegel.[10] The unmasking of the Romantic ideal as a historically-generated discourse rather than a transcendent truth was begun by Marxist critics who attacked it as a bourgeois construction. The German Critical Theorists, in particular Theodor Adorno, have claimed the idea of 'the creative genius' diverts attention from society and its repressive mechanisms. The idea of the 'creative subject' is seen by Adorno as in harmony with 'vulgar bourgeois consciousness' for two reasons:

> One, it glorifies pure creation by human beings without regard to purpose and thus feeds into the Bourgeois work ethic; and two, it relieves the viewer of the task of understanding the artistic object before him, giving him instead a surrogate – the personality of the artist, or worse, trashy biographies of him.[11]

In other words, art objects are perceived in terms of the mind of their 'creator' rather than material objects in their own right. Not only are the social relations of production (and therefore questions of domination and social inequality) masked but the ability to criticise and reveal the nature of social reality – which Adorno believed Modernist art could show if properly apprehended – is also denied by way of the dominance of the Romantic ideal.

Adorno and Williams have pointed out that Romantic conceptions influenced psychoanalytic positions on the question of creativity. Indeed Trilling argued that psychoanalysis is one of the culminations of the nineteenth-century Romantic movement in literature.[12] He identified a shift away from the Hobbesian conception of the utilitarian ego towards the idea of the anarchic and self-indulgent id, the 'divided self' which obsessed many in the Romantic movement and which provided the intellectual context for Freud's theory of the pre-conscious mind. Freud introduced the idea of fantasy as an intrinsic component of creative thinking – a replacement of Platonic divinity with the unconscious. The same psychoanalysts tend to regard works of art as essentially projections of the unconscious mind or 'day dreams'. (The most self-conscious example being the works by the surrealists who produced their various paintings and writings in accordance with Freudian principles.) Fantasy, in the Freudian model, is seen as part of the sublimation of repressed instincts – the product of a neurotic or psychotic mind. But Trilling argues that in regarding the artist as a neurotic Freud was merely adopting a popular belief of his age – an expression of industrial rationalisation and bourgeois philistinism.[13]

In relating the creative powers of the artist to neurosis, Freud is effectively providing what amounts to a medicalised re-reading of the Romantic agony. Moreover, Adorno notes what he sees as an essential similarity between the writings of Freud and the idealist philosophy of Kant. Both reduce art to 'an absolutely subjective system of signs denoting drive states of the subject'.[14] Adorno criticises both Kant and Freud for conceptualising art as existing *only* in relation to the individual who produced or contemplated a particular work. The objective role of social conditions and the process of production itself are practically ignored. In other words, creativity in idealist philosophy and psychoanalysis alike is resigned to the realm of the subject alone.

However, Freud's legacy was subsequently carried over into various streams of thought including the critical theory of the Frankfurt School of which Adorno was a part. In his seminal book *One Dimensional Man*, a damning critique of modern 'mass' society, Herbert Marcuse employs a concept of 'repressive desublimation' in order to explain how apparent advances in personal liberties and prosperity in modern society actually involves a negation of opposition and consequently a reinforcement of capitalist domination. Marcuse and other Critical Theorists are highly concerned about the ways the 'culture industry' has appropriated and effectively neutralised the oppositional culture represented by artistic Modernism. This process, Marcuse argues, involves a sweeping desublimation. As he writes:

> Artistic alienation is sublimation. It creates the images of conditions which are irreconcilable with the established Reality Principle but which, as cultural images, became tolerable, even edifying and useful. Now this imagery is invalidated. Its incorporation into the kitchen, the office, the shop; its commercial release for business and fun is, in a sense, desublimation – replacing mediation by

immediate gratification. But it is desublimation practiced from a 'position of strength' on the part of society, which can afford to grant more than before because its interests have become the inner-most drives of its citizens, and because the joys which it grants promote social cohesion and contentment.[15]

The oppositional culture so incorporated by contemporary mass culture is the culture which the Frankfurt School argued 'represented the last preserve of human yearning for that "other" society beyond the present one' – the possibility of an emancipated society. Mass culture, on the other hand, served a new political function in that it reconciled the mass audience to the status quo by way of creating, and subsequently appearing to satisfy, false wants and needs. Artistic endeavour no longer involved a struggle for truth which transcended the smoke-screen of ideological representation but rather became part and parcel of the dominant ideology. It is in this way, within Marcuse's Marxian/Freudian framework, that sublimation is transformed into repressive desublimation.

If we return to Adorno and Williams, however, we find in both a more challenging view of creativity in the post-Romantic age. Williams's approach to creativity is to democratise it, to locate it in the activity of every human mind by relating it to perception. Every individual learns how to perceive the world, but such learning must be in relation to existing cultural rules. For Williams, human beings learn to perceive a thing by describing it. Description involves interpretation in relation to general social rules which determine whether a description is novel or consistent with current understandings. Description and interpretation are, in turn, functions of communication. Williams argues that we learn to perceive something by describing it to others – by conveying a particular experience. The arts, for Williams, are examples of intense forms of communication and it is the shared communication which represents the social basis of artistic creativity:

> The artist shares with other men what is usually called 'the creative imagination': that is to say, the capacity to find and organize new descriptions of experience. Other men share with the artist the capacity to transmit these descriptions which are only in the full sense descriptions when they are in a communicable form. The special nature of the artist's work is his use of a learned skill in a particular kind of transmission of experience. His command of this

skill is his art . . . . But the purpose of the skill is similar to the purpose of all general human skills of communication: the transmission of valued experience.[16]

In this view, art relies on a working communication being reached between artist and audience in order to succeed. Communication is an activity in which both artist and spectator/reader/listener actively participate. The artist encodes an experience within the formal properties of the work and this experience is decoded by the viewer or reader. If this transmission breaks down then the art-work has failed:

> To succeed in art is to convey an experience to others in such a form that the experience is actively recreated . . . all else is failure . . . . The failure of art is the failure of communication.[17]

This implies that successful communication depends on certain criteria of competence which, for socio-structural and not organic reasons, is not uniformly distributed throughout society. Most modern art can, following Williams's argument, be seen as elitist because the members of society competent in the skills of reading or 'actively recreating' the experiences conveyed in the literary works of Kafka or Beckett, the paintings of Klee and Mondrian, the music of Schoenberg or Cage, or the Modernist cinema of Antonioni, Bertolucci or Godard, are the minority who have been educated in such competence. Those who do not possess these skills are likely to regard such works in negative terms ranging from bewilderment and boredom to outrage and hostility. In this context the art has failed because communication has failed. Yet it is doubtful that even Williams would deny the stature of the artists mentioned. In his attempts to democratise creativity Williams tends to neglect the structural inequalities so crucial to the patterning of artistic production and reception. As the Critical Theorists would see it, he fails to perceive the truth-content of modern art which is located precisely in its refusal to be the midwife of communication and, by implication, the inherently repressive nature of mass communication in contemporary society.

The way in which Williams relates creativity to communication is radically challenged by the aesthetics of Adorno. Williams and Adorno conceptualise the dynamics of the creative process in very different ways. First Williams:

It is neither subject working on object, nor object on subject: it is, rather, a dynamic interaction, which is in fact a whole and continuous process. The man makes the shape and the shape makes the man, but these are merely alternative descriptions of one process, well known by artists and in fact central to man himself.[18]

The subject/object relationship at the heart of the creative dynamic is seen here as more or less harmonious. But Adorno is much less humanistic, and his work has a more pessimistic conception of the human subject.[19] He regards the subject/object relationship in terms of a 'precarious balance', rather than an 'identity of the two' as Williams does. Adorno tends to stress the importance of object over subject by arguing that the subject is simultaneously always an object while an object need not also be a subject. He develops instead a concept of 'precarious balance'; of the dialectical relationship between subject and object in the process of artistic creation:

On its private side, the subjective process of creation is irrelevant. It is the objective side of the process that constitutes the precondition for the realisation of its internal logic of development. Subjectivity comes into its own not as communication or message but as labour. The work of art aims at the balance between subject and object without any assurance that it will succeed. This too is an aspect of the illusory quality of art. The individual artist functions as an executor of that balance. In the productive process he faces a task that has been posed for him, rather than one he poses for himself. In every block of marble and in every keyboard, a sculpture or a musical composition respectively, seems to be waiting to be set free. Artistic tasks tend to contain their objective solutions, not of course in any mathematically precise sense, not like univocal solutions to equations. The artist's absolute act is of minuscule importance. He mediates between the problem he confronts as given and the solution as it potentially inheres in his material. If a tool can be called an extension of the human hand, then the artist is an extension of a tool that is engaged in making possible the transition from potentiality to actuality.[20]

Here Adorno argues that alleged creative freedom is illusory in that art-works express objective social tendencies *unintended* by their creators. The so-called spontaneity of subjective creativity can only realise itself through objectification, which means working with materials already filtered through existing social matrices. Intentionality is fundamentally non-identical to content, and may fail to actualise itself in the structure of the work:

> Objective forces beyond the control of mere intention determine whether a creative dynamic is set free in the work.[21]

And again:

> Design is not an absolute constant . . . for it is almost always subject to change in the process of realisation and implementation. Indeed it is almost a mark of objectification for a work to have departed from its overall conception under the pressure of its immanent logic.[22]

The subject is seen by Adorno as 'under the sway' of the art-work. In order to explain this process Adorno utilises the concept of 'immanence'. He argues that immanent analysis involves the use of categories intrinsic to the object rather than externally imposed upon it. In this way any moment or truth value within the object will be perceived undistorted by external social categories, preserving the germ of optimism and possible social emancipation in the face of large-scale incorporation and repression by the forces of mass culture. While critical theorists such as Adorno and Marcuse regard mass or popular culture as necessarily repressive, Williams takes a rather different view, believing that popular culture itself contains the seeds of opposition to capitalist incorporation.

What conclusions with regard to the question of creativity can be drawn from this consideration of Williams and Adorno? Firstly, it foregrounds the question of intentionality and its realisation. While Williams tends to overstress 'communication', at the expense of the objective forces at work in production and reception, Adorno tends to obliterate intentionality altogether. By doing so, he renders artistic activity problematic since purpose becomes obscured and we are forced back on to the Freudian question of the motivation of the subject. Secondly, difficulties also arise when we consider the problem of innovation versus repetition within the art-work. The concept of creativity embraces both categories. An object which can be said to have been generated by way of a creative process or act may, on the one hand, represent a tangible innovation: an expansion in human resources, formal properties or knowledge, and involving a moment of non-recognition. On the other hand, the object may be a novel combination of identifiable techniques, observations, ideas already in existence which have been repeated in a different form. The latter is the form of writing favoured by the proponents of intertextuality. As Roland Barthes suggests, the 'text' represents 'a multi-dimensional space in which a variety of writings, none of them original, blend and clash'.[23] Thus recognition, on the audience's part, is ultimately not a problem in such accounts as innovation consists of a new combination of existing, and recognisable, elements.

In different ways both Williams and Adorno would seem to come close to endorsing this view. In Williams's case the stress placed on communication would seem to work against genuine innovation, which could seriously run the risk of communication breakdown. While Williams concedes that the art-work can serve on the frontiers of knowledge, particularly in disrupted and rapidly changing societies, it also serves at the very centre of society – the artist being regarded as 'the voice of the community'. This serves to downplay genuine innovation and change. The majority of artistic activity in Williams's model is therefore only creative in the restrictive sense, involving elements of recognition and not genuine innovation. While this may be an accurate reflection of actual conditions, and is certainly the case with regard to the following analysis of current British cinema, it does not provide a full theoretical explanation of true innovation which at some point must involve a moment of non-recognition both on the part of the audience and the artist.

Adorno, on the other hand, does concentrate on the dynamics of the process but his argument too has its difficulties. As pointed out, Adorno utilises a concept of 'immanence' to explain socially critical creativity. He builds a problem-solving conception of the creative process with both the problems and the solutions located as external to the subject. This renders the artistic task as one of finding the solution rather than creatively solving the problem in hand. By locating both problems and solutions in objective conditions, Adorno is, in a sense, arguing that the concepts which make the future are concepts belonging to the present, not to the future. A certain inevitability that solutions will be found is implied in Adorno's thesis and this would appear to preclude any genuine novelty. While this implies some connection between Adorno's position and the semiological notion of intertextuality, in terms of an apparent common strain towards the idea that 'everything is repetition', we must be careful not to equate the two. Adorno, despite the problems generated by his dialectical approach, genuinely believes in the dissonant force of innovation – 'the shock of the new', to borrow Robert Hughes's term, being one of the strengths of Modernist art.

If we turn our attention towards the question of creativity in the context of cinema the issues of innovation and repetition are a crucial consideration. Given the commercial imperative which informs most film-making, it is not in the interests of film-makers to alienate their audience. Therefore the general pressure is towards the creation of cinematic fictions which may be novel at the level of storyline but which tend to conform to general expectation with regard to formal construction and narrative development. This ensures that an active communication in Williams's sense, with its attendant categories of description and interpretation, is achieved between film-maker and audience.

Robert Philip Kolker makes a distinction between Melodramatic and Modernist cinema.[24] The Melodramatic aesthetic applies to classic Hollywood cinema and its variants, including most British cinema, and is characterised by repetition, assurance, security, emotional safety and the reinforcement of generally-held beliefs and values. Modernist cinema in contrast, seeks to question and challenge assumptions, both about the world and the nature of cinema itself. It seeks to be socially and politically critical and denies its audience the security of recognisable characters, events and outcomes. If Hollywood, and by extension British, cinema provides an example of Williams's communication, then the formal and political strategies of European Modernist cinema are much more akin to Adorno's conception of the function of the art-work. However, Modernist cinema can still be seen in terms of communication, albeit a more open form which demands a greater participation on the part of the audience than melodrama does.

It is unsurprising that Williams's model of artistic production and reception should have an affinity with the dominant aesthetic mode of British cinema as he and the producers of that cinema share a common liberal-democratic cultural background. Both Williams and the postwar British cinema have displayed a profound interest in issues of lower-class culture and social justice in advanced capitalism. The British realist aesthetic has continually displayed a progressive political stance in gradually extending the cinematic franchise to examine the lives, aspirations and problems of ordinary people in modern society. Cinematic communication in this context is underpinned by a desire to address contemporary social experience in a manner which may be thought-provoking and politically progressive, but without recourse to the Modernist formal devices of audience dislocation and self-reflexivity.

The tension between subjective intentionality and the objective structuring, lying at the heart of the creative process, will be examined, with specific regard to film production, in Chapter 1. This will involve a reconstruction of the creative subject in the film-making process which considers the issue of film-making as an essentially collaborative undertaking. But firstly we must consider how the concept of creativity has been utilised in film theory and criticism.

# 1 Creativity and Cinema

## THE QUESTION OF AUTHORSHIP

The dominant approaches in film theory and criticism tend to treat creativity as virtually synonymous with authorship. Here film is conceptualised in terms of a conscious communication; a statement directly attributable to the film-maker concerned. The general thrust in film studies has been to move away from the notion of the film-maker as an author standing behind the film, and towards the idea of cinema as a process of spectating in which the film-maker becomes merely one element. The original conception of conscious creativity has been gradually shed along the way – firstly in terms of a shift towards the notion of authorship as an unconscious structure, and subsequently, of a general valorisation of the spectator at the expense of the film-maker/author.

These shifts reflect the desire to ground film studies in a materialistic framework, and to locate film-makers (and subsequently audiences) within objective social structures and processes. The result has been an increasing marginalisation of the issue of creativity to the point where it is no longer recognised. Yet film-making, like all spheres of human endeavour, is an ongoing process in which creativity plays an integral part: whether it is in terms of the creation of new cinematic fictions, or the expansion of film language and modes of communication, which utilise the medium in new ways. In addition, the general thrust of film theory has tended to displace critical debate further and further from the object in question – cinema, entering instead into the more abstract realms of semiotics and psychoanalysis. As a result many of the articles which have appeared in journals such as *Screen* have contained little reference to film-making practices, preferring to concentrate on linguistics, ideology, Lacanian psychoanalysis and general theories of representation and perception.

This chapter will document some of these developments in order to show how the issue of creativity has become effectively negated and the implications this negation has for current explanations, particularly those which are heavily influenced by the writings of various French 'structuralists' and 'post-structuralists': intellectuals such as Christian Metz, Jacques Lacan, Louis Althusser, Michel Foucault, Roland Barthes, and Jacques Derrida. I shall conclude by drawing out the productive strands of the debate – in particular the desire to place the study of film and film-making within a social context – while avoiding the pitfalls: namely the abandonment of the creative principle and the neglect of film-making practices.

## THEORIES OF AUTHORSHIP

The first systematic commitment to the film-maker as author is generally attributable to the writers associated with the French journal *Cahiers du Cinéma* during the fifties. While the spiritual guru of the *Cahiers* group was the theorist André Bazin, the major voices, who formed *la politique des auteurs*, were François Truffaut, Eric Rohmer, Jean-Luc Godard, Claude Chabrol and Jacques Rivette, all subsequently to become 'New Wave' film-makers in the sixties. As Edward Buscombe points out, the (loosely) collective *Cahiers* position was never proposed in terms of a coherent *theory* as such:

> The Politique, as the choice of term indicates, was polemical in intent and was meant to define an *attitude* to the cinema and a *course of action*. (My emphases)[1]

*Cahiers*' achievement in inaugurating the '*politique*' was to shift the locus of the authorial signature in cinema from the writer and, in the case of Hollywood, the producer, to the director. However, not all directors qualified as auteurs. An important distinction was drawn between the true '*auteur*' – a film artist who works on material in such a way as to transform it into his or her own personal vision, and a '*metteur en scène*' – a craftsman who, no matter how skilled, can only adapt the concepts of others. This distinction presupposes a writer/director distinction and was based on the working practices of American cinema, dominated by a studio context in which directors were hired to tackle particular scripts, rather than the European work of Renoir, Cocteau, Dreyer or Bergman, which gave an ostensibly freer rein to personal vision and control.

In lionising not only Hitchcock, Welles, Hawks and Ford, but also Preminger, Walsh, Boetticher and Fuller, the *Cahiers* critics were committing themselves to the idea that all cinema, even the most routinised and commercial, contained a 'space' amenable to directorial self-expression. Such a conception has its roots in Romanticism's stress on 'natural genius', 'the creative imagination' and 'emotional spontaneity'. These were the unique properties of the artist or poet, as a figure often isolated from, and at times in conflict with, society.[2] Auteur criticism was subsequently developed by Andrew Sarris in America, and critics writing for the British journal *Movie* – such as Robin Wood, Ian Cameron, David Thompson and Victor Perkins. The criteria and interests of the *Movie* group were broadly similar to that of *Cahiers* in that they regarded auteurism as a critical tool rather than a coherent theory. Sarris, on the other hand, was more grandiose in his theoretical pretensions. He saw the 'auteur theory' as being grounded in three basic premises: 'the technical competence of the director as a criterion of value, the distinguishable personality as a criterion of value', and the rather vague notion of interior meaning, 'extrapolated from the tension between a director's personality and his material'.[3]

The central weakness of this scheme, according to Edward Buscombe, is that the simultaneous use of auteur theory as a method of classification *and* as a criterion of value leaves no room for films which are distinctive as the work of a particular film-maker but inferior at the same time. I would, for example, argue that the work of the British director Terence Fisher for Hammer Films between 1951 and 1973 displays (particularly from *The Curse of Frankenstein*, made in 1956, onwards) a consistent use of themes and 'mise-en-scène'. Yet I would also argue that Fisher's view of the world is trite and reactionary, his style turgid and stagey. The use of individuality alone as a test of cultural value was something Bazin warned against, since it destroyed the whole validity of auteurism.[4] Sarris seems to have ignored such advice to his peril.

Sarris's conception of the subject of the auteur theory, the film artist, is also flawed. He uses the term 'talent' unreservedly and without clarification. He also questions what he identifies as Bazin's 'historical determinism', replacing it with what can only be described as a naive idealism:

> I suspect somewhat greater reciprocity between an artist and his zeitgeist than Bazin would allow. He mentions, more than once, and in other contexts, Capitalism's influence on the cinema. Without denying this influence, I still find it impossible to attribute

X directors and Y films to any particular system or culture. Why should the Italian cinema be superior to the German cinema after one war when the reverse was true after the previous one?[5]

This argument is absurd. The historical moment of German Expressionism and later of Italian Neo-Realism is fundamentally related to cultural conditions and social processes: the artistic and social climate of Weimar Germany and the dominance of a leftist aesthetic in Italy after the Second World War which could never be replicated in occupied West Germany. Clearly Sarris's idealism is untenable as a theoretical framework for auteurism and his notoriety has tended to tarnish other auteurist writings. Yet both the *Cahiers* and *Movie* groups were aware of the limitations of auteurism and regarded its usefulness primarily as a critical, rather than a theoretical device.

The sixties witnessed a desire to ground the study of cinema within a more scientific framework. One of the pioneers of this approach was Christian Metz who applied the principles of structural linguistics to film in order to demonstrate that it operated like a language. This can be seen in part as an attempt to transcend the subjectivity of auteur theory and to construct an objectivist film theory. However, it also led to the development of 'auteur-structualism', a combination with the auteur principle: the film-maker as centre, with the ideas of the French anthropologist Claude Lévi-Strauss, in particular his writings on myth and meaning. Auteur-structuralism was developed by the writers associated with the British publication *Screen* in the sixties: Geoffrey Nowell-Smith, Peter Wollen, Jim Kitses, Alan Lovell and Ben Brewster, and was founded on the belief that the defining characteristics of an author's work are not always those most readily apparent. This is where structural analysis, with its focus on the *structural* relations of myth rather than their ostensible content, comes into play.[6] Auteur-structuralism can be regarded as an attempt to transcend the problems generated by the Romantic conception of auteurism. Nowell-Smith writes:

> The purpose of criticism becomes therefore to uncover behind the superficial contrasts of subject and treatment a structural hardcore of basic and often recondite motifs. The pattern formed by these motifs, which may be stylistic or thematic, is what gives an author's work its particular structure, both defining it internally and distinguishing one body of work from another.[7]

The most formidable exponent of auteur structuralism is Peter Wollen, whose book *Signs and Meaning in the Cinema* applies auteur-structuralism to the films of Howard Hawks and John Ford.[8] In each case Wollen extrapolates either a hard core of motifs, with regard to Hawks, or in the case of Ford, a series of shifting antinomies, the major being that of wilderness/garden. Wollen argues that Ford's work is structurally 'richer' than Hawks's by virtue of the greater depth constituted by the series of shifting relations revealed by structural analysis, compared to the more straightforward set of common motifs identified in the films of Hawks. This, for Wollen, makes Ford the greater artist. His original (1967) position regards the auteur as the structuring principle. While he does acknowledge the 'noise' of camera style and acting, Wollen reaffirms the 'mind (conscious or unconscious) of the auteur' as the source of coherence and unity within auteur-structuralist analysis.

Wollen subsequently altered his position by way of his rethought conclusion to *Signs and Meaning*, added to the main text in 1972. This involved a shift, which Brian Henderson claims was not explicitly acknowledged by Wollen,[9] from the notion of the film-maker as a structuring presence, to the idea of the film-maker as merely one structure (or code) among many. Wollen writes:

> The film is not a communication but an artefact which is structured in a certain way. Auteur analysis does not consist of retracing a film to its origins, to its creative source. It consists of tracing a structure (not a message) within the work which can then post factum be assigned to an individual, the director, on empirical grounds.[10]

Wollen is moving towards a position similar to that of Adorno in the sense that the art-work is now seen in primarily objective terms with the consequent relegation of the auteur to a secondary position in the process. As the issue of conscious communication finds itself being pushed out of the picture, creativity as a meaningful category is abandoned. No attempt is made to find a more adequate account of the process of initiation and development to replace it. Since creativity is seen as a Romantic conception, the ideas of conscious communication or intentionality are also abandoned.

The failure to propose an alternative to Romantic conceptions of initiation and change renders auteur-structuralism a rather static perspective: a charge anticipated and conceded by Nowell-Smith who claimed the approach was prone to reductionism since it neglected the possibility of structures being variable and non-constant, that the work of film-makers could develop and change over time.[11] Indeed, Nowell-Smith could not find a simple and comprehensive structure in his study of Visconti precisely because of the film-maker's constant development. This problem was rooted in the privileging, within the structuralist method, of the synchronic over the diachronic which renders the method blind to developmental processes. A related problem, suggested by Nowell-Smith and expanded by Caughie,[12] is that auteur-structuralism massively privileges thematics to the detriment of style and mise-en-scène which, after all, are a demonstration of a particular film-maker's individual utilisation of the medium.

Another criticism levelled at auteur-structuralism is that none of its critics directly questions the applicability of the ideas of Lèvi-Strauss to film. Brian Henderson attacks Wollen for avoiding crucial questions: whether films are like myths and whether methods of examining myths are applicable to film study. He suggests that Wollen's inability to dispense with the subject – the structures attributed as 'Hawks', 'Ford' or 'Hitchcock' – means that his claims cannot be grounded in Lévi-Strauss who deliberately and systematically omits any theory of the subject: 'the ultimate goal of the human sciences is not to constitute man but to dissolve him', proclaimed Lévi-Strauss in his conclusion to *The Savage Mind*.

The structuralist technique did, however, prove itself to be a useful tool of analysis in terms of uncovering thematics and consistencies in the work of film-makers, or in the study of a particular genre, as Will Wright has shown with reference to the Hollywood Western.[13] A positive development would have been the attempt to relate internal structures within the work to external social structures in order to resist charges that films were taken as given objects or closed systems, while at the same time allowing for a greater consideration of issues of individual style and *mise-en-scéne*. This may be one way of tackling the problem of the relationship between subject and object within the context of a creative process. This extremely important question will be returned to in due course, but first of all I shall briefly examine the direction taken by theoretical debate in the light of post-structuralism.

## POST-STRUCTURALISM AND FILM THEORY

In common with structuralism, post-structuralist critics also find they are unable to dispense with the figure of the author as easily as they would wish. In an attempt to demonstrate the textual system at work in the Hollywood film, Stephen Heath chose, perhaps wrongly, to analyse Orson Welles's *Touch of Evil*.[14] In spite of his claim that the author 'Orson Welles' is only of interest in the sense of being 'an effect of the text', many of the codes which Heath articulates as components of the textual system of *Touch of Evil*: camera movement, lighting, dialogue, music, action, characters, etc. are demonstrations of the (more or less) intentional creativity of Welles and his collaborators on the film. The narrative information these 'codes' or 'cinematic devices' convey to the audience represents a demonstration of a film-maker who understands the conventions of film production and (more importantly) reception. Such conventions are locatable within clearly-defined social and aesthetic structures.

Moreover, Orson Welles dominates the film from start to finish, both stylistically and physically, in terms of his presence in the fiction as police-chief Hank Quinlan. The 'textual system' of *Touch of Evil* is not a closed one, but many of the external reference-points which inform it share a common denominator: Orson Welles, the man and his work. Geoffrey Nowell-Smith, arguing against the notion that in the textual process an author can return as a fiction (i.e. one code amongst many), suggests that, with specific reference to John Ford:

> the 'fiction' of the author enables us to locate an 'author of the fiction' who is by no means dispersed but who in 'his' notional coherence provides the means for us to grasp the text in the moment of its production before us.[15]

Nowell-Smith is sensitive to the different ways a film-maker like Ford (or Welles, or Hitchcock) can inscribe himself in the text which goes beyond the notion of an author as subcode. He argues that either we must say that there are several authorial subcodes – of expression, content and so on, or we must see the author as criss-crossing the text and marking it at various levels, in which case it would be better to talk of the author, rather than the text, as system. Again this would only apply to certain film-makers whose presence, both internal and external, in relation to the film is strong enough to inscribe itself in the text and so provide the coherence enabling the audience to grasp the text in a certain way and recognise it as, in Nowell-Smith's term, 'authored discourse'.

A final criticism of Heath's approach to *Touch of Evil* is articulated by Pam Cook.[16] She argues that Heath demonstrates a tendency to concentrate only on formal strategies at the expense of extratextual references to history, politics or economics which may in fact play some part in these textual strategies. In this way the textual system remains uncontextualised. This is a fundamental weakness of many 'textualist' writings where the text is seen as the be-all and end-all and any references to an extratextual reality are omitted. In this way the text becomes a 'given' in the way that auteur-structuralists were criticised for treating film.

The concept of the author, and by extension creativity, has been forcefully rejected by post-structuralist critics.[17] In general they have shifted the focus of attention away from production towards analyses of the process of spectating. However, the figure of the author has proved rather difficult to dispense with. The desire to reconceptualise the spectating subject in terms of the idea of cinema as discourse, and spectating as an active process, reintroduced the figure of the film-maker as a creative manipulator of the spectator's response.[18] The application of the theory of the enunciating subject to particular films has produced interesting results.

Sandy Flitterman, in an article concerned primarily with the problematic 'look' of the male director *vis-à-vis* the filmic image of woman, concentrates on Hitchcock's film *Marnie* by way of reference to Raymond Bellour's essay 'Hitchcock the Enunciator'.[19] Flitterman argues that a film-maker appropriates and then designates the 'look' in a specific way and it is this which 'characterises a particular director's system of enunciation, the way the look is organised to create the filmic discourse'.[20] Bellour's article is used as an illustration of how the director uses his privileged position to represent his own desire through the image he constructs and, in Hitchcock's case, by delegating the look to his fictive subjects: male characters in the film. In addition, the film-maker is endowed with the capacity to *create* discourse.

A second example is Nick Browne's analysis of structures and strategies which give form to the action of the narrative and at the same time determine the locus of the spectator in their viewing of the film.[21] Browne analyses Ford's *Stagecoach* and attempts to show that the spectator's relation to the fiction and the characters within it is subject to a constant shifting. Each camera set-up, Browne argues, is a marker of the enunciation. Some set-ups implicate the spectator in the action by closely identifying him or her with a character in the fiction, while other set-ups involve a more detached identification with the (essentially voyeuristic) camera.

What is common to both Flitterman and Browne is the unacknow-ledged idea of the manipulation of the audience's gaze. Such manipu-lation is directly attributable to the film-maker but in focusing on the psychological and political implications of the gaze, Browne and Flitterman ignore the vital issues of creativity and intentionality which their analyses uncover. In both case studies indicated above – *Marnie* and *Stagecoach* – the viewer becomes involved in a complex process of manipulation and identification. This is a creative process, attributable to a specific film-maker, an indication of that individual's ability to direct an audience's emotional (and sometimes intellectual) response by means of a constant positioning and reposi-tioning of the very look or gaze – the essence of the process of enunciation as explored by writers such as Flitterman and Browne. It is interesting that a theoretical line of enquiry which began with such a radical decentring of the author should end up reaffirming the idea of a conscious originator standing behind the text.

In this respect, cinematic creativity can be said to have a central core which is represented by the intentional utilisation of materials in order to produce a desired response. This can range from the unambiguous audience responses to a thriller by Hitchcock, to the more open-ended ambiguous response generated in relation to a film by Resnais or Antonioni. An uncharacteristic example from recent British cinema is Derek Jarman's *The Last of England*:

> *The Last of England* is not as manipulative as a conventional
> feature . . . my audiences have much greater freedom to interpret
> what they are seeing, and because of the pace, to think about it.[22]

This is consistent with Buscombe's attack on Wollen's notion of the film-maker as a post-factum structure. Buscombe writes:

> It is possible to reveal structures in Hitchcock's work which are by
> no means unconscious, such as the use of certain camera angles to
> involve and implicate the audience in the action.[23]

This is exactly the 'creative manipulation' referred to critically, but unacknowledged in such terms, by Flitterman and other writers such as Laura Mulvey,[24] in their examination of the objectification of women in Hitchcock's films and its relation to the pleasures of the 'male gaze'.

This insight demonstrates further the applicability of Williams's idea of communication to cinema. An active communication between film-maker and audience is achieved, ranging from conventional cinema, which can justifiably be described as 'closed' communication to a greater or lesser degree, in which the audience is guided by various cinematic cues or prompts, to the more open-ended dialogue of film-makers like Derek Jarman:

> For me the voice of the audience is interpretive, teaching me what I've done. I don't work for a passive audience. I want an active audience.[25]

But even more traditional film-makers value response, true communication never being merely one way. As Stephen Frears comments: 'Most film-makers develop the style of their films in a relatively instinctual way and need critical feedback.'[26]

The question of intentionality is worth considering. The endorsement of communication implies an acceptance of subjective intentionality, yet Adorno's idea of the creative process involving a necessary departure from original design carries some weight. The pre-filmic idea always undergoes a transformation from words on a page to a series of sounds and images. In addition, original ideas can be changed through the process of editing: emphases can be altered, the chronology of events disrupted, the whole meaning of a film transformed. What appeared to work on paper might not hold together in the same way on screen. Occasionally, financiers will demand the right of final cut which may disrupt the intentionality of the film-maker.

While acknowledging the structuralist critique of the film author, Paul Coates has argued that any revised theory must insist on the presence of individuality:

> The various structuralisms maintain that individuality has been shattered. Shattered individuals, however, still remain individuals: a bullet has pierced the single pane and rayed it with splinters, but a frame – society – holds it in place, retaining it as a building block in its structure. Considered from without, the splintered pane remains a unit (within an overall structure).[27]

Coates suggests that an individual film-maker imposes his or her 'mark' on a film in terms of what he refers to as 'obsession, mannerism or style', which imposes a pseudo-unity or coherence. However, and this is crucial, against this individuality there is opposing material, what Coates refers to as 'a fire to test the concepts of the director'. This opposing material includes the key collaborators on the film, the script, and the source material (if any); in other words, the material context of the production. Coates argues: 'If either the directorial strength or the frictional opposition is absent, the film is without its individuality.'[28] Coates's argument implies a real sense of a productive engagement between film-maker and context: posing questions, limiting possibilities, suggesting solutions. In doing so he integrates the subject and objective processes as interdependent categories within authorship.

He also raises the question of creativity as an individual or collective endeavour. Films by Hitchcock, Welles or Godard, all rely heavily on the skills and contributions of key collaborators and many 'auteurs' have consistently worked with the same creative personnel. The question that must be asked therefore, is can cinematic creativity be justifiably assigned to a sole individual or should the process be seen more in terms of a collective endeavour? The idea of a collective film-making subject is extremely interesting given the logistics of the film-making process which render it impossible for a sole individual to make a film.

Coates's conception of 'opposing material' can be expanded to a consideration of a variety of contexts which combine to shape the creative process in hand, suggesting possibilities, providing resources and imposing constraints on the film-maker. Before turning to an examination of such contexts with regard to current British cinema I shall briefly consider other pertinent theoretical questions: the rather problematic issue of realism and the medium of cinema and what implications this has for an understanding of film-making as a creative process.

## CREATIVITY AND REALISM

One of the key debates in film theory concerns the question of realism. At the centre of the debate lies the assertion by some critics of a unique mimetic relationship between cinema and reality by virtue of the principles of photographic reproduction. In his early essay 'The Ontology of the Photographic Image', André Bazin sees photography in terms of 'a process of mechanical reproduction from which man is excluded'.[29] If we extend this argument, cinema, as the medium of the moving image, is essentially a transparent medium, a window opening out on to the world. For this reason film enjoys a special affinity with the classical conception of art as mimesis.

The question now raised is whether film, as a process of mechanical reproduction, can also be a creative art-form in the manner of other, more abstract or conceptual art-forms. Rudolph Arnheim, an early proponent of expressive film-making, argues that if cinema were simply the mechanical reproduction of reality then it could not also be an art form.[30] Consequently, he urges film-makers not simply to copy but to originate, to interpret and to mould; to exploit the possibilities of the medium in a creative manner in order to keep alive the possibility of film art.

Much of the early debate on film realism was informed by value-judgements about the true nature of the medium of film; what kinds of films should be made and which aesthetic principles should be followed in the process. Such 'manifestos' were written in the face of a heterogeneity of filmic practices ranging from documentary to fantasy, and dating back to the experiments of the French pioneers Lumière and Méliès. Subsequent contributors to the debate attempted a synthesis of both realist and expressive insights; to preserve the 'scientific fact' of photography and consequently the cinema's privileged representation of the real world, while creating space for the idea of film as symbolic and expressive.

Bazin, who along with Siegfried Kracauer has been regarded as the major champion of cinematic realism, attempted to adhere to a realist position while considering film to be an expressive form. In one of his later essays he claims that film could be regarded as art because film-makers needed to enlist artifice in order to create the illusion of transparency which generated a creative tension crucial to the work of art. Literal mimesis would result only in a flat and unheightened naturalism.[31] Such a statement explains Bazin's enthusiasm for fictional realism as opposed to documentary on the one hand, and his enthusiasm for the Modernist features of Bresson's film-making on the other.[32]

One contemporary British film-maker who shares Bazin's view of film as an essentially mimetic form is Bill Douglas, writer/director of the autobiographical trilogy: *My Childhood, My Ain Folk, My Way Home* and *Comrades*, the story of the Tolpuddle Martyrs. Douglas explains his philosophy in the following manner:

I'm very admiring of what the camera can do. The camera can reveal a great deal without words. It can reveal the inner soul of people. If you rush through words and rush images you don't get into the heart of human beings. In life I remember there were moments when I sat looking at people when they were in repose, and there was a beauty about them, and a stillness. And when I came round to look through a camera perhaps one was looking for that moment I saw in life.[33]

This is the reason Douglas has tended to concentrate on working-class subjects, placed in environments of great poverty and hardship. Through the poverty and the misery the nobility of the human spirit survives.

Returning to the theoretical debate, another interesting attempt to resolve the realism/creativity contradiction was made by the American avant-garde film-maker Maya Deren.[34] Deren believed strongly in the transparent nature of the photographic medium while still seeing film as a creative form. For her, creative activity can occur at the 'pre-photographic' stage. She describes cinematography in terms of a 'controlled accident'; the maintenance of a delicate balance between what is there spontaneously and what is deliberately introduced into a scene. As she puts it:

Only in photography – by the delicate manipulation of what I call controlled accident – can natural phenomena be incorporated into our own creativity, to yield an image where the reality of a tree confers its truth upon the events we cause to transpire beneath it.[35]

Creativity refers in this context to actors, to action and to production design although Deren does not mention these specifically. She does not, however, consider environments, such as studio sets, which escape her categorisation as 'what is there spontaneously' or 'natural phenomena'.

While touching briefly on the capacity of photography to alter reality by means of slow, fast and reverse motion and telescopic projection, Deren explicitly warns against overt manipulation of the image since it destroys the reality which remains 'the building block for the creative use of the medium'. Filmic creativity for Deren lies not in the image itself as an end but in the assemblage of such images – the editing or 'post-photographic' stage. As she puts it: 'All invention and creation consists primarily of a new relationship between known parts.[36] Deren identifies a creative input at the pre- and post-photographic stages of the film-making process, which can be extended to the actual photographic stage itself. Despite the mechanical nature of the photographic reproduction process, the technology of cinematography offers film-makers a great deal of scope for intervention; to creatively manipulate the image in order to create a desired effect. The initial choice of framing and camera angle are the first examples of image manipulation. These do more than simply render an image in the camera viewfinder. They can generate particular emotional or intellectual responses on the part of the spectator depending on whether a subject dominates the frame or is dominated by other elements in the frame, whether the subject is in close-up or long shot, whether the shot is a low angle, high angle, slightly skewed or positioned at eye-level. All of these techniques impart different meanings in line with codes of representation. For example, tightly-framed, low-angle shots of a figure imply dominance while high-angled shots of a figure dominated by the surrounding landscape imply a certain vulnerability. The shifting of camera positions as we have seen also implicates the spectator in the narrative in terms of the process of enunciation discussed above.

We can now turn to the choice of lenses, lighting, filters and film-stock. These all imply some manipulation of the image whether in terms of the focal plane (either deep or shallow), the lighting of a scene (hard or soft, low-key or high-key, natural or artificial), the colour of that light and the characteristics of the negative in terms of colour or black and white, light sensitivity, grain and contrast. Each of these possibilities can be utilised to convey certain information and guide an audience's response: shallow focus concentrates the aud- ience's attention on particular objects or characters, hard low-key lighting is more mysterious than soft high-key lighting.

Beyond this there is the whole realm of trick photography and optical effects, and finally, the issue of film being an aural as well as a visual medium, which opens up a whole new area for creative manipulation. Film soundtracks bring together a variety of natural and artificial sounds including dialogue, ambient sound and music which can be used to underscore the images or, in some cases, to generate emotions which run counter to those created by the visual information, to introduce a vague sense of unease into a scene.

This discussion raises the question of the importance of technology to the creative process under examination. The creative choices described above are all in relation to technical possibility. Technology represents the 'tools of the trade' which enable film-makers to creatively intervene at each stage of the process. Consequently, the whole question of technology as a resource deserves to be examined in depth, going far beyond a simple consideration of the utilisation of technology with regard to current British cinema, to embrace wider theoretical concerns such as the relationship between technological and aesthetic development.

# 2 The Question of Cinema Technology

If film-making can be seen as a creative process structured and constrained by the availability of particular material resources, it follows that we must consider those elements which set its parameters, which effectively constitute the 'space' within which it occurs. There are two major examples of a tangible material resource necessary for film-making: finance and technology. Films cost money, often quite substantial amounts of money to develop and produce. In addition, of all the arts, film is the most dependent on technology, or more precisely a whole range of technologies: mechanical, optical, chemical and electronic, for its existence and development.

At the level of cinema as an institution, both resources are equally important and much has been written about the economics and technology of film-making since its birth at the end of the nineteenth century. However, in the case of any particular project, the question of finance will generally tend to overshadow that of technology, given the notorious difficulties associated with raising money for film production. In addition, the size of the production budget effectively determines what uses film-makers can make of available technology. Does the budget make provision for the hire of sophisticated remote-control camera systems or special effects? Even the type of film stock used will depend on the money available. The hire of equipment and processing facilities can also be problematic when budgets are limited. It is not surprising that the most spectacular uses of cinema technology in Britain tend to be limited to American productions made in British studios or big-budget projects, like Terry Gilliam's *Brazil* and *The Adventures of Baron Munchausen*, with North American backing. A two-million-pound British film will usually be modest in its utilisation of technology.

The question of the financial structure of the British film industry will be tackled later. My primary interest in this chapter is to examine the issue of film technology on both a theoretical and a substantive level. Technology represents the 'tools of the trade' and therefore is a crucial consideration in any examination of film-making as a creative process. I shall look at the relationship between technology and aesthetics and then at how existing technology can be utilised in innovative ways, with particular regard to British cinema history – a national cinema not normally noted for its innovative uses of film technology. Finally, the issue of film technology in relation to current production will be explored: the resources available and expanding applications of video technology.

## THE CRITIQUE OF TECHNOLOGICAL DETERMINISM

The historical process of technological invention and innovation and its relationship to issues of film practice and aesthetics has generated great controversy in recent years. Some writings on technological innovation and development are very much influenced by the 'Romantic ideal'. Robert Allen and Douglas Gomery have referred to such approaches as the 'Great Man' theory of film, where technological development is explained in terms of individual genius.[1] On the other hand, along with other recent commentators, they have also set up a critique of *technological determinism*. This approach sees technology as a self-generating, autonomous process which, in turn, determines the nature of film practice and aesthetic preference. Raymond Williams goes further and argues that technological determinism represents the orthodox view of technological development, not only with regard to a specific practice or institution such as cinema or television, but in the general context of technology and social change. He describes the position in the following way:

> New technologies are discovered by an essentially internal process of research and development which then sets the conditions for social change and progress.[2]

If we substitute the phrase 'aesthetic development' for 'social change and progress' we have in effect a statement of the technological determinist view of the relationship between technology and cinema.

Williams goes on to identify a distinct but similar general perspective of technological development and society which, like technological determinism, also regards technology as essentially self-generating. In this case, however, the significance of technology lies in its uses, which are held to be symptomatic of wider society and processes of social change. Technology no longer determines social change but rather is absorbed in the process of change in a more marginal way. Williams is critical of both technological determinism and this alternative perspective which he calls *symptomatic technology*, because both abstract technology from society. By giving it a self-generating status they effectively state its autonomy as a process. As a result, Williams argues, most histories of technology are written from these assumptions. This argument is supported by other writers such as Stephen Heath, who makes use of Williams's categories in order to demonstrate that most historical considerations of technology and technological development regard their object in terms of

> an evident reality of functioning progress (invention, modification, improvement and so on) analysable in terms of and with the factual guarantee of scientific development.[3]

Consequently technology becomes isolated as a 'self-generating instance'.

Williams extends his critique of technological determinism in a later article, published in 1983, concerned primarily with the question of film history.[4] He argues that any historical consideration of issues of technology should make a firm distinction between the concepts 'technology' and 'technical invention'. The latter concept is described by Williams in terms of 'a specific device, developed from practical experience or scientific knowledge and their interaction'. But this does not adequately explain the significance of technology with respect to a specific institution such as cinema. However, as Williams explains, technical inventions are brought together by a process of 'exclusion, selection and improvement' into a 'systematic technology'. This implies the operation of factors other than technology. Furthermore, Williams stresses that a history of cinema cannot simply be reduced to a history of technical inventions or even technologies. Even in the earliest years of cinema the basic technology was being used in radically different ways and for different purposes, within the same cultural context. Louis Lumière was developing a highly realist approach to film at the same time George Méliès was experimenting with the possibilities of using film to create illusion and fantasy.

The whole question of the relationship between cinema technology and cinema practice is opened up further if we consider the arguments of film historian Barry Salt. Salt sums up his position in the following manner:

> Now that some interest has arisen in the history of the influence of film technology on the form of films there has been an unfortunate tendency to exaggerate its importance, whereas in truth it appears that, as far as the more interesting aspects of movies are concerned, technology acts more as a loose pressure on what is done rather than a rigid constraint.[5]

Salt tends to see technology as responding to the determination of aesthetic demands, rather than vice versa. For example, he identifies the stylistic trend towards longer shot-lengths in 1940s Hollywood cinema which generated the requirement for increased camera manoeuvrability. This led to the introduction of the Houston crab dolly in 1946 and the Selznick crab dolly in 1948. The introduction of these specific pieces of equipment, Salt argues, represents 'a clear-cut case of film technology meeting purely aesthetic demands'.[6] This argument is problematic in that the demands Salt identifies as 'aesthetic' could also be seen as 'commercial' in the sense that Hollywood tended to compete, both internally and in the international market, on a basis of technical quality. Inventions such as the crab dolly contribute to the expansion of technical possibility by making the camera more mobile but, in keeping with the dominant Hollywood aesthetic, not more obtrusive. In this sense the economic can be seen as constraining the aesthetic. In addition the idea of technology responding to aesthetic demands, if taken as a general statement of the relationship between technology and film aesthetics, gives rise to a new form of idealism with the motor of change located in the imagination of the film artist. If technological determinism is guilty of abstracting technology from its social context then aesthetic determination is equally guilty with respect to abstracting either aesthetics or the mind of the artist.

Salt does not fall into the trap of aesthetic determination, however, since he also identifies instances where new technological developments apparently have little or no direct relationship to aesthetic demand. Perhaps the classic case in point is that of the lightweight hand-holdable camera. The first portable Arriflex camera was introduced in Germany in 1937 but was hardly used in fiction film-making until well after the Second World War although its weight, portability and quick-change magazines made it an ideal combat camera. It also boasted a reflex viewfinder which enabled operators to, in effect, see through the lens and this represented a major breakthrough in camera optics. The Arriflex became part of the Allies' booty after the war and was soon available in Hollywood. (Other significant pieces of technology were also captured from the Germans, such as the magnetic tape recorder which was subsequently to revolutionise the sound-recording process, and the first single-strip colour process developed by Agfa which led to the development of Eastman colour in America, which in turn superseded three-strip Technicolor as the dominant system in Hollywood production.) However, the application of the Arriflex was extremely limited, due in part to the American preference for synchronised sound. One early example of its use cited by Salt was the subjective sequences of Delmer Daves' 1947 film *Dark Passage*, with Humphrey Bogart. In general Hollywood continued to use bulky Mitchell studio cameras which were much more in line with institutional practices at the time.

A similar situation existed in France and elsewhere. The Eclair Cameflex had been introduced in France in 1948. This was a lightweight camera which, Salt suggests, was an improvement on the Arriflex in that its viewfinder design made for steadier handholding. Once again the immediate effects of this piece of technology on film practice was virtually zero. The aesthetic possibilities inherent in such equipment remained largely unexplored in France for over a decade until the rise of the 'New Wave': in particular the experiments of directors like Jean-Luc Godard and François Truffaut and cinematographer Raoul Coutard.

We can therefore conclude that the existence of a particular technology does not necessarily guarantee its take-up by film-makers. This understanding works against both technological and aesthetic determination respectively. Other factors affect the initial technical innovation and the pattern of its take-up and utilisation in film-making practice. The economics of an institutionalised studio system, in the case of Hollywood, can have an enormous effect on technological development and utilisation. Gomery and Allen develop an economic explanation of technological change in the American cinema. For them, new technologies are developed in the drive for higher profits in a highly competitive market situation, with both internal competition between studios and external competition between cinema and other leisure pursuits such as radio and (later) television. They utilise a model of invention–innovation–diffusion to examine the introduction of sound technology, its initial association with Warner Brothers, one of the minor studios at the time, and its eventual adoption by all the studios.[7] A relatively stable economic environment also creates the conditions whereby the time and money required for technical innovation can be made available. It is not surprising that the majority of the major technical breakthroughs occurred in America and Germany, during the domination of that industry by UFA, the only European studio which came close to matching the Hollywood majors in the interwar period. Economic factors, as well as providing the necessary impetus for innovation, can also delay the take-up of a particular new technology. Returning to the issue of sound technology, it is interesting to consider that although magnetic tape was available in Hollywood after the war – representing a major advance in terms of sound technology and opening up the possibility of multi-track recordings, stereophonic sound and later Dolby – the deployment of new sound systems was delayed for economic reasons, in particular the cost of converting theatres.[8]

The issue of technological advance in one area leading to retrenchment or retreat in another area is also worth consideration. The classic example in this context is that of the introduction of sound recording, which had certain well-documented knock-on effects, often with negative implications. The carbon lamps which were standard Hollywood lighting at the time were too noisy and had to be replaced by tungsten incandescent lights which produced much lower levels of illumination (they were also at the red end of the spectrum so the old orthochromatic film stock, which was blind to red, had to be replaced by panchromatic stock) and to compensate, cinematographers had to open up their lens apertures to very wide settings which reduced depth of field, creating the 'soft look' which was the dominant visual aesthetic in Hollywood during the thirties. In this way a technical breakthrough in one area can have significant repercussions in other areas. Thus Peter Wollen writes of 'the way in which innovations in one area may help to produce conservatism or even "retreat" in another . . . '.[9] Rick Altman gives other examples of sound technology affecting image technology: the introduction of sound forced film-makers indoors because the early microphones picked up wind and other unwanted sounds. This led to research on back-projection techniques to simulate exteriors in the studio.[10]

The influence of non-cinema factors, particularly on the generation of technological innovations, is another interesting consideration. Raymond Williams argues that the necessary conditions for technological development to occur include resource investment and official sanction. It is no surprise therefore that numerous technological developments have occurred in the contexts of industrial production or military technology.[11] As Gomery and Allen point out, some of the initial technical inventions which facilitated the birth of cinema occurred in an existing commercial context.[12] They also point out that

> the invention and innovation of certain pieces of technology necessary for what was to become 'cinéma verité' film-making resulted from certain military needs during and immediately following World War II.[13]

Wollen gives several examples of technological innovations originally generated in a military context which were subsequently adapted for cinema.[14] These include panchromatic film stock, originally developed for reconnaissance fog photography, and projection systems such as Cinerama, derived from aerial gunnery simulation, and CinemaScope, from tank gun-sighting periscopes. This interrelation between the technologies of warfare and cinema has been recently explored by Paul Virilio.[15]

What preliminary conclusions can we draw? The general tendency in recent work has been to stress heterogeneity of factors determining developments in cinema technology. Wollen stresses 'the heterogeneity of the economic and cultural determinants of change'.[16] Steve Neal writes:

> just as the economic, psychological and aesthetic factors involved in the cinema cannot be reduced to the technology fundamental to them, so technology and its development cannot be simply reduced to the status of an effect produced by the economic, psychological or aesthetic factors or processes. The history and current state of the cinema rather involve an uneven and often complex interweaving of all these elements each conditioning but not fully determining, or explaining, the others.[17]

Heath talks about a cinema history in terms of

> determinants which are not simple but multiple – interacting, in which the ideological is there from the start – without the latter emphasis reducing the technological to the ideological or making it uniquely the term of an ideological determination.[18]

Neale and Heath are strongly influenced here by the ideas of Jean Louis Comolli. Comolli, the leading figure in the *Cahiers du Cinéma* group since the late sixties, stresses the importance of economics and ideology in relating to issues of cinema technology. He makes the following introductory point in his seminal article 'Machines of the Visible':

> the historical variation of cinematic techniques, their appearance–disappearance, their phases of convergence, their periods of dominance and decline, seem to me to depend not on a rational-linear order of technological perfectability nor an autonomous instance of scientific 'progress' but much rather on the offsettings, adjustments, arrangements carried out by a social configuration in order to represent itself, that is at once to grasp itself, identify itself, and itself produce itself in its representation.[19]

In this way cinema, for Comolli, is not only socially determined but also helps society define itself through representation and identification.

Comolli, like Williams, makes a distinction between technical inventions and their being brought together in a systematic way to form what he calls the 'cinema machine': an economically and (particularly) ideologically determined configuration. The machine, Comolli stresses, is always social before it is technical. The immediate social context for the birth of cinema was generated in the late nineteenth century – a period characterised by an obsession with 'the visible' and representation. Hence cinema was constructed as a social machine in very particular ways.

The ideology of realism is also important according to Comolli, in terms of explaining patterns of innovation and development in cinema technology and technique. The initial predominance of deep focus, the introduction of sound and colour are all explicable in terms of the cinema as an approximation towards the dominant codes of photographic realism. This may appear to have similarities with Bazin's notions of an evolutionary process towards what he calls 'the myth of total cinema', but whereas Bazin had an idealistic belief in the 'truth' of reality, Comolli sees it in terms of an illusion created by an ideological process concerned with the suppression of difference and the desire for identity.

While theorists like Comolli have been correct in attempting to locate such issues in relation to social structures and to criticise idealist notions of the natural evolution of technology, there is a tendency to subsume all analysis under a bludgeoning conception of ideology (or more specifically bourgeois ideology): an all-embracing category which, as Gomery and Allen argue, is used to 'sweep all western civilisation into one concept'.[20] Such an abstracted category cannot provide the basis for a sufficient explanation of a phenomenon as tangible and materially constituted as technology.

Perhaps a more productive point of departure would involve a consideration of the basic mechanism of innovation and change as it applies to technology. The development of new technology occurs, as we have seen, in a variety of contexts. However, what is consistent to all is a notion of necessity. Innovations occur in relation to specific problems of a practical nature, be they in the field of commercial entertainment or military technology. The solutions to specific problems constitute themselves in terms of technical innovations and inventive applications of such innovations in terms of cinema practice: innovations at the level of technology and technique respectively. There is also the issue of novel applications of existing technology, the best examples being those of spin-offs from military and industrial technology. Existing technology, in its broadest sense, also helps to constitute the context within which innovation occurs, representing resources upon which individuals can draw, presenting a series of possibilities. Hence the applications of broad technologies such as electronic technology or chemical technology to particular problems generated within the specific context of film-making.

It quickly becomes apparent that this process is similar to that of artistic creativity. The material context essentially determines the nature of problems and provides particular resources and constraints within which solutions may or may not be generated. Creativity in the field of technology is therefore similar to that in film-making itself, structured by constraints and possibilities. Such a conception of technological innovation avoids the slide into seemingly limitless heterogeneity and indeterminism which characterises much current thinking.

## TECHNOLOGY AND BRITISH FILM

The relationship between technology and the exploration of aesthetic possibility is worth examining in greater detail. While most film-makers adhere to orthodox practices in terms of technological possibility, some particularly innovative and ambitious individuals will attempt to set themselves technical problems which can only be solved in terms of novel applications of existing technologies. This may involve the discovery of new possibilities inherent in the technology or deliberate misuse of technology. It is important at this stage to make a distinction between 'technology' and 'techniques'. The former facilitates and underpins the latter which constitutes the creative domain of the film-maker. It is at the level of techniques that film-makers can be described as innovators.

A classic example of such an innovatory approach to film-making is described by Robert Carringer with regard to the remarkable creative collaboration by director Orson Welles and cinematographer Gregg Toland on the production of *Citizen Kane*. Carringer writes:

> Welles not only encouraged Toland to experiment and tinker, he positively insisted on it . . . . Those involved say there was a kind of running game between the two with Welles coming up with one farfetched idea after another and challenging Toland to produce it and Toland delivering and then challenging Welles to ask for something he could not produce. Some of the devices Toland came up with he had already used in other films but others were new or used in significantly new ways in *Citizen Kane*.[21]

The work of innovators like Welles and Toland is explicable within the paradoxical context of a studio environment which on one hand generated a profound conservatism but also, by virtue of the economic strength and security of the studios at the time, could provide film-makers with the 'space' and resources required for innovation to take place. Welles and Toland were able to use these advantages to the full. However, Welles was never afforded the same freedoms by Hollywood again, being too much of a maverick for the studios to cope with.

If we move on to consider British cinema, we find that, as in Hollywood, production was dominated by a studio system until the late fifties. This implied certain standardised working practices but also occasionally provided the resources for innovative uses of technical facilities. The studio-based Technicolor productions of Michael Powell and Emeric Pressburger, financed by the Rank Organisation in the late forties, including *A Matter of Life and Death, Black Narcissus* and *The Red Shoes*, stand out as perhaps the zenith of that kind of film-making in this country with their elaborate sets, vivid colour-schemes and optical trickery. *Black Narcissus* is particularly interesting with its effective and convincing use of glass shots disguising the fact that the Himalayan locations were actually a lot at Pinewood studios. At the same time one of the best British examples of expressionistic cinematography was produced, namely Carol Reed's *The Third Man*, shot on location in Vienna by Robert Krasker.

As in America and France, the British studios and their practices effectively blocked the take-up of certain technological possibilities. John Ellis notes that at Ealing studios, experimentation with lightweight cameras was non-existent despite their being ideal for location shooting.[22] Film-makers at the studio did tend to shoot exteriors on location but this was done using a solid, static camera style which complemented the dominant studio aesthetic. Ealing had invested heavily in plant and machinery (including bulky studio cameras) during the thirties and forties and such investment had to be justified in terms of maximum utilisation.

Experimentation with lightweight cameras, such as the Arriflex, occurred mainly in a post-studio environment as the old structures began to break up and film-makers became more and more interested in location filming. The British cinematographer Walter Lassally, who worked closely with the film-makers of the 'Free Cinema' documentary movement and their subsequent 'graduation' to feature films, used Arriflex cameras on *A Taste of Honey* and *Tom Jones*, both directed by Tony Richardson in the early sixties. The former film is important in that it was the first British feature to be shot entirely on location: the size, weight and portability of the Arriflex enabled Lassally to shoot in real locations including cramped interiors.[23] Richardson was particularly pleased with the production process of *A Taste of Honey* in terms of the freedom the shooting style afforded him. Lassally used three different kinds of film stock on the film including the high speed Ilford HPS (400 ASA) stock which, as he explains, was previously considered suitable only for newsreels and documentaries. This enabled Lassally to shoot at very low levels of light including one close-up shot in a cave lit by one solitary candle – fifteen years before Stanley Kubrick's celebrated use of candlelight in *Barry Lyndon*.

*Tom Jones*, on the other hand, was in colour, but Lassally shot it in a style similar to that of *A Taste of Honey*. Despite its being a period-piece it was decided that the film could be shot in a thoroughly modern fashion on location using Arriflex cameras, often handheld to create a 'new wave' sense of excitement and movement. The hunt sequence in particular provides ample evidence of the success of the technique on a film which remains one of the major achievements of the British cinema, evoking the cultural ambience of the 'swinging sixties' far more effectively than any of the contemporary dramas which were to follow.

As I noted earlier, the question of technology as a resource is closely linked to financial resources and most British productions, being low-budget, are highly constrained in terms of what technological devices and processes are possible at that level of production. However, even in the case of such modestly budgeted production, film-makers are presented with a set of basic choices with regard to technology. These include choice of camera, film stock, sound equipment and editing machines. With regard to cameras, one of the great standards in the industry is the Panavision Panaflex. The Panavision system is built around the Mitchell movement: a dual-pin register system which holds film stock very steady when it is exposed. An alternative to the Panaflex is provided by the Arriflex 35 BL camera. As cinematographer Michael Coulter (Director of Photography on *No Surrender*, *Heavenly Pursuits*, *The Good Father*, *Housekeeping*, *The Dressmaker* and *Diamond Skulls*) explains, the Arriflex system is smaller, more flexible and incorporates a different system of registration to the Panaflex:

> for me it's like the difference between a BMW and a Renault 4: the BMW is solid and very comfortable but the Renault 4 is a bit more adaptable, you can put down the back seat, shove ladders on the roof and things like that.[24]

Cinematographers are also closely involved with laboratory technology, particularly the developing and printing processes. Roger Deakins, the lighting cameraman on a host of recent British films including *Another Time, Another Place*, *Nineteen Eighty Four*, *The Innocent*, *Defence of the Realm*, *Sid and Nancy*, *Personal Services*, *Shadey*, *White Mischief*, *The Kitchen Toto*, *Stormy Monday* and *Pascali's Island*, explains that on the production of *Nineteen Eighty Four* a colour-desaturation process was used to produce the desired 'look' of the film. As Deakins explains:

> Kays came up with this system a couple of weeks before we started shooting whereby they leave the developed silver on the print and

this acts as a black and white layer so you get 50 per cent colour. So we got the idea of semi black and white but we had to make it more brown and this was done mainly in the printing and a bit with filters on the camera. Also the colours of the sets in some instances – because the colour was drained by this process some of the sets were really brightly-coloured so that in the final process they would still look as colourful as they normally would but other things would look semi black and white.[25]

The same desaturation process was used on Terence Davies' film *Distant Voices, Still Lives* but in a slightly different way. On *Nineteen Eighty Four* the final result had tended towards blue tones, while this time the tonal emphasis was towards browns. In each case the technology contributed significantly to the visual impact and atmosphere of the film.

Moving on to editing equipment, the basic choice is between the upright Moviola, originally developed in Hollywood, and flat-bed editing tables such as the Steenbeck with was first introduced in Germany during the 1930s but did not become popular in America until the late sixties. While the flat-bed is argued to be more versatile and easier to use, many established editors prefer the Moviola. Tom Priestley (an editor active in the British industry for over thirty years) favours the Moviola because it runs at the same speed (24 frames per second) all the time both backwards and forwards:

because it's running at the same speed you are actually learning the rhythms of the shot . . . . On the table like the Steenbeck, it has variable speeds and often as not you go fast through the bits you don't want to look at so the rhythm gets lost. I think there's a tendency in Steenbeck editing for there to be more emphasis on the point of cutting and less on the overall rhythm.[26]

It is interesting to consider that as a resource, film technology is subject to constant development and expansion. Cameras and camera systems are becoming increasingly mobile and versatile, for example 'floating' camera systems such as 'Steadicam' and 'Panaglide', the remote-controlled camera systems mentioned above, snorkel lenses and fibre-optic photography and an increasingly versatile range of dollies and crane arms. Film stocks are becoming faster without dramatic quality reduction in the image. Sound recording and reproduction technology is improving in the wake of Dolby systems.

And in terms of image quality, high-band video is fast approaching 35mm film without the problems of colour fading over time and dramatic quality reduction from master print to release prints, as I shall explain in some depth in the next section of this chapter. Such innovations and improvements are gradually absorbed into mainstream practices, becoming commercially available for hire from the major equipment suppliers and laboratories which serve the various film industries around the world.

Film-makers are constrained by the limits of currently available technology. This may seem an obvious or even facile point but it is an important consideration in the sense that the limits of current technology and technological possibility effectively constitute the parameters within which creative film-making can take place.

## NEW TECHNOLOGY IN THE VIDEO AGE

Despite major advances in certain aspects of cinema technology, particularly in areas such as mobile camera systems and special effects, the basic apparatus remains largely unchanged. Cameras may be lighter, lenses and film-stocks faster, but the technological process is still predicated on the same basic principles which underpinned the technical developments brought together to form a systematic technology by the pioneers of cinema in the late nineteenth and early twentieth centuries.

Perhaps the most exciting developments which have occurred in the general area of motion picture technology over the last two or three decades have been those in the field of electronic, as opposed to optical, systems of recording and playback: in popular terms, 'the video revolution'. One must agree with Roy Armes's assertion that a full and adequate understanding of video

> demands that it be seen within the whole spectrum of nineteenth and twentieth century audio, visual and audio-visual media includ-ing radio and photography, the gramophone and the tape recorder.[27]

I shall not examine this spectrum in the very thorough manner Armes does, although I shall touch upon some aspects of the relationship video technology has to other media. What is important is that video should be seen neither as an isolated technology distinct from other media, nor as a stage in some audio-visual evolutionary process running from cinema to television to video. The relationships between the three are much more complex than that; indeed the roots of video technology are very closely connected to major developments in other media.

The initial context for the birth of video was generated by the development of magnetic sound tape in Germany during the thirties. As I have noted elsewhere, magnetic tape, which was invented by Fritz Pfleumer and manufactured by BASF, was part of the spoils of war appropriated by the Allies and quickly introduced into the United States. The first video tape was developed in America in the 1950s, with Ampex demonstrating the first broadcast standard video recorder in 1956. These early developments in video technology must be seen in relation to the new broadcast medium of television which at the time, if not in its infancy, was still very much in its early childhood. As Stuart Marshall explains, the development of video technology was largely supported by the broadcasting industry because it was complementary to the needs of that industry. Video-tape technology would enable the broadcast industry to cut costs, to dispense with rigid schedules, to enable studio productions (which had previously been broadcast 'live') to be repeated without being recreated, and to build up an international market in studio productions as programmes on tape could be sold to foreign broadcasters. Marshall writes:

> The drive behind the research was therefore towards both increased efficiency in production and resources and the creation of more marketable products.[28]

The development of video technology therefore should not be seen in some technologically deterministic way. It did not occur in some autonomous sphere, but rather was developed at the time and in the manner it was because of wider social and economic factors. Marshall is always at pains to place his analysis in a context which relates technological process to perceived needs on the part of those in society who have the power to sanction and encourage development and investment. This is very much the case with video technology.

After the initial North American impetus the location of most of the major breakthroughs in video technology shifted to Japan, led by the introduction in 1965 of the Sony Portapak system. This was a black-and-white portable reel-to-reel video system using half-inch tape. Broadcast systems at the time required two-inch video tape and the cameras were very large and cumbersome. Consequently, the Portapak system effectively liberated video technology from being the sole preserve of the broadcaster in a similar way that the development of lightweight 16mm film cameras liberated film-makers from institutionalised studio-based film-making. However, the quality of the Portapak system came nowhere near to meeting the broadcast format because it featured an inferior 'helical' scanning system as opposed to the 'quad' system of standard broadcast video. But the significance of the Portapak lies in its breaking of the broadcasters' monopoly over video technology, which in turn set the agenda for further research and development.

Sony again broke new ground in 1970 with the introduction of the three-quarter-inch U-matic format which for a while represented the standard industrial (non-broadcast) format. However, since then the rapid pace of development in electronic systems has effectively brought industrial video up to broadcast standard: in particular the introduction of high-band U-matic and Sony's Betacam system, introduced in 1982, which has proved very popular in the field of documentary and news reporting. Betacam is not only high-quality; it is also extremely portable, being based on the domestic Betamax system and utilising half-inch tape. The domestic sphere was initially served by the Phillips system introduced in 1972. However, this was quickly eclipsed by both Betamax and VHS with the latter coming to dominate, in Britain at least, in the wake of the domestic video boom in the early eighties.

The importance of video to film-makers lies in its accessibility. Roy Armes sees video as part of a wider development which has occurred in the postwar period which he describes in terms of

a democratization of the media akin to that allowed by celluloid in the 1890's with individual control, access, and even creative production available.[29]

While film-production, at least in the American context, remains, for Armes, dominated by multi-million dollar production, television created a demand for developments in 16mm film technology (for drama and documentary since, until recently, video cameras were too bulky and inflexible for location work other than outside broadcasts of sporting and ceremonial occasions), which in turn led to a massive upsurge in independent film-making. Similarly, the development of sound tape created the conditions for the birth of low-cost independent record companies. Video, Armes argues, represents:

> a key continuation of this democratizing tradition, as a system which allows personal recording and creative production as well as the consumption of pre-recorded, pre-packaged material.[30]

While it is true to say that video has made 'film-making' more accessible, in that it is basically a low-cost recording medium, it is still structured in terms of a cost-related hierarchy which effectively separates domestic video-users from professionals in both the industrial and broadcast spheres. As Armes points out, costs rise enormously at the post-production stage (vital to all video outside the basic domestic 'snapshot' sphere) due to the expense of post-production hardware such as editing facilities, and computer graphics. The range and quality of post-production facilities, particularly in the light of recent advances in digital post-production, has made video very attractive to the professional film-maker and although costs are high they are not as high as similar post-production processes for film.

While video remains almost exclusively a television medium as far as film-makers are concerned, a few experiments have been carried out by directors whose domain is very much the cinema. One of the first films shot on video with the intention of giving it some sort of theatrical release was Michelangelo Antonioni's *The Oberwald Mystery*, made in 1980. Since directing *The Red Desert* in 1964, Antonioni had been interested in manipulating colours – to make 'a violent attack on reality' as he puts it.[31] In this film Antonioni physically painted the landscape. By the time of *The Oberwald Mystery* technology could enable him to be rather more sophisticated. Video facilitated colour correction at the post-production stage with the opening sequence being shot in a wood at night and subsequently 'corrected' to the colours of sunset. The ability to experiment with colour after principal photography had been completed also attracted British experimental film-makers Peter Wollen and Laura Mulvey to video. They shot *The Bad Sister* on video in 1982 for Channel 4 but unlike Antonioni's film it was never shown in the cinema.

Next to Antonioni the other major film-maker who has experimented with video is Francis Coppola. In his studio-based production *One From the Heart*, Coppola utilised a process called 'pre-visualisation' which involved recording the action, music and dialogue on video before actual photography (on celluloid) began. This process allows the director to make and see the completed work prior to shooting, enabling the major creative decisions to be made without exposing thousands of feet of film. Many American film-makers tend to 'cover' a scene excessively, leaving the creative decisions to the editing stage – a technique involving substantial waste. The aim of 'pre-visualisation' was therefore to cut production costs.[32] The process led to savings of $2 million on the production. However, the decision to shoot the film on studio sets costing between $4 and $5 million effectively negated this economy and put an end to Coppola's experiments.

The first British feature-length drama made on video for both cinema and television was *Out of Order*, directed in 1988 by Jonnie Turpie for the Birmingham Film and Video Workshop on a budget of £380 000, around a quarter of the cost of a typical low-budget production shot on film, provided by Channel 4 and the BFI Production Board. The film was shot using a Betacam CCD chip camera which was ideally suited to the film-makers' needs. As Julian Petley explains:

> Such cameras are more robust, use less power and have greater light sensitivity than conventional video cameras, and are also free from magnetic and electrical interference.[33]

The only problem encountered was that the system produced an image not considered fully up to broadcast standards by the IBA. However, special dispensation was sought and given enabling *Out of Order* to be made. It is inevitable that more productions along these lines will be produced.

Despite the significance of these experiments, video remains very much a medium of the future. In terms of the production process itself, video incorporates a single camera system similar to film but with the added facility of instant playback and remote monitors. However, video monitors and playback facilities are now being used by film-makers shooting film in order to help certain decisions to be made: what the image looks like, which takes to print and so on. At the moment video is markedly inferior to film in terms of light sensitivity and image definition. As cinematographer Michael Coulter, who has worked in both media explains:

With video you need more light. There's not the latitude, you can't let the shadows go the way you do in film. It also tends to be very flat . . . . It's hard to get contrast into it because the minute you raise the contrast level from highlight to shadow the shadow fills in so much that the video signal needs you to pump more light into the shadow . . . . I've tried various things such as hard rim light to try and pull it apart because it's such a flat image.[34]

These problems tend to make cinematographers rather unenthusiastic about using video. Roger Deakins, for example, states that:

Until video gives you the possibilities at the moment you have on film: the flexibility and the sharpness and the quality, until it does that I don't really want to know.[35]

Another problem with video technology as far as film-makers are concerned is the process for transferring video to 16 or 35mm film for projection purposes in cinemas. It is significant that Antonioni and Jonnie Turpie have both suggested that the least satisfactory aspect of making a feature on video was the tape-to-film transference technology. However, new technology is being developed which will enable video to be transferred to 35mm film by means of a laser system with significantly better results than previous transference technology. On a domestic television screen, video and film can be practically indistinguishable, as the BBC television series *Boys From the Blackstuff*, written by Alan Bleasedale and directed by Philip Saville, demonstrates. One episode of the five was shot on film, the others on video with little difference in terms of image quality.[36] As Roy Armes notes:

Video cannot rival film in respect of the powerful impact unique to the projected big screen theatrical film presentation, but it can match it perfectly if the outlet is television broadcasting and the domestic receiver.[37]

This is the state of affairs as the eighties draw to a close but, given the rate of advance in video technology, it is only a matter of time before electronic technology gains the ascendency in the image as well as sound, as Wollen predicted more than a decade ago.[38]

As I have already pointed out, it is the benefits afforded by video at the post-production stage which are the most attractive to the film-maker, although even here opinions are divided. Armes argues that video editing is less flexible than film in that it involves transferring shots to a new master tape, with subsequent editing decisions requiring the construction from scratch of a new master. Film does not present this problem as it is physically cut and spliced together and can be rearranged without replicating entire sequences. However, even editors who prefer working in film argue that video has its benefits. Tony Lawson, for one, prefers the hands-on, tactile nature of film-editing but he suggests that:

> What is good about video is that it's fast . . . particularly if there's a lot of footage. It's much easier to handle that kind of thing on video than in physical terms . . . . You can also try out opticals instantly which you can't do on film.[39]

Despite his reservations about editing in video, Armes does concede that in terms of the entire post-production process, the video director has much more personal control than the film director. Every aspect of the process takes place in the director's presence, unlike the lab situation in film which is noted for its 'opacity' by Peter Wollen.

Perhaps the most interesting and innovative production which has made use of video technology as a post-production facility is Derek Jarman's *The Last of England*. What makes this film all the more remarkable is that the images were generated on Super-8 film – until recently considered to be an amateur format. Jarman began his experiments in Super-8 during the long-protracted process of raising finance for his biographical study of the Italian painter Caravaggio. His early works in Super-8 were transferred to U-matic video for editing purposes before being blown up to 16 or 35mm release prints. These included *The Angelic Conversation* and *Imagining October* and cost a fraction of what a normal 16 or 35mm film would cost. They were also much looser in narrative terms, being more akin to poetry than prose as Jarman himself puts it. Technological advance combined with more generous funding enabled Jarman and producer James Mackay to embark upon more ambitious and visually inventive projects. The promo films they made for the rock band The Smiths – entitled *The Queen is Dead*, featured a range of optical effects including the superimposition of black and white and colour images and in effect was a dry run for the first full-length feature to be shot in Super-8 in this country: *The Last of England*, with its impressive combination of the poetic aesthetics of the Super-8 medium combined with sophisticated video post-production techniques.

The promos made by Jarman for The Smiths created a vogue for Super-8 pop promos with some film-makers going so far as to denigrate other formats to achieve the grainy 'look' associated with Super-8. but this is necessarily to take a rather limited view of a format which is far more flexible and capable of producing a rich, heavily-saturated colour image. So while others were copying the visual style of *The Queen is Dead* and other Jarman promos – grainy black-and-white image, shaky hand-held camera, rapid cutting, Jarman and his collaborators were aiming for a higher-quality image approaching that of 35mm. This development is demonstrated in the back-projection footage shot for The Pet Shop Boys' 1989 tour. The 40-minute film which accompanies eight of the group's numbers was generated primarily on Super-8 and after video post-production, including very convincing blue-screen superimpositions, blown up to a 70mm print for projection. Even more impressive is Jarman's next feature *The Garden*, a follow-up to *The Last of England*, which mixes 16mm and Super-8, and is constructed in the same rather freewheeling fashion with no formal script.

James Mackay, the producer of all of Jarman's work in Super-8, is particularly enthusiastic about the benefits of video and its future potential. In addition to the post-production possibilities opened up by video technology, he also cites the possibilities of electronic technology overcoming the problem of colour fading which still affects film negatives – the only solution at present being the manufacture of preservation masters which, as Mackay explains, is a phenomenally expensive process. He makes his case for an alternative:

> Video does not fade. Digital video can be copied onto punched tape if necessary. It can always be reconstructed. As a process, electronics is always in a state of progression, as we have seen. So all those films will go orange while mine won't. The prints you see the first time round are the same you will see in the cinema. Each new transfer from tape to film will be better than the last. I can only see advantages.[40]

The future looks very exciting indeed as far as the extension of video technologies, and the possibilities this will create for film-makers, are concerned. Video is becoming more accessible all the time, providing more opportunities for people who are interested in film and video making but who are devoid of production finance to acquire some 'hands-on' experience using high-quality equipment.

What is interesting is that there are sources of finance who appear willing to back film-makers experimenting with new technology, Channel 4 and the BFI Production Board being the most notable examples. Alan Fountain, the Commissioning Editor, Independent Film and Video, at Channel 4, welcomes the uses of new technology:

> One of the things we've always been interested in is trying to work with people who don't want to work in a purely conventional way with the image, who want to think more in terms of what I'd call the cinema-aesthetics of film-making: people who want to experiment with different technologies and to try to push the limits of technology forward. I'm all in favour of that.[41]

As we have seen, Channel 4 have been involved in several of the innovative works mentioned in this chapter: *The Bad Sister, Out of Order, The Last of England* and *The Garden*. The Channel have also screened Super-8 and video work by film-makers from all over the world. This is exactly the kind of interest and encouragement that film-makers with ideas and the inclination to experiment with the new technology would appear to need.

Despite these significant developments, Video has some way to go before it begins to replace film. Celluloid remains central to the cinema process. However, things may change with the development of High Definition Television (HDTV) systems which represent a huge leap in terms of image quality and flexibility – precisely the reasons given by film-makers for not using video. The HDTV equipment is rather cumbersome at present but, as with 35mm film and earlier video systems, research and development will inevitably lead to the introduction of more portable and flexible equipment. An early example of a British production using the system is the BBC's drama serial *The Ginger Tree*. However, at the moment the major benefits provided by video tend to be in the field of digital post-production, where manipulation of the image has reached a highly advanced stage of sophistication, extending the range of creative possibilities for film-makers in the process.

# 3 The Financing and Production of British Films: Historical Background

> . . . all facts and personages of great importance in world history occur, as it were, twice . . . the first time as tragedy, the second as farce.
>
> Karl Marx, *The Eighteenth Brumaire of Louis Bonaparte.*

Despite the generally positive evaluation in this book of the vibrancy and commercial astuteness of production companies, sales agents and distributors currently active in British cinema, one overriding fact must not be overlooked. The financial structure of British film-making is inherently unstable and the amount of production finance made available to film-makers in this country in any one year is pitifully meagre given the popularity of film as a medium. Compared to the American film industry, Britain has no industry as such. As Steve Woolley puts it:

> it's like comparing the space programme with people in the Hebrides knitting scarves . . . . We are crofters over here. We have the technology and we have the brain but we don't have the money.[1]

Part of the problem is the greater potential cinema audience in North America. In Britain most of the population prefers to watch films on television or video cassette rather than in the cinema. But they do watch them; there is a tangible demand for film in this country. Part of the problem is that the resources generated from this popularity are not fed back into the domestic production industry to the extent they might be. Neither video nor TV companies at present

50

pay a fair price for the films they exploit commercially. Given the general lack of resources, life for film-makers and companies alike is a constant struggle for survival. One major financial slip-up could spell disaster for even an established and successful film company – Goldcrest being a classic example as I shall explain later. This is the major economic reality which characterises film production in Britain today.

Before examining the structures of finance, production, distribution and marketing which shape the film-making process in Britain, some background detail is necessary to show why things have turned out the way they have, why the British film industry is so small and unstable, and why British film-making is frequently described as being in a permanent state of crisis. Here I shall concentrate on two distinct but historically interlocking issues: the relationship between the British and American film industries and the question of state support for film-making in this country.

The British film industry has never been able to come to terms with the existence of its American counterpart. Hollywood has dominated the British market since the days of silent film due to its size, commercial strength, the quality of its product and the publicity and glamour generated by its star system. In a strictly economic sense, Hollywood always had an advantage. The American market was large enough for films to recoup their costs at home, enabling their producers to sell them abroad at very favourable rates, undercutting their competitors in foreign markets. American products also tended to be far superior in terms of quality.

Britain, on the other hand, was slow off the mark in terms of developing its film industry. Despite the fact that by the end of the First World War demand for film was high, investment in the UK tended to be directed towards exhibition rather than production. As Michael Chanan observes:

> profits were to be made from showing American films, which, as a result of the enforced curtailment of production in Europe during the war, were now a long way in the lead on British screens.[2]

Government intervention in cinema also tended to be in the sphere of exhibition. The question of censorship arose very early on with the emergence of the conception of cinema as a public sphere which was subject to public regulation.[3] While much of the early legislation related to safety matters the British establishment was also interested in the moral well-being of the lower classes who formed the majority of cinema audiences. To avoid any overt form of state censorship, the film industry initiated its own scheme with the setting-up of the British Board of Film Censors (BBFC) in 1912. In theory film-makers were at liberty to make any film they wanted, but in practice a BBFC certificate was required before a film could be distributed and exhibited. In the 1930s there was a shift towards pre-censorship with scripts being sent to the BBFC for approval before production commenced. This was a financial necessity for many producers who could not run the risk of costly re-editing or having their film rejected by the board.

The 1926 BBFC report set out seven general categories which were deemed justifiable grounds for censorship: religious, political, military, social, questions of sex, crime and cruelty.[4] So the list of restriction was extensive, effectively constraining film-makers in terms of their choice and treatment of subject matter. It is interesting to consider that European films such as Murnau's *Nosferatu* and Eisenstein's *Battleship Potemkin* were initially banned by the British censor. However, by the late thirties a general process of relaxation had begun, although progress was often slow. Even such innovative films as Karel Reisz's *Saturday Night and Sunday Morning*, made in 1960, were significantly compromised in order to satisfy the censor.[5] Although Hollywood also employed a code of censorship it can be argued that the Hays Code was generally less stifling than its British counterpart.

During the formative years of the British film industry the Americans had also become actively involved in distributing product in Britain: Vitagraph (subsequently Warners) had registered a British company in 1912, with Fox, in 1916, and Famous Lasky Film Service (Paramount), in 1919, following suit. Direct US involvement in the British film industry served to exacerbate the inequalities originally created by the Americans' structural advantages. The Hollywood subsidiaries in Britain employed tactics such as 'block' and 'blind' booking – the former forcing an exhibitor to accept a package of films in order to obtain the desired major features, while the latter was a similar practice but involving product which was still in the process of being made. Either way such tactics meant that screens were booked up months in advance, making it difficult for British producers to acquire a 'window' for their films in what was after all their own home market. As a result many were forced out of business. By 1926 only four per cent of all the films shown in British cinemas were home-produced while the American share stood at ninety-two per cent.[6]

It was in response to this state of affairs that the British Government finally bowed to pressure and became involved in the film industry in a financial, as opposed to a restrictive or censorial, sense with the implementation in 1927 of minimum quotas for British films. These were initially set at 7.5 per cent for renters and 5 per cent for exhibitors, with both figures planned to rise to 20 per cent by 1938. This act amounted to a mild form of protectionism in a period when free trade was the norm in commercial enterprise. Film-making was officially regarded by the government as such an undertaking and consequently responsibility for administering the quota was given to the Board of Trade. A significant precedent had been set.

The 1927 Act which established the quota had two major consequences. Firstly, the emergence of the 'quota quickie' – cheap, low-quality films produced to satisfy the quota, which was unforeseen, and secondly, implicit in the drafting of the Act and regarded as highly desirable by the Board of Trade, the beginning of a form of vertical integration along the lines of the Hollywood studio system with production, distribution and exhibition brought together in large film-making combines. Simon Hartog argues that an implicit pact was made between the Board of Trade and the Federation of British Industries (FBI, a forerunner of the CBI) that in return for the implementation of the quota the FBI would encourage the creation of at least one major British combine.[7] The emergence of such an organisation was regarded as the only way British films could possibly compete with Hollywood both at home and abroad: to play the Americans at their own game. Arguably this ethos has guided certain producers ever since, giving rise to cycles of expansion – assault on the American market – ultimate failure – heavy losses and retrenchment/bankruptcy: a context of recurring financial crises, infuriatingly similar in character yet seemingly insufficient to force certain aspiring British producers to exercise caution or consider alternative strategies.

The mid-thirties witnessed the first premeditated assault on the American market by British film companies. This followed the unexpected international success of Alexander Korda's *The Private Life of Henry VIII* in 1933, a film which cost £94 000 and earned over £500 000.[8] Korda's film was backed by United Artists, an important factor because this gave him access to American distribution. He subsequently attempted to emulate this success with a series of big-budget historical epics, as did the Gaumont-British Picture Corporation which, along with the Associated British Picture Corporation, had emerged as a major vertically integrated British film company. GB had an American connection through Fox who had a major stake in the company. The outcome for both Korda and Gaumont-British was disastrous: distribution proved to be a major problem and even the prestige British productions tended to lag behind American product in terms of production quality. As a result both suffered heavy losses and a subsequent weakening of their position within the British industry. This inadvertently created the conditions for the rise to power of the most famous British studio boss: J. Arthur Rank.

Throughout the thirties, Rank had been steadily building up his film empire and by 1941 the Rank Organisation was established as the most powerful vertically integrated film combine in Britain owning two of the three major circuits: Gaumont-British and the Odeon cinemas, controlling an assortment of established production companies including GB and Gainsborough and General Film Distributors (GFD), the biggest distribution company in Britain. Rank also had a stake in two major studios: Pinewood, which he had helped to build in 1935, and Denham, which he acquired from Korda. In addition, Rank had a close link with several key independent producers including Michael Powell and Emeric Pressburger, David Lean's company Cineguild, Frank Launder and Sidney Gilliat, Filippo del Guidice's Two Cities Films and Michael Balcon's Ealing studios. At its height, the Rank Organisation was as large and powerful as any of the American majors. By virtue of his substantial stake in British exhibition, Rank was in a position to bargain with the Americans. forcing them into giving him access to their home market. So began the second British attempt to conquer the American market but one, like Korda and Gaumont-British before him, doomed to failure. This time, however, the reasons were rather more complex.

Rank had rather more substantial US connections than his predecessors. He had inherited the Fox connection from Gaumont-British, he had a link with United Artists via Alexander Korda, and a substantial interest in Universal through the General Film Finance Corporation which he established along with other leading industrialists in 1936. Universal was to become Rank's main distribution outlet in North America. The second-largest British film combine, Associated British, had also acquired a major US connection with Warners, buying a 25 per cent stake in the company. These Anglo-

American connections, plus the fact that the three major circuits in Britain were controlled by two companies (the establishment of the duopolistic situation which remains today), began to cause concern at home in that independent British producers had to maintain a favourable relationship with at least one of the 'big two' in order to ensure their films would be exhibited. In addition, the fact that both Rank and Associated British, by virtue of their US connections, had a standing commitment to show Hollywood product on their circuits suggested that such interests might be protected at the expense of the British independents. Such concerns resulted in the drafting of the Palache Report in 1944 entitled 'Tendencies to Monopoly in the Cinematograph Industry', which was to provide the basis for a vigorous campaign in favour of state intervention in the film industry.[9] However, when the report was published, the Board of Trade declined to act on its recommendations. Rank continued with his plans to take the postwar American market by storm when suddenly a major crisis occurred.

In 1947 the Labour Chancellor, Hugh Dalton, imposed a 75 per cent ad valorem duty on imports, including films, and the Americans immediately responded by placing an embargo on Hollywood films exported to Britain. The Government's decision damaged Rank's reputation because, as Robert Murphy points out,[10] the Americans tended to equate Rank's position with that of the British government, whereas in reality the Labour administration were hostile towards staunch Tories like Rank. The US backlash materialised in a fall-off at the American box-office for British films. At home production was increased to fill the gap created by the embargo but the embarrassed British government quickly reached an agreement with the Americans over the repatriation of dollars earned in Britain, resulting in the removal of the duty and the lifting of the embargo. This let in a flood of American films including the pick of the previous year's releases. The rush of unexpected competition caused many British productions to flop, creating a major crisis which, Dickinson and Street argue, nearly killed the British production industry, because in spite of significant increases in production standards in the home industry, American films were still more popular with British audiences. In any case Rank's films began to fail commercially both at home and in the American market. In addition, he lost money on ventures such as children's films, full-length cartoons and experiments in cinema technology (the 'independent frame' process). The net result was a major retrenchment for the

Rank Organisation, a cut-back in production and a rationalisation plan. The bubble had burst and the British film industry was to feel the effects for years to come.

Not surprisingly, other producers suffered badly in the wake of the Dalton duty. Korda, who had attempted a comeback after buying British Lion in 1946, once again found himself in severe financial difficulties. However, in the wake of the Palache (and subsequently the Plant) report, there was substantial pressure on the government to do something to help the industry. The most direct response was the setting up of the National Film Finance Corporation (NFFC) in April 1949. The NFFC was inaugurated by Harold Wilson who was President of the Board of Trade at the time. It was established as a kind of film bank, rather than a direct form of subsidy, with an initial revolving fund of £5 million, which was increased to £6 million the following year. Its brief was to supplement rather than replace private capital and it tended to spread its resources rather thinly over a wide range by providing the 'end money' – the last 30 per cent normally not covered by distribution guarantees of a film's budget.

It is important to stress that the NFFC was not intended as a major government initiative to alter the structure of film financing in Britain. Film was still regarded as primarily a commercial undertaking, unlike broadcasting and the arts in general which had both benefited from public assistance in the form of the British Broadcasting Corporation funded by the license fee and the Arts Council respectively. Neither model was seen as appropriate for the film industry. While the NFFC did help to fund more than 750 films in 35 years, including such notable productions as *The Third Man*, *Saturday Night and Sunday Morning*, *The Servant*, *Gregory's Girl* and *Comrades*, it did end up losing a lot of money. This is not surprising as the NFFC's stake in films tended to be high-risk and the last to be recouped. £3 million was initially lent to Alexander Korda who promptly lost the lot, mainly due to factors beyond his control such as the major decline of the cinema audience in the fifties.

In addition to the NFFC, the postwar Labour Government further attempted to help the film industry by means of the introduction of the Eady Levy, devised by Wilson and Sir Wilfred Eady and based on existing schemes in France and Italy. Julian Petley describes the levy in terms of:

A voluntary arrangement . . . whereby, in return for a reduction in Entertainments Duty, exhibitors agreed to pay a levy on the price of each cinema ticket: this levy was paid into a fund which was subsequently shared out among producers of British films in proportion to their box office earnings.[11]

The scheme was made statutory in 1957 but unlike those in Italy and France, the levy was not used to encourage certain kinds of production. Instead it tended to attract more American companies to set up production units in Britain in order to qualify for Eady money.

The decline of the cinema audience in the fifties enabled the major exhibitors to consolidate their domination as independent cinemas began to close. The gap created in production by the retrenchment of Rank and the second demise of Korda could only be filled by companies strong enough to survive the decline in the cinema's popularity. The only companies which fitted the bill were the American majors. Over a period of twenty years from the early fifties onwards, the American share of British distribution increased from 10 to 60 per cent, while US financing of British films increased substantially, reaching a peak in the late sixties when between 80 and 90 per cent of all British productions were backed by American studios. In a financial sense at least the British film industry had become what it had fought to avoid. As Dickinson and Street put it:

> after 1961 it became increasingly difficult to define any part of the industry as British rather than Anglo-American. There was too much working against the British independent companies: the monopolistic structure of the industry, the lack of alternative sources of finance, the weakness of the NFFC, and the willingness of producers to accept American backing.[12]

Important films were made during this period but ultimately it was the Hollywood executives and their ambassadors who pulled the strings and when the Americans withdrew on a major scale in the early seventies British film production collapsed. The US withdrawal was prompted by several factors including the fact that the majors had overspent and overstocked with films made in Britain at a time when US audiences were turning towards more modest American films like *The Graduate*, *Bonnie and Clyde* and *Easy Rider*. In any case, the American withdrawal left the British bereft of a major part of its production finance.

The financial crisis of the early seventies led to a strong call for an increase in state aid to the film industry, including some demands for nationalisation. These fell on the deaf ears of the 1970 Conservative administration which demonstrated its lack of interest in film-making by allocating the NFFC only £1 million of the £5 million promised by the previous Labour Government. By 1974 the Labour Party had returned to power and Harold Wilson appointed the Terry committee to look at the problems faced by the film industry. The major proposal which came out of this period was the idea to set up a British Film Authority. Like so many other recommendations made by film committees in the past, this plan never got off the ground.

The late seventies witnessed yet another attempt on the part of certain British production companies to take the American market by storm. The chief protagonists this time were Lew Grade's Associated Communications Corporation (ACC), an offshoot of his massive interests in commercial television, and EMI, chaired by Grade's brother Bernard Delfont, which had begun life in the music industry and since diversified, buying the Associated British Picture Corporation in 1969. In 1976 EMI acquired the British Lion Company and with it Barry Spikings and Michael Deeley – two particularly ambitious film producers. At British Lion they had produced Nicolas Roeg's film *The Man Who Fell to Earth*, which was made entirely in America. This gave them the idea to make American films for American audiences, and with the financial muscle of the EMI corporation behind them this is what they set out to do. After a successful start with *The Deer Hunter* Deeley left the company and Spikings embarked on a series of expensive flops including *The Jazz Singer*, *Can't Stop the Music* and *Honky Tonk Freeway* which alone lost £25 million. Spikings' policy, which involved rejecting British script ideas as well as concentrating on American ones, was a total disaster and it was left to the giant Thorn company to take over EMI in order to keep it afloat.

Lew Grade's venture was somewhat similar. He was determined to conquer America on a massive scale and become the biggest film producer in the world but unfortunately his knowledge and expertise did not match his ambition, regardless of his success in television. Grade was essentially a salesman and his technique was to pre-sell films around the world, using the advances or guarantees to make the film. For this strategy to work his reputation had to remain untarnished. He embarked upon a series of big-budget films in the late seventies and into the eighties, using well-known actors and choosing what appeared to be 'safe' subject matter: best-selling novels and remakes of old classics. The results, however, were generally bland

and unpopular with audiences and Grade began to lose money. His last spectacular loss-maker was also his biggest: *Raise the Titanic* which cost $35 million and failed spectacularly at the box-office. Grade was forced to close down AFD, the American distribution company he had set up with Delfont in 1978 and he was subsequently replaced as head of ACC by the board.

At the time of Grade and EMI's collapse, the British political situation had changed again with a new Conservative administration swept to power on a monetarist free-market philosophy mandate. In 1981 it was announced that the NFFC should be funded by Eady, linking its future to a levy which had greatly diminished in significance in line with the general audience decline in Britain. Calls were made by the Association of Independent Producers, the ACTT and other industry bodies to supplement Eady with a levy on blank video cassettes and charging television companies substantially more for the right to broadcast films. These calls were rejected and in 1985 the government announced that it was abolishing the levy and the NFFC with it, replacing the latter with the British Screen Finance Consortium.

One move by the Conservative government which did help to stimulate production, albeit for a short period only, was the introduction of Capital Allowances in 1979.[13] This effectively meant that for tax and depreciation purposes films could be treated in the same way as plant and machinery. The asset resulting from expenditure – the master print of the film – was considered 'plant' and could therefore qualify for 100 per cent Capital Allowance, enabling financiers to write off their entire investment in a film in the first year. This in turn opened up the way for the operation of leaseback deals structured around a seller – the production company, a lessee – a distribution company and a lessor – the investor. The role of the lessee was to guarantee the lessor a return on its investment over a fixed number of years, effectively taking on the risk. This system is a reflection of the traditional method of financing films in this country with a film being pre-sold to a major distributor (usually North American) who will guarantee a major part of the budget, enabling the rest to be raised from commercial or, in the case of the NFFC when it was in existence, subsidised sources.

Unfortunately, the government decided to phase out Capital Allowances between 1984 and 1986. While they were undoubtedly an encouragement to potential investors to put money into film-making and contributed in part to the 'revival' in British production in the early eighties, it is difficult to assess how much of a negative reaction their phasing-out caused. Some producers who acknowledged the incentive provided by Capital Allowances were not too distraught at the removal of this enticement. As Al Clark of Virgin Vision put it in 1985:

> What was good about Capital Allowances was that it encouraged companies or provided extra incentives for companies, that had previously nothing to do with films, to give it a shot . . . . What it created was at least a potential for a much wider range of investment in films . . . . There's no question that Capital Allowances were at least a factor in encouraging us because they are of great value to any company with a large tax bill. But once you've been bitten you tend to stay with it, which is what we've done and will continue to do whether there are Capital Allowances or, as is the case, not.[14]

Despite Clark's assertions it is interesting to note that there have been relatively few newcomers to the production scene since Capital Allowances were phased out, compared to the early eighties which saw the emergence of the likes of Virgin and Palace. It is difficult at this stage to make any definite statements either way, but the removal of any incentive in an industry as starved of resources as British film production is bound to have negative consequences.

In their major study of state intervention in the British film industry, Margaret Dickinson and Sarah Street conclude that the withdrawal of state support would leave the British film industry exposed to market forces. While conceding that the system of state support was never designed to replace or compete with commercial finance it did reverse the trends towards internal monopoly and American control and opened up certain limited opportunities for film-makers:

> Even the modest funds available to the NFFC and the BFI Production Board have enabled a few films to be made which would probably never have been scripted if the initiative had been left entirely with the dominant media groups. The change of policy will therefore almost certainly lead to a decline in all film activity not promoted by major commercial interests. It will also mean that in the future there will be nothing to prevent these commercial interests from choosing to supply their captive market entirely with

imports. Against these odds British film production may finally lose its protracted but tenacious struggle for survival.[15]

This rather grim prophecy has not been borne out by events in the years following the 1985 Films Act. British Screen has contributed to a wider range of product than the NFFC ever did, including more experimental work, despite its more overtly commercial brief. Interesting work continues to be financed by the BFI Production Board and Channel 4. Despite its rhetoric, the government still contributes to film production through British Screen and the BFI, and it continues to support the National Film School, albeit in each case this aid is in partnership with private interests.

Significant state support would be most welcome but, given the current political and economic climate, it is better to accept the realities and direct one's energies into exploring ways of making 'free enterprise' work in favour of innovative film-making. This requires the industry to be extremely astute in preserving existing markets and in developing new ones. The bulk of British production continues to be substantially financed by way of North American pre-sales and distribution guarantees but this need not always involve the degree or order of compromise implied in Dickinson and Street's conclusion. It is significant that quintessentially 'British' films such as *A Room With a View* have found an audience in the States in recent years. British producers apparently seem to be heeding the lessons of the past – not attempting to beat the Americans at a game which they effectively invented and have controlled ever since. However, there is still the problem of over-reliance on American finance. The slump in production suffered by the British industry in the summer of 1989 was the direct result of a drop in American investment with even successful British producers finding it difficult to secure North American funding.

On the other hand, there would appear to be increasing opportunities for the development of strong ties between British producers and their European counterparts. The need to develop such links in the face of the Anglo-American problems outlined above was recently underlined by Simon Relph, the head of British Screen Finance, in an article in *Screen International*.[16] There have been several recent British productions which have European backing, including all of Peter Greenaway's films from *A Zed & Two Noughts* onwards, Derek Jarman's *The Last of England*, Ken McMullen's *Zina*, David Hare's *Paris by Night*, Terence Davies' *Distant Voices, Still Lives* and

Andi Engel's *Melancholia*. In addition, Channel 4 have invested in a range of European co-productions including foreign-language films. European co-productions tend to be more formally innovative given the substantial interest in film as art in countries such as West Germany, Italy, and France. This is certainly true of the 'British' projects which have attracted European investment. The open market of 1992 may provide even greater opportunities for British film-makers working within a European, rather than a transatlantic context, encouraging the development of a greater variety of projects and aesthetic approaches to cinema.

# 4 British Feature Film Production

If there is one point on which most 'independent' film-makers in Britain tend to agree unanimously, it is that raising the money to make a film is the most difficult stage of the entire process. This seems to hold true regardless of topic, scale or size of budget. If film-making can be seen as a process structured by constraints, then top of the list of constraints must be finance, or more precisely the lack of it. It is interesting here to consider the description 'independent' as it is applied to film-making activities in this country. The term tends to be used rather vaguely and ambiguously in the literature dealing with British cinema. On one hand it is applied to small-scale non-commercial film-making carried out in the context of regional workshops. More frequently it is used to describe the work of those producers and directors who do not have access to a regular source of finance; who are not under contract to a major studio. This effectively extends the description 'independent' to cover practically all indigenous film-making in this country. As one film journalist recently commented: 'The only independence British film-makers have regularly enjoyed is independence of a regular source of funds.'[1]

Several reasons have been suggested for the continuation of this rather depressing state of affairs: the high risks involved in film financing coupled with the weakness of the home exhibition market, the refusal of successive governments to take cinema as an institution seriously, to recognise its cultural significance and support it with public money; and the parasitic relationship between cinema and the small screen media: television and video. These media have traditionally relied on film-makers to supply them with popular product while refusing to recognise that importance by paying competitive rates for that product. This has led to calls on the government by the Association of Independent Producers (AIP) to introduce a levy on blank video tapes and to force the television companies to pay rates for feature films which reflect their value and popularity within the schedules. These are all important issues and are worth examining closely. However, the major concern of this chapter is the identification and examination of the handful of relatively stable sources of film finance which exist for independent film-makers in this country. I shall also compare the fortunes of these relatively successful companies and others which have encountered severe financial problems in recent years, in the attempt to identify reasons why some companies have failed while others have been more successful in their operations. This will hopefully enable me to make some tentative statements regarding the structuring of constraints affecting independent film-makers in terms of the kinds of projects which receive funding, what conditions are attached to funding agreements and what bearing these processes have on cinematic creativity in general.

One preliminary point which should be made when considering the question of film production in Britain is that the annual feature-film output of this country is very small. In 1988 fifty-six feature films were made, instigated or financed in Britain. Not all of these will formally be recognised as British films, however, because American producers still favour UK studios such as Pinewood and Elstree as a production base. Of the fifty-six, fourteen were fully funded by American sources. Examples of such features include *Indiana Jones and the Last Crusade* and *Batman*. The figure of fifty-six films produced is actually the largest number for ten years although it is not spectacular in that the average for the past five years has been around fifty-one features a year.[2] So the industry we are dealing with is a relatively small one.

In May 1987, *Screen International*, the major trade paper of the British Film Industry, ran a series of articles on film finance. The current situation in the UK was covered by Simon Perry, a leading independent producer responsible for such films as *Another Time, Another Place, Loose Connections, Nineteen Eighty Four, Nanou, Hotel Du Paradis* and *White Mischief*. Perry writes:

> The main issue for independent producers in 1987 is the lack of companies interested in financing independent feature film production in the UK.[3]

This was in spite of the hard work done by producers in recent years: the nurturing and development of projects and the close creative involvement at every stage in the process. It was this kind of effort which, in Perry's opinion, ensured the critical and commercial success of films like *Chariots of Fire, Company of Wolves* and *My Beautiful Laundrette* among others. As he writes:

Independent producers are the cornerstone of the new industry, yet many of them, with good projects, cannot raise finance.[4]

In the 1982 AIP handbook thirty companies were listed as worth approaching for potential finance. By 1987 the situation was rather less favourable with only a handful of realistic possibilities. At the top of Perry's meagre list were British Screen, Channel 4, and Zenith. A further company which Perry declines to mention but which should be considered on a par with the others is Handmade Films. Together these companies comprised the financial backbone of indigenous British cinema in 1987, and by and large continue to do so, with the addition of a handful of ITV companies making tentative forays into the world of feature films. Their collective importance, particularly in the light of the recent decline of Goldcrest, and less significantly Virgin Vision, cannot be overestimated.

## THE FUNDING PROCESS

Basically there are two types of film finance: the presale to a distributor and/or broadcaster and the equity investment. Films can be wholly financed by either method or, and this is the most common procedure, by a combination of both. A presale takes the form of either a cash advance against specified distribution rights in the finished film or a distribution guarantee which can be discounted by a bank which provides funds, in the form of a loan, to the film-maker. A broadcaster participates in a similar fashion: either advancing cash against broadcasting rights or providing a licensing agreement for broadcasting rights which can be discounted. The equity investor on the other hand is entitled to recover the investment plus interest, and to participate in the net profits of the film, usually in direct proportion to the scale of the original investment. The four companies listed above represented practically the only realistic sources of equity finance available to independent film-makers in Britain in the late eighties.

In *Raising Production Finance*, an information pack aimed at independent producers and published by the AIP in 1986, the following examples of what are described as 'typical co-financing structures for a low budget British film', are set out:[5] (The average low-budget British production at that time cost in the region of one to two million pounds.)

|     |                                                              | %   |
| --- | ------------------------------------------------------------ | --- |
| (1) | Equity Investor A:                                           | 30  |
|     | Equity Investor B:                                           | 20  |
|     | Presale to UK TV:                                            | 15  |
|     | Presale to all foreign (excl. US, France and Germany)        | 35  |
|     |                                                              | 100 |

Here the equity investors A and B recoup from revenues accrued in the USA, France and Germany (all media) and UK theatrical and video.

|     |                                             | %   |
| --- | ------------------------------------------- | --- |
| (2) | Equity investment and right to sell foreign: | 50  |
|     | Presale US rights:                          | 30  |
|     | Presale to UK TV:                           | 20  |
|     |                                             | 100 |

In this case the equity investor recoups investment from all foreign rights, excluding US distribution revenue.

|     |                        | %   |
| --- | ---------------------- | --- |
| (3) | Presale all UK rights: | 20  |
|     | Presale all US rights: | 50  |
|     | Equity investor:       | 30  |
|     |                        | 100 |

Here the equity investor recoups from all foreign sales, excluding US and UK territories.

Several issues are raised by the above examples. The importance of the North American market, even in the case of low-budget British features, is obvious. Medium- and high-budget films rely even more on this source of finance: for example, Terry Gilliam's *Brazil*, budgeted at £9 million, was financed via presales to Universal and Twentieth-Century Fox for the North American and the rest of the world distribution rights respectively. Similarly, John Boorman's production *Hope and Glory* was backed by Columbia and Nelson Entertainment to the tune of $7 million.

The importance of the presale to UK television is also indicated with 15 per cent of example (1)'s budget and 20 per cent of example (2)'s attributable to this source. Basically UK television means Channel 4 in these examples. The channel pays in the region of £250 000 for the broadcasting rights to a British feature: a significant and often vital contribution to a low-budget production (although the price is still very cheap for one-and-a-half to two hours of quality drama). Not only does this represent an acknowledgement on the part of British television of the value of feature films in terms of ratings figures, it also marks the entrance of television into the field of feature film production: paying up front before the film is made, rather than after the event.

The overall importance of the presale *vis-à-vis* equity finance is worth considering in depth. This importance is a reflection of the lack of equity finance in this country on one hand, and the size (and therefore importance) of respective markets on the other. Although in example (1) above, the equity investors will be entitled to recoup from North American revenues, the general preference in the industry is to presell projects to an American distributor for a sizeable percentage of the total budget. This reduces the risk factor for potential equity investors and makes such investments easier to secure. This is a reflection again of the size and importance in revenue terms of the US market. As Margaret Matheson, the former Director of Productions at Zenith, explains:

> In theory you could raise one hundred per cent of the money in the UK and earn seventy per cent of it back from outside the UK . . . but in practice you are more likely to raise it in the market where the money is more likely to be earned back . . . . In an ideal world we would like to raise sixty per cent of a budget on a US distribution deal and put up the balance of forty per cent ourselves for the rest of the world.[6]

Ancillary markets – video and television – are also very important in terms of securing rights and once again the significance of the American market looms large. As Al Clark, former head of production at Virgin Vision, a distribution and, until recently, production company, explains, video and television rights are so important now that in North America a theatrical release is virtually considered to be an ancillary market:

> it exists to create enough attention for a film for its video release to be profitable if the theatrical release is not, in itself . . . . Generally when an American Independent company does its calculations it calculates at best break-even on theatrical with all profits coming from video and television.[7]

Gareth Jones, the Head of Business Affairs at Handmade Films, explains the importance of the ancillaries with respect to the European markets:

> it used to be that video was sold separately from video and television rights. Now companies are wanting all of it and the way this has moved is quite unusual in that video companies, for instance in Scandinavia and Germany, have actually grown to the extent that they've actually moved into theatrical distribution . . . . What they want out of it is video and TV sales, but they will put it out in a decent theatrical exhibition because that showcases the movie for the secondary, but very lucrative, rights.[8]

However, the video boom has not benefited the British production sector as much as some would have hoped. Simon Relph of British Screen argues that the problem with video deals is that they were originally set up along the lines of book publishing with the producer earning a royalty (20–25 per cent) on *wholesale* prices. At the time no one could predict how well the video companies would fare. But, as Relph points out, video distributors' retail income in 1987 was more than £200 million: 'If only ten per cent of that had found its way back into UK production that would have been incredibly significant.'[9] Relph is particularly annoyed that he has to keep running to the government for handouts when there is enough revenue being earned in the various media which depend on film product to support a healthy production programme in this country.

Basically the presale/equity split signifies the ownership of the film, or at least the rights relating to where and how it can be sold to the public and the right to recoup from these sales. Ownership also implies control, not only at the level of distribution and marketing but also at the production and even pre-production stage. Distribution companies and equity investors will only back projects they consider to be viable propositions. This involves notions of commercial viability as every distributor and every equity investor (with the possible exception of the BFI Production Board) must be commercially oriented to survive in what is a highly competitive market situation. And it is probably fair to argue that the larger the company, the more conservative its investment decisions tend to be. Part of the reason for this is that film-making is a high-risk business and the larger the budgets involved the greater the risk. Consequently risk tends to be minimised by companies 'playing safe' with subject matter; by using tried and tested formulas, employing 'name' directors and stars. In other words, American distributors will only pre-buy rights to British films if they are reasonably confident that these films will make money in the American market. This strategy encourages repetition of successful formulas and works against experimentation and innovation. Formulas can vary from the medium- to large-budget 'prestige' film like *The Killing Fields*, *Gandhi* and *A Passage to India*, popular with American audiences in the first half of the eighties, to the subsequent vogue for smaller-scale, more parochial (but still able to attract an international audience) productions like *My Beautiful Laundrette*, *A Letter to Brezhnev* and *A Room With a View*. In the 1988 *Screen International* survey of British production referred to above, of the fifty-six films produced in Britain that year, thirty-one were in the low-budget category (up to £2 million), seventeen were medium-budget (£2–5 million), and eight were classified as big-budget (over £5 million).

But such a situation may change in the near future. There may be a series of low-budget failures and the money might dry up as a consequence. Sarah Radclyffe of Working Title, the company responsible for *My Beautiful Laundrette*, *Personal Services*, *Sammy and Rosie Get Laid*, *Wish You Were Here* and *A World Apart* has put it this way:

> If you have a year when all the films, or 50 per cent of the films, you presell to America turn out to be things which should have been made for television, the following year when companies like ourselves go back to America to try and pre-sell, we are going to get that much less . . . . We are in distinct danger of what happened to the Australian film industry. Australian films were really 'in' in the States five or six years ago, they did really well. Then they had a couple of years producing films which weren't up to standard, not many came through as really working and the

price of Australian films just plummeted. We've got to be careful that doesn't happen here.[10]

In a sense, the heart of the problem is the geographical and cultural divide which separates financial source from production context. This leaves independent film-makers in this country at the mercy of the whims and short-term decision-making of American executives who have the power to decide whether or not British films are worth investing in, in that year (as indeed seems to have been the case in 1988 with ten UK/US co-productions as opposed to twenty in 1987) or, even when investments have been made, to pull the plug at any moment. An example of the kind of situation that can arise is the Mike Radford/Simon Perry production *White Mischief*, which was in danger of folding when Canadian distributors and cinema-owners Cineplex Odeon pulled out along with half of the film's $7 million budget. It was fortunate that Columbia and Nelson Entertainment were on hand to bail the production out. Columbia also rescued Bill Forsyth's film *Housekeeping* which Cannon had abandoned after the proposed star Diane Keaton decided at the last minute she didn't want to do the film. Cannon were only interested in the production as a vehicle for Keaton, not as the latest project of one of Britain's most original and successful film-makers.

The implications of these observations serve to place a heavy burden of responsibility on British sources of finance, in particular equity investors, who are in a position closer to the independent film-maker than the American distributor and may be prepared to trust the judgement of producers and take risks on inexperienced film-makers with innovative ideas. British equity financiers share a common cultural context with the film-makers they are, in a sense, employing and this may encourage them to make rather bolder investment decisions than their American counterparts. However, it must be remembered that the four equity participants mentioned all operate within a commercial context (even Channel 4, which is not in the same direct relation to box-office receipts as the others but which must continue to satisfy its shareholders by maintaining reasonable ratings figures) and none can afford to take reckless decisions by abandoning commercial considerations altogether.

The preceding comments relate to the orthodox and highly predominant methods of financing films in this country. There are however, occasional exceptions to the rule, circumstances where the cultural importance of the project overrides its commercial potential. In such rare circumstances financial packages may be cobbled together from a multitude of sources, including private individuals with a desire to see the particular project realised. One example from the past ten years is Ron Peck and Paul Hallam's film *Nighthawks*, a chronicle of the London gay scene in the late seventies. The project began under the auspices of Four Corners Films, a London-based workshop and after failure to secure finance from the BFI and the NFFC the producers advertised for private sponsorship. A wide range of individuals assisted the project, including film-makers such as John Schlesinger, Don Boyd, Lindsay Anderson and Tony Garnett plus some wealthy members of the rock industry. These investments amounted to around half of the final £60 000 budget, enabling the rest of the money to be raised from more conventional sources including the German television company ZDF. Such a funding process is probably less likely to occur today in that Channel 4 and/or the BFI Production Board, which now has a greater commitment to narrative feature films, most likely would have been interested in the project.

Before taking a closer look at the major companies currently involved in the funding of feature films in Britain, it is worth considering briefly the issues of development finance and budgeting a production. Development is the money which gets any project off the ground in the first place, and includes expenses such as commissioning a writer to produce a screenplay, securing an option on a book or a play and legal fees incurred at this stage. As Bancroft and Davies have noted, only a tiny proportion of screenplays that are developed each year are actually produced as films. Development finance, therefore, is regarded as a particularly high-risk investment and is consequently the hardest money to raise.[11]

The four major British equity investors are also important sources of development finance. Zenith (who have 'a substantial development fund', according to Margaret Matheson), Channel 4 and Handmade all provide in-house development – although Gareth Jones of Handmade stresses that the company did not formally put money into developing projects until quite recently. British Screen, on the other hand, is linked to the National Film Development Fund (NFDF) which has annual resources of £500 000 a year, provided by the government. To qualify for an NFDF loan – maximum £24 000 – a project must satisfy the conditions of eligibility set out in the 1985 Films Act. For a film to qualify as British:

1. It should be made by a British producer.
2. If a studio is used it should be in the UK or Commonwealth or the Republic of Ireland.
3. A substantial proportion (approximately 75 per cent) of total labour costs should be paid to British persons employed on the film.

Even if these requirements are satisfied the film will not qualify if 20 per cent of the total playing-time is shot outside the UK, unless

a) All the preparatory work was carried out in the UK.
b) The normal lab processing incidental to the making of the film was carried out in the UK.
c) At least 50 per cent in terms of the value of the technical equipment used was provided from sources in the UK.[12]

Other sources of development finance in the British industry include the BFI Production Board, which has resources to develop and produce two or three full-length features a year on a non-commercial basis, TV offshoots Granada International and Euston Films (wholly owned by Thames Television), who have recently moved into feature film-making, and established production companies like Palace Productions who have developed projects like Neil Jordan's *Mona Lisa* which was produced by Palace with finance from Handmade Films. Steve Woolley of Palace has explained his company's position in the following way:

> Palace doesn't have resources to put up their own money to fund films. We are not a company that has millions of pounds tucked away somewhere that we can invest in movies. We are primarily a distribution company that grew from being initially a video company. Due to a string of successful theatrical releases and video releases we built up a good cash flow and were able to develop films a little bit . . . . Palace don't have a development fund as such. We have money from the bank which we use across the board – acquisitions, development. We are an amorphous kind of company . . . so what we do, if we want to develop something, we find it from our own resources and sometimes that means going into partnership with somebody . . . . But if we really believe in it we'll develop it ourselves.[13]

Working Title are another production house (as opposed to equity financier) who have their own development fund and, as Graham Bradstreet of WT explains, their own credit line negotiated with a Dutch merchant bank.[14] This gives the company at least some security, enabling them to maintain a suitable flow of projects. They are also determined to keep costs down whenever possible, as Sarah Radclyffe explains:

We don't waste money on development. In America development is such a big industry, there are so many people employed to develop films whose salaries have to come out of some-where – they usually get tacked onto budgets . . . '.[15]

Development may not automatically lead to production but the in-house development policies carried out at Zenith, Channel 4 and Handmade do produce much higher take-up rates than the NFDF funded projects, for example, which according to recent figures have at present a take-up rate of one in eight projects going into produc-tion. (This itself represents an improvement from one in seventeen in 1980.)[16] David Rose, the Chief Commissioning Editor for Fiction at Channel 4, and his assistant Karin Bamborough, receive forty scripts and treatments a week. Approximately half of these are selected for development each year and all of these would be expected to go into production, with producers seeking co-finance from other sources if necessary. Zenith and Handmade operate under similar conditions: expecting to take most, if not all, of the projects they have developed into production.

In 1989 a new potential source of development finance for British film-makers appeared in the shape of the European Script Fund. The Fund, presided over by Secretary General Renée Goddard, has £1.3 million to spend in its first year. Applicants must be nationals of EC member states and the maximum which can be granted to any individual writer or director/writer team is approximately £24 500.

The issue of realistic budgeting is understood by all the major players in the finance game. The size of any film's budget should be directly related to its estimated market value (i.e. estimated sales revenue). As Alan Stanbrook has pointed out, it is suicidal to do the opposite: that is, make a film for whatever it costs and then try to sell it to as many people as possible.[17] Basically what it boils down to is judging the commercial potential of a particular project; what its market value would appear to be and attempting to make it at a budgetary level which reflects its worth, within an overall strategy which attempts to keep costs down as much as possible. As Sarah Radclyffe states:

> Our above-the-lines (what goes to director, producer, writer and stars) are always kept to the absolute minimum . . . very much in ratio to what everyone else is getting.[18]

Patrick Cassavetti, the producer of *Brazil*, *Mona Lisa* and *Paris By Night*, points out that the third of these films, written and directed by David Hare, was initially judged to be budgeted at a level which was more than the film was worth in market terms so the project was adjusted accordingly.

Stanbrook points out that film budgets fall into three parts:

1. Above-the-line items: fixed costs such as the director, producer and leading players' fees.
2. Below-the-line items: variable costs such as studio, labour, transport, hotels, etc.
3. Indirect costs: the financial and legal fees incurred.

In America the above-the-line costs normally amount to 50 per cent of the total budget while the comparative figure for a British production is 15–20 per cent. A final important item is the involvement of a 'completion guarantor' in the project. The completion guarantor is effectively an insurance policy: guaranteeing, for a premium, the funds to complete a film should the production go over budget. Some financiers will only commit themselves to a project once a completion guarantee has been secured.

The importance then of the key decision-makers at British Screen, Channel 4, Zenith and Handmade, in terms of choosing which projects to develop and produce and which to reject, is considerable. Between them they largely determine what British cinema is from one year to the next. This has important implications for the creativity of writers, directors and producers and can be seen in terms of a set of constraints. Once a financial commitment is made, a complex process of consultation and the monitoring of production in creative and financial terms is set in motion. In this way the company involved has direct access to the decision-making process at every stage, subtly affecting the final outcome. Over and above these direct and tangible forms of intervention, the prevailing relationships which characterise British film-making also serve to affect the creativity of those engaged in the generation of new ideas prior to the raising of production finance. Film-makers and scriptwriters may internalise notions of what a viable idea for a film may be by constructing these notions in line with existing funding practices as carried out by these companies at present under discussion. This process may not be fully conscious but it serves to preserve a continuity in terms of subject matter and style, and is, I would wish to argue, a fundamental element of the structuring of creativity in the film-making process.

This is very close to Williams's discussion of the organisation of market processes in the field of cultural production and in particular, the shift from producer-originated work to market-originated work. He writes:

> In sophisticated market planning, a certain type of work can be selected at so early a stage, on the basis of a few examples or of some calculated or projected demand, that production, from that stage, no longer originates with the primary producer but is commissioned from him . . . . On the other hand, the contrast between market-originated and producer-originated cannot be made absolute, once market conditions have been generalized. For producers often internalize known or possible market relationships, and this is a very complex process indeed, ranging from obvious production for the market which is still the work the producer 'always wanted to do', through all the possible compromises between the market demand and the producer's intention, to those cases in which the practical determinations of the market are acknowledged but the original work is still substantially done.[19]

This comes very close to a description of the processes involved in British cinema. All of the companies I have mentioned, with the exception of British Screen, often initiate ideas by commissioning a screenplay from a writer. Also, film-makers will not normally approach a particular company with an idea which is radically different to the kind of project the company have, by virtue of their track-record, shown themselves to be interested in. This is not to suggest that these companies impose rigid 'house styles' upon film-makers they fund in the way certain Hollywood studios tended to do – for example Warner Brothers in the 1930s. However, there are lines of similarity which can be traced through different companies' outputs. Furthermore, in an age of increased co-financing it is perhaps more appropriate to talk about an overall British film-making style. While the questions of aesthetics this suggestion raises will not be tackled in this chapter, I shall attempt to identify the different ways financiers like Channel 4, British Screen, Zenith, Handmade, the BFI Production Board and one or two production houses like Palace and Working Title impinge upon the creative process by looking at the working practices of each and the rationale behind their investment decisions.

## CHANNEL 4

Undoubtedly the major player in the game of financing indigenous British production in the eighties has been Channel 4. In the first six years since commissioning operations began, the channel contributed to over 120 films. In 1987 David Rose had a budget of £9.5 million to invest in film production – a figure representing between six and seven per cent of the channel's total programme money. This high priority strategy, as has already been suggested, amounts to an acknowledgement by a British television company that feature films are a highly significant and popular form of programming and should be paid for accordingly.

David Rose, in his capacity as Chief Commissioning Editor for Fiction, was able to make three different types of investment in feature films which will enjoy at least some form of theatrical release. (The Channel has also produced films specifically for television like Stephen Frears' *Walter* and most of the 'First Love' series made for Channel 4 by David Puttnam's Enigma company.) Firstly, Channel 4 can finance a film fully. Examples include *My Beautiful Laundrette*, *The Good Father* and *Ping Pong*. This gives the company sole rights and the option of distributing the film through Film Four International, their sales arm. However, as film-making has become more expensive and financial deals more complex, this type of total involvement in a cinema film is no longer a realistic proposition.

In the second instance, Channel 4 have co-produced feature films with other companies. For example, Zenith approached Rose with David Leland's project *Wish You Were Here*. The script had been developed by Zenith and the production budgeted around £1 million. Rose proposed that Channel 4 supply 75 per cent of the budget with Zenith coming up with the rest. However, the 75 per cent included the British television licence which, as has already been pointed out, amounts to around £250 000. This meant that Channel 4's equity stake in *Wish You Were Here* was £500 000 to Zenith's £250 000, a ratio of two to one rather than three to one. In terms of recoupment this is very favourable to Zenith who only provided one-quarter of the budget. In this way Channel 4 is able to use its special position within the industry to the benefit of its partners. This type of involvement is also perhaps the most common, given the current state of British production. It is also significant that Channel 4 has been involved in almost all of British Screen's projects since that company began operations in 1986.

A third option at the channel's disposal is the provision of a television licence only, plus perhaps a little extra money when the rest of the budget is in place. This may amount to only a small percentage of the budget but given the general lack of resources, such small investments can be a vitally important link in the financial chain. A recent example of such a limited involvement is *Sammy and Rosie Get Laid*, written by Hanif Kureishi and directed by Stephen Frears. Purchasing the television rights to a film basically means that Channel 4 will screen the film perhaps three times over seven to ten years. The first screening should ideally be at the point when the film appears to be running out of steam at the box office. But, as Rose points out, this has to be negotiated in practice. Then there is the Cinematograph Exhibitors Association (CEA) to confront and they operate a policy of barring films from being broadcast for three years. However, Channel 4 negotiated a deal with the CEA allowing any film costing less than £1.25 million to be exempted from the statutory three-year holdback. This shift in policy has obviously been an important factor in attracting more television companies to become involved in film production. At present the average holdback for features which escape the CEA's statutory requirements is between twelve and eighteen months. The situation was opened up even further in September 1988 when it was announced that films costing under £4 million could now be televised at any time after their theatrical release and that this figure would rise with inflation or £300 000 a year, whichever was lower. This move is highly beneficial to Channel 4 and other television companies who have become more and more involved in putting money 'up front' for film production.

As far as the selection of projects goes, David Rose claims that he is interested particularly in original screenplays because he feels audiences will recognise originality and respond to it.

I tend to resist adaptations of novels, but then again there are exceptions. I think a recent exception would be *A Month in the Country* which was written by J. L. Carr and is a very slight novel which is one of the reasons it worked . . . . It was adapted by Simon Gray and Pat O'Connor has made a very distinguished film . . . . But my feeling is that with almost any adaptation the writer starts with a burden really. It was written as a novel and if it's a good novel then it's not a screenplay.[20]

This is an important point given the strong literary bias and the frequency of adaptation in British cinema throughout its history.

Rose is also interested in originality in a wider sense:

If you pick up a script and you immediately feel you have been there before; that it's derivative, then I would rather find something else.[21]

The ability of the script to engage the reader is a further key consideration:

I want a script where I'm compelled to turn the page and it holds me. That first reading is absolutely crucial. If it doesn't engage me, I'm thinking, however brilliantly it's cast or directed or whatever, there's something wrong here.[22]

This attitude may go some way towards accounting for why so many Channel 4 films have a literary feel, regardless of whether they are adaptations or not. If the written word on the page is so important to Rose this does seem to concede ground to those critics who claim that Film on Four projects are merely glorified television dramas. TV drama has traditionally relied on strong scripts rather than visual technique and as Rose's background is in television drama his preferences are not altogether surprising.

Once a financial commitment has been made, Rose and his colleagues keep very close tabs on the production. The company has approval of all the key appointments: director, line producer, lighting cameraman, editor, designer, composer and leading players. In addition, the accountant working on the film has to be approved and while Rose and Karin Bamborough monitor the creative aspects of the production – viewing the rushes, particularly the first few days' work, visiting the shoot once or twice – cost accountant Therese

Pickard keeps an eye on the daily cost returns. Any alterations to the schedule have to be approved by Pickard as the schedule represents a meticulously prepared breakdown of the production budget and any changes are bound to alter costs.

Once shooting is completed Rose views the rough cuts and the fine cut and makes comments and observations which he would expect the film-maker to listen to and discuss with him. Although the channel do not have the right to determine the final cut – that is the director's privilege – it does have approval of the final sound mix, something Rose considers to be 'absolutely crucial'. Finally the prints are graded to both Rose and the film-maker's satisfaction and a low-contrast print is delivered to Channel 4 for future broadcasting. The input and influence of Rose and his team is very substantial at every stage of the process.

Although the company is protected from the harsh realities of commercial film-making – they invest in films to provide the channel with high-quality drama programming, not to make money – their trading performance has improved markedly since they began in 1982. Although at present only a handful of films backed by Channel 4 are into profit, the status of Film Four International is growing in the international marketplace. As Rose comments:

Five years ago at Cannes no one knew who Film Four International were. Now we have a high profile and therefore people are more attracted to Bill Stephens [FFI's sales manager for overseas sales outside America] when he's promoting our films . . . . There is hardly a territory left which is not covered.[23]

As Georgina Henry pointed out in an article on Film Four International published in *Producer* magazine, in the year to March 1987, the sales department at Channel 4, which was about to be merged with the acquisitions department with Colin Leventhal at the head, earned £5 million in sales revenue. When one considers that £4 million was spent that year on acquiring the television broadcasting rights for Film on Four and David Rose's annual budget currently standing at around £9 million, then one can see that the Channel's film budget has been effectively balanced for the first time.[23] The bulk of the £5 million sales figure was made up of the deals struck with distributors for the rights to *Wish You Were Here*, *A Month in the Country* and *Rita, Sue and Bob Too*. Business had been particu-

larly good in North America where FFI are very ably represented by
Joy Pereths.[24]

What all this amounts to is a realisation of the fact that as things
presently stand, Channel 4 is the major bulwark of the low-budget
British film industry, having a stake in roughly half of all the feature
films produced in Britain in any one year. The company have taken
on a responsibility for ensuring the ongoing health of independent
film-making in this country. Rose is very much aware of the
company's position in this context:

> I think it would be irresponsible if our board, who have been
> extremely supportive, putting quite large sums of money into Film
> on Four, were to, perhaps in the next couple of years, think that
> drama should be doing something different . . . . So in a way I
> think we have brought upon ourselves a responsibility. But we
> didn't set out to.[25]

Nevertheless that responsibility is considerable by virtue of the
amount of money they have been prepared to invest in film-making
activities. On top of David Rose's budget the Channel have an annual
subvention to the BFI Production Board of £500 000. In return they
automatically get the UK TV licence on all BFI product. Channel 4
are a major shareholder of British Screen, providing the consortium
with £300 000 a year. The company also play a major role in the
financing of independent British feature films through a department
other than David Rose's. This is the 'Independent Film and Video'
department which is run by commissioning editor Alan Fountain,
assisted by Rod Stoneman and Caroline Spry. Fountain's brief covers
three main areas: the 'Eleventh Hour' slot which is a window for both
British and foreign experimental and non-commercial product, the
access documentary slot 'People to People' and also the Channel's
commitment to the franchised film and video workshops around the
country. In 1988 Channel 4 invested £1.5–2 million in fourteen
workshops.[26] Fountain describes his particular role within the Channel in the following way:

> In some ways my job initially was defined as much around a
> production sector as it was around a particular area of television.
> What that came down to . . . was crystallised around certain slots.
> One was the 'Eleventh Hour', which had, and still has, a brief for
> complementing to some extent, what isn't on the rest of Channel 4

or even on the rest of British Television . . . in terms of experimental work, in terms of work from outside the UK, both
documentary and fiction, political documentaries which don't
necessarily observe the conventional codes of balance and so
forth . . . . So it's a very eclectic spot, really. What we have taken
for it is often defined by the fact that we think it's worth doing, but
no one else will take it for whatever reason.[27]

The 'Eleventh Hour' budget in 1988 stood at around £2–2.5 million
and this went towards the occasional commissioned piece of work,
purchasing of completed programmes and presales, enabling features, shorts and documentaries to get made in the first place.
Fountain stresses that the amount he is able to put up as a presale is
less than that offered by David Rose's department, at between
£10 000 and £50 000 per project.

Fountain is able to finance feature films through the 'Eleventh
Hour' budget and the franchised workshops. As he explains:

Some of the workshops have developed to do fiction and more and
more of them want to. What we've tended to do there is to allocate
them their basic money, which is normally on a sort of rolling
contract, or a fixed contract over three to five years. Sometimes,
where they are doing a more expensive production . . . whether it's
'Frontroom' or 'Amber' or 'Black Audio' or whoever. What we've
tended to do is boost their budget up against a particular production which is normally fiction . . . . We've also contributed to, or
directly commissioned, other fictions from outside the workshops.
Examples are *Zina*, *Ghost Dance*, *Empire State*, *Business as
Usual* – a number like that. Not as much as we'd really like to, but
a number of that sort.[28]

Other notable features in which Fountain's department have been
involved, include workshop productions like *Acceptable Levels*, *The
Love Child* and *Out Of Order*, and independent features such as
*Ascendency* (Edward Bennett), *Burning an Illusion* (Melenik Sha-
bazz), the Terence Davis trilogy, *The Gold Diggers* (Sally Potter) and
*The Last of England* (Derek Jarman).

With regard to the differences between Fountain's and David Rose's
departments, apart from the obvious difference in the size of each
department's annual budget, Fountain comments:

Generally, I would say that we tend to be looking for projects which aren't straightforwardly conventional in formal terms – which are more risky aesthetically and relate to different sorts of traditions. We tend to support some film-makers who probably work in a much more European tradition, whereas David has taken a bit of a distance from that sort of tradition. I think the other factor that comes in is that we've taken risks on people who haven't necessarily shown they can do it already. David's tended to go with people who are known more, they've had more experience and are tending to work in, generally speaking, a more conventional area. Generally there's a budget difference – *Empire State* was as expensive as a lot of the projects David's doing but it's one of these ones which started out as being much lower-budget and then as the thing was talked about and developed the budget went up and up.[29]

Ron Peck's film is unique in that it was eventually backed by money from both Fountain's and Rose's departments: the latter responding to a plea from the Channel's head at the time, Jeremy Isaacs, who was keen for the film to be made. Fountain is also interested in film-makers who utilise new technology or existing technology in innovative ways. Productions like Derek Jarman's *The Last of England*, shot on Super-8, and *Out of Order*, the first British feature intended for the cinema shot on video, testify to this.

As far as the production process is concerned, Fountain and his assistants will, if the Channel is developing a particular project, work closely with the film-maker at this stage of the process. During production someone will pay a visit to the shoot, or be on hand if any problems arise. Rushes and assemblies are viewed whenever possible but the overall supervisory role is less intense than with David Rose's department, for example. As Fountain explains:

It depends on different projects; how it's going, what the film-makers want . . . . For instance on *Zina* I saw a lot of versions before it was completed. On some of the other productions I've only seen a couple of rough cuts . . . . But the idea is to follow it along as closely as we can.[30]

Fountain has cooperated productively with other financing bodies like the BFI production board, British Screen and occasionally, a foreign investor such as ZDF – the German television company who invested in *Zina* and *The Last of England*. However, he is cautious about the possibility of more frequent European co-production as he argues that by and large most European companies don't want to get involved in work which they see as primarily 'British'. Film-makers like Derek Jarman and Ken McMullen are exceptions to the rule. Being funded by the Channel guarantees films an audience. Fountain points out that while all the film-makers he has worked with are keen to have their work screened theatrically, even on a bad night the television audience will be greater than the number who would pay to see it in cinemas.[31]

David Rose's department has also experienced problems regarding the theatrical exposure of certain films, particularly in the early days when some Channel 4 films performed particularly badly at the box office while others did not even make it to the cinema screens at all. One of these films was Charlie Gormley's *Living Apart Together*. As Gormley explains:

> Basically, what happened was that they (the Channel) were really short of product and the deal was struck. I was shooting super 16 . . . and we'd agreed to make a theatrical product – it would get some kind of window and then it would go. But they had to close down the window because they ran out of road; they just had to stick the movies on television.[32]

In these ways then, Channel 4 make their very considerable contribution to a whole range of low-budget film-making in this country, from the (often) highly conventional drama of 'Film on Four', to the more experimental and off-the-wall production featured in the 'Eleventh Hour' slot. For many film-makers the Channel has been a godsend, enabling them to realise projects they probably would not have done otherwise. Ron Peck for one openly admits that had it not been for Channel 4's interest in his second feature *Empire State*, he probably would have had to attempt to finance it in a similar way to his first film *Nighthawks*, which was made possible only through the benevolence of the individuals who contributed to the £60 000 budget.

Other film-makers have encountered certain problems in their dealings with the Channel. Charlie Gormley, for example, was told privately that *Heavenly Pursuits*, his follow-up to *Living Apart*

*Together* almost missed a theatrical run, such as its predecessor had. Gormley describes his relationship with the Channel in the following way:

> it is a slightly uncomfortable partnership but it's the only partnership available to you unless you can hack it with an American major and that's murder.[33]

Derek Jarman is another film-maker who feels that, however well-intentioned the people at Channel 4, the fact that they are now the dominant source of finance for 'independent' film-makers has created problems for himself and others. As he explains:

> Channel 4 came in with an idea that they were going to create a low-budget cinema as part of their project and the problem with this is that the people who were actually in charge of it had no knowledge of cinema whatsoever – not the low-budget British cinema in any case. They had knowledge of, presumably, European art cinema but they weren't prepared to see film-makers like myself in any way comparable to anything that might be done in Germany: Fassbinder or Herzog or anyone like that. At the same time they had a problem on their hands because they arrived at the moment Margaret Thatcher was about to launch herself into her second term and the world that they came from was under attack, or at least their liberal sixties views . . . Channel 4 never funded the independent British film-makers who were around at the time they started, with the exception of Barney Platts-Mills who made a film in Gaelic. In my case they turned down *Caravaggio* and I suddenly found myself in a new world which before, in the seventies, it was the wild west so you went where you went. But now if you went to anyone they would say, 'Well, we'd love to make a film with Channel 4.' Now this was great as long as Channel 4 wanted you. Channel 4 would say, 'Well, we did want you because we bought your three films.' I just want to put something quite down the line here. Channel 4 bought my three films: *The Tempest* for £12 000, *Jubilee* and *Sebastiane* for eight grand each. So this is a very cheap one-and-a-half hours of television . . . . They also discovered that they couldn't perhaps show them because 'Good heavens! Help! We have to establish ourselves and be seen to be fairly good before we show all this problematic stuff by

film-makers like Derek.' It wasn't as if they didn't like me, it was just I was a problem so they buried me for five years.[34]

Jarman's films were eventually shown on the Channel once the initial hysterical outcry from the tabloid press and certain sections of the Conservative party, which greeted the plans to screen them, along with Ron Peck's *Nighthawks*, had died down.

However, Channel 4's broadly successful operations in the area of fiction have helped to encourage other television companies to become involved in the financing of feature films, albeit rather tentatively as yet. There are numerous examples, including Euston, an offshoot of Thames Television, who began making the odd cinema film in the seventies (usually spin-offs of popular television series produced by the company like *The Sweeney*) but became more substantially involved in films like *A Month in the Country*, *Bellman and True*, *The Courier*, *Consuming Passions* and *Dealers*. Granada International have put money into *The Magic Toyshop*, *The Fruit Machine*, *Tree of Hands*, *Joyriders*, *My Left Foot* and *Strapless*. TVS have backed *The Innocent* and *The Simon Wiesenthal Story*. London Weekend have a stake in Working Title's *The Tall Guy* and *A Handful of Dust*. STV and Thames have recently invested in *Killing Dad* and *Danny the Champion of the World* respectively. Finally, Anglia and HTV have announced plans for development and production investment.

In addition to the ITV companies, the BBC have recently become involved in independent film production, partly as a result of Government pressure on the BBC to commission a certain amount of independent product. The new head of drama at the BBC is producer Mark Shivas who has made both television drama and features. Lynda Myles (co-producer of *Defence of the Realm*) was appointed Commissioning Editor, Independent Drama Productions. The Corporation has invested in several features, including *White Mischief*, *Loser Takes All*, *War Requiem*, *Fellow Traveller*, *Dancing Thru the Dark* and *Poison Candy*.

These developments demonstrate a long overdue acceptance, on the part of the television companies, of the popularity of film on TV and an acknowledgement of the price that must be paid to maintain a steady flow of new and interesting film drama on our screens. In addition, the securing of rights in a particular film, with the possibility of recoupment, is an added financial incentive for the television companies to become involved in the funding process. The one danger: that of compromise in line with what is deemed suitable for television compared to cinema does not worry film-makers like James Mackay who produced Derek Jarman's *The Last of England*, part-funded by Channel 4. Mackay explains that there is no reason that money from television should offer more of a compromise than money from merchant banks. He argues that neither *Empire State* nor *Caravaggio* could be described as hugely compromised films:

> It's very difficult to get away from any kind of compromise. I think we were lucky on *The Last of England* simply because we made it before they gave us the money . . . . I think there is always compromise when someone else is giving you the money but it seems to me the important thing is these films are being made even if they do have an element of compromise. I don't think those films would have been funded a few years ago.[35]

However, the threat of political censorship has raised its ugly head more than once in the last few years and this is something which worries the more progressive elements in British television. Further problems were created by the changes to the ITV levy system (a supertax on the ITV companies which amounts to a form of monopoly rent) in 1989 by the government which resulted in the ITV companies having to pay more to the Treasury. This development led to Euston Films suspending their investment in feature films, although in general reactions to the changes have been mixed, with most ITV film arms sticking to their original plans. It is difficult to predict future developments in this area given the present moves to deregulate the broadcasting industry. At the moment Channel 4 is safe until 1992, but what will happen after that is impossible to determine.

## BRITISH SCREEN

If Channel 4 can be regarded as the brightest star in the sky then following closely behind are the British Screen Finance Consortium (British Screen), under the control of Chief Executive Simon Relph. Relph is an experienced independent producer who understands the intricacies of the film-making process very well indeed. His production credits include *The Return of the Soldier*, *Privates on Parade*,

*Secret Places*, *The Ploughman's Lunch*, *Wetherby* and *Comrades*. Despite the initial pessimism which surrounded the setting up of British Screen as a replacement for the National Film Finance Corporation, the achievements of the new organisation have, to date, been very encouraging. Basically the consortium is a semi-privatised concern (the NFFC had been publicly funded), its income being made up of an annual government grant of £1.5 million a year, £300 000 from Channel 4, £300 000 from Cannon and £250 000 from Rank. The government and Channel 4 are committed for the first five years of the consortium's life while Cannon and Rank are entitled to withdraw after three years if they wish to do so. On top of this funding, British Screen also receives any income still being generated by past NFFC investments. This was originally estimated to be in the region of £500 000 but so far the assets have been worth closer to £1.2 million.

In its first year of operations, commencing January 1986, British Screen committed nearly £3.7 million to seven features. This involvement comprised equity investments in six films: *Personal Services*, *Belly of an Architect*, *High Season*, *Empire State*, *Rita, Sue and Bob Too* and *The Kitchen Toto*, and the provision of a distribution guarantee to complete the financing of a seventh: *Prick Up Your Ears*.[36] In the second year the company were in a position to invest £5.6 million in thirteen films.[37] As Guy Phelps suggests, Relph's position at British Screen was different in some very important ways to that of Mamoun Hassan at the NFFC.[38] First of all, Relph assumes total responsibility for investment decisions; he is bound to confer with his chairman only if any single investment exceeds £500 000. Hassan, on the other hand, could only advise the NFFC's board which was made up of members with strong personalities and often major differences of opinion. This occasionally led to bitter disagreement and infighting. Relph can avoid such problems. As Phelps explains, as a result decisions can be made quickly and firmly, according to consistent and identifiable criteria.

More importantly, British Screen have a much more appropriate policy on the terms of their investments and right to recoup than the NFFC ever had. For example, Relph's investment decisions are subject to producers having the bulk of their budget already in place. The NFFC often found themselves being the first to commit funds to a project and in many case the rest of the budget was never found and consequently the films affected did not get made. As Phelps points out, the Corporation found itself in the position of asking the government for more money while having £5 million in the bank – all committed to projects which had not yet found their balance.

British Screen insist on recouping their investment at least *pari passu* with other equity investors. The NFFC on the other hand traditionally supplied producers with 'end money'; that is, they were the last in the queue to receive payment, making their investment the most risky. Relph is determined to run British Screen along more broadly commercial lines than the NFFC. All investments are made with the likelihood of recoupment firmly in mind. As the company puts it in its guide to producers approaching the consortium for finance:

> There must be a considered relationship between the cost of a film and its income potential. Unfortunately this means with most films that they must have commercial appeal outside this country.[39]

Relph has also explored other ways of maximising returns and minimising the time they take to reach British Screen. Along with Zenith and Palace he has set up 'The Sales Company' headed by Carole Myer, formerly of Film Four International, to reduce the costs of recovering investments in the markets they are entitled to exploit. Instead of the usual 15–20 per cent, British Screen and their partners only pay $5-7\frac{1}{2}$ per cent, to use their own sales facility. This policy has enabled British Screen to claw back half of the funds they committed in 1986 through presales and distribution guarantees. This in turn has enabled the company to invest more money in production in its second year of operations: between £4.5 and £5 million in twelve features and a number of short films.

In terms of investment decisions British Screen operate a set of loose criteria. As has been mentioned, projects must have a degree of commercial appeal in terms of the relationship between the proposed budget and potential audience. This need not discourage innovation in the way 'commercial considerations' are normally perceived as doing. For example, as Phelps points out:

> British Screen's approach allows it to support projects as experimental as Derek Jarman's *The Last of England*, a riskier prospect than anything the NFFC was in a position to back, but within the limits of its budget perfectly commercial.[40]

British Screen expect submitted projects to be 'quality' films and to
aspire to the highest standards'. They can be in any genre, as the
company is, in Relph's words 'trying to support the whole spectrum
of British film-making'.[41] Projects have been as diverse as Jarman's
experimental film, a Comic Strip film, a horror film and contemporary social drama. The only kind of film the company explicitly rejects
is the exploitation production. If the director and producer are
inexperienced, British Screen may suggest that the film be made
under the guidance of an experienced executive producer. The length
of a film must also be carefully considered, as in British Screen's
view, too many scripts are overlong. Finally, the more cinematic a
project is considered to be, the more likely it is to receive support.

Once production begins, Relph, like his counterparts at Channel 4,
has approval of the schedule and budget, the key personnel involved
and the cast, as well as the production cash-flow and insurance
arrangements. He pays close attention to the first few days' 'rushes'
until he is confident that the production team can be left to get on
with it. He also tries to visit the shoot at least once. Relph describes
his involvement in the following way:

> I have to keep in touch with the economic progress of the film so
> that they keep within the budget, and if they don't, that the
> completion guarantors are on top of it and things aren't damaging
> the film . . . . The time I get most involved with films is at the
> editing stage, which is the most exciting. In nearly every film I do
> there is a Zenith or a David Rose whose interest, if you like, is the
> editorship of the film; to be the studio effectively. I don't tend to
> do that. I tend to be there more or less for the producers to use as a
> counsellor, but I don't get over-involved. British Screen was set up
> not to become a major studio, but to be an organisation which
> exists to help in the fertilising of the film-making spectrum in
> Britain – to help it and assist it but not to tell it what to do. I want
> to respond to what it wants to do.[42]

Relph is also busy in his attempts to attract more resources to
British Screen. This demonstrates his awareness of what changes are
affecting the industry and what practical possibilities for development
exist. He was only too aware that at the end of 1988 both Rank and
Cannon could withdraw from the company if they wished to do so,
which they in fact did. Consequently, Relph put a great deal of effort

in attempting to attract new shareholders for the company and in November 1987 it was announced that Granada Television had agreed to inject £250 000 a year for three years into British Screen, becoming a major shareholder in the process. As Relph explains:

> I see that as being a very important part of the job – to try and build up the resource we have to invest in British films and I hope that I can succeed in that. I've been waiting to do a year's work and show them (current shareholders – particularly the government, and potential shareholders) how we are going to operate. It's much easier to get people to give you money if you say, 'Well, there's the record.'[43]

As it stands, Relph's record is impressive and already the company are involved in a significant percentage of all low-budget British production. British Screen are much more finely tuned to the economic realities of film-making than their predecessor and as a result they are able to back not only more films but also a wider range of films. The major problem lies in whether or not the government will continue to contribute its annual grant to British Screen. If this funding is withdrawn the company would probably fold as it is not yet in a position to become fully self-supporting. If this were to happen a vitally important source of production finance for British film-makers would disappear.

## ZENITH PRODUCTIONS

The third of the four major equity financiers active in British cinema is Zenith Productions, which was originally a wholly-owned subsidiary of Central Television. According to the company's former production chief Margaret Matheson, who had previously been the production controller at Central, Zenith was set up initially as a profit centre, rather than Central being enticed into film production by the success of Channel 4. It perceived growing opportunities for international co-financing of prestigious drama: along the lines of Central's mini-series *Kennedy*, which Matheson produced and which was financed via a major presale to the NBC network in the United States. In 1984 Central also financed a low-budget feature film: *The Hit*, which was subsequently transferred to the Zenith catalogue. The availability of international co-finance opportunities could not be

taken up by Central itself because such involvement required operations on a much more flexible basis than the in-house productions to
which Central were accustomed. So the company decided to organise
the setting-up of what Matheson describes as: 'a low overhead,
small-staffed, fast-thinking, flexible outfit that could respond to this
international opportunity'.[44]

As has already been pointed out, Zenith have a commitment to
development as well as production. Matheson explains that the
company receive:

> a phenomenal amount of submissions at various stages, from an
> idea over a drink, through to a treatment, through to a final
> script . . . . Apart from the fact we are receiving an endless
> barrage of proposals in various forms we also originate things
> ourselves . . . .[45]

The provision of equity finance for a project is linked to specific
rights, in particular the right to allow the Sales Company to handle
the film in the relevant territories. Matheson claimed to be interested in projects with a high profile and strong subject matter. Several
have been loose 'biopics' on characters like Cynthia Payne, Sid
Vicious and Joe Orton, which Matheson claims, have some sort of
contemporary resonance even if they are slightly period pieces. The
company have made films with controversial film-makers like Nicolas
Roeg and Alex Cox along with more mainstream 'British' directors
like Stephen Frears, Alan Clarke and David Leland, whose films are
closer in look and feel to those associated with Channel 4. Perhaps
more significantly, projects must be capable of being made on a
budget of $5 million or less for Zenith to be interested. This is a
reflection of the company's awareness of the difficulties associated
with recouping funds on large-budget productions *vis-à-vis* low-
budget films. A film must earn two-and-a-half times its negative cost
(the cost of production up to the printing of the final negative) in
order to break even. The higher the budget therefore, the more
difficult breaking even, let alone going into profit, becomes. Although productions are closely monitored by the company throughout, in both creative and financial terms, it is the pre-production
stage which Matheson identifies as being the most crucial:

> I feel strongly that the most important creative work is in the
> preparation . . . of the script, in the casting, in the choice of

director and in the director's choices . . . . If you've got something wrong once you're turning over there's not a lot you can do about it.[46]

On the financial side, once a budget and a schedule have been prepared, the package is sent to a completion guarantor and the Sales Company for a forecast of the project's sales potential throughout the world. The sales forecast for these markets must be close to the proposed cost of production or Zenith would not go ahead with it. The next step is the organisation of an American distribution deal which Matheson would hope to be in the region of 60 per cent of the budget. In November 1987 Zenith entered into a joint venture with the American company Atlantic, giving three Zenith productions: *Patty Hearst, For Queen and Country* and *The Wolves of Willoughby Chase*, guaranteed North American distribution. The company operated a $5 million budget ceiling in order to lower the financial risk and to enable a higher proportion of the budget to be raised in the UK. Matheson herself is acutely aware of the importance of wise investment decisions and good marketing. As she puts it, the key to successful operations lies in 'knowing what you've got to sell' and 'careful consideration of the best form of advertising depending on the particular audience you think will go for it'.[47]

By and large, Zenith's performance has been impressive in the production of both theatrical features and TV mini-series. The features Zenith have been involved in include *The Hit, Wetherby, Insignificance, Billy the Kid and the Green Baize Vampire* (the only real disappointment according to Matheson), *Sid and Nancy, Personal Services, Prick Up Your Ears, Wish You Were Here, Sour Sweet, For Queen and Country, The Wolves of Willoughby Chase, Paris by Night, The Dead, Slam Dance*, and *Patty Hearst*: the last two being ostensibly American films but similar in style and scale to the British projects. As Matheson explains:

because of the size of the American market it's bound to be attractive to make American subjects. But I wouldn't want to make any old American subject. I'd like to think that with anything we do we bring some unique characteristic, unique point of view . . . . So if it's an American subject I'd like to think it's something that we would treat differently than an American production company might.[48]

The solid critical and commercial success represented by this output has earned the company a great deal of praise. Graham Wade, for example, writes:

> The healthiest of the new breed of company appear to be those like Zenith Productions . . . . Zenith is confidently expected to earn considerable revenue for its parent company from a number of film and television projects which are mostly co-produced. Its successes depend on careful selection of property, backed by sophisticated marketing techniques which squeeze every penny from complicated patterns of release, covering the whole range of outlets from cinemas to video cassette. The key to successful production in the last part of this century lies in this new, complicated mix of media outlets.[49]

On 1 October 1987 Carlton Communications paid Central £6.3 million for Zenith and right away merged the company with their own production unit The Moving Picture Company, who, under producer Nigel Stafford-Clark, had been responsible for feature films such as *Parker*, *The Assam Garden* and *Stormy Monday*. Stafford-Clark consequently moved over to Zenith to work as a producer under Mathieson. Carlton Communications are a £600 million listed concern and this should make it easier for Zenith to attract City investors. In November 1989 Paramount acquired a 49 per cent stake in Zenith, giving the company access to Paramount's distribution network in North America. Zenith have tended to concentrate recently on television projects but there are plans for further feature production. In April 1989 Zenith announced three new feature projects, each budgeted between five and eight million dollars, marking a break from their previous $5 million limit. These projects are deemed to be more 'transnational' in appeal, an indication of a change of policy at the company after a period of consolidation and market assessment in the wake of the Carlton take over.

## HANDMADE FILMS

Handmade Films were set up in 1978 by ex-Beatle George Harrison and his business manager Dennis O'Brien to rescue the Monty Python film *The Life of Brian*, which had been abandoned by EMI.

Initially the company tended to concentrate on comedy subjects like *Time Bandits* (which grossed over $45 million in North America), *Privates on Parade*, *The Missionary* and *A Private Function* – all involving members of the Monty Python team – and two films from the Dick Clement/Ian Le Frenais partnership: *Bullshot* and *Water*. They have subsequently broadened their field to encompass a whole range of projects including Neil Jordan's *Mona Lisa* and Nic Roeg's *Track 29*. As Margot Gavan-Duffy, script editor at Handmade explains:

> It started very much with the 'Pythons' and that was the reason George Harrison and Dennis O'Brien moved into film-making. And for some years comedy was the guiding factor . . . slightly off-the-wall mainstream comedy, quirky, oddball films. I think probably the first one to break the mould was *Mona Lisa*, which was a difficult decision because it was a different sort of territory . . . . Since then we've made a number of films which are more serious . . . . I think people here feel easier with comedy, feel they have a surer touch – *Mona Lisa* was obviously successful, some of our other straighter films seem less so . . . . I guess really the guideline is work quality and anything that's unusual or interesting.[50]

Gareth Jones explained that Handmade tend to finance their films on a debt financing basis by borrowing money from a bank – usually an American bank which has a department specialising in film finance – against presale guarantees. As Jones puts it:

> We obtain pledges of advances. Those advances are in turn pledged to the bank . . . . We borrow the money against the security of the film itself and the sales.[51]

Handmade attempt to presell their films one hundred per cent, through a network of sub-distributors. They operate output agreements with distributors with the latter party agreeing to take a certain number of Handmade films over a specified period, thereby ensuring a continuity of finance.

> We have guaranteed distributors who will take a number of our films and pay you a set level which is based on a percentage of the budget. This might only be between two and six per cent . . . quite

small amounts. Obviously the more output deals you have in different territories the more it contributes towards your budget. [52]

Most Handmade films are budgeted at £2–3 million, which, as Jones explains, tends to be the level at which there is a good chance of breaking even, even if the film doesn't perform spectacularly at the box office. Jones suggested that a certain level of income could be gleaned by idiosyncratic films in Europe and the UK but in the US this was rather less certain: 'with a *Mona Lisa* you make money, but for certain other movies you might not'.[53] Therefore, budgets are kept low whenever possible. As Jones, explains the company are not prepared to pay the kind of huge fees that mainstream directors can command. People have to be prepared to work within Handmade's budgets. However, the company is prepared to move into bigger-budget film-making if the material is broad in its appeal and there is a star attached. The largest project Handmade have been involved in to date is perhaps their most unfortunate experience: *Shanghai Surprise* starring Madonna and Sean Penn which crashed at the box office. Despite the well-publicised difficulties on set with Penn, and the film's commercial failure, Handmade covered their own costs through presales, leaving the distributors to bear the loss.

Potential projects are discussed by a committee within the company, but final decisions to proceed are taken by Dennis O'Brien in consultation with George Harrison. As far as monitoring production is concerned, Handmade appoint a line producer to the project to attempt to keep the production on budget and on schedule. Jones explains that most of the company's British productions tend to be based at Shepperton studios where Handmade have an office and a full-time production accountant who liaises with the line producer on a day-to-day basis during the production process. Over and above this daily supervision, the company have weekly production meetings where problems can be aired. As Jones explains:

> It's really a case of: if things start to go astray, people are alerted very quickly . . . . Our main concern is when budgets start not to be adhered to and that's something you can see happening very quickly – even if you go half a day over. It's something that's stepped on and rectified as quickly as we can do it.[54]

In terms of issues of creativity and freedom, Handmade have lengthy conversations with the director before the project commences principal photography. As Jones explains, the shape and the feel of the project is discussed and once the script is in a form that the company finds acceptable production proper will begin. The film-maker is then more or less left to make the film on his or her own, providing prior agreements are adhered to regarding script, budget and schedule. However, what distinguishes Handmade from the other companies mentioned so far is their demand of final cut. Jones explains: 'We are a fairly tough company when it comes to creative controls . . . . We want final cut, it's as simple as that.'[55] It is partly because of this that Handmade have seldom ventured into the realm of co-production. Jones also admits that the final-cut policy can cause resentment at times.

Like one or two other British production companies, Handmade have recently begun to produce films in North America. Margot Gavan-Duffy explains that while British films sometimes work in America, they frequently don't and producers stand a better chance in that market with American films. The US productions to date include *Track 29, Five Corners* and *The Pow Wow Highway*, Dennis O'Brien has argued that these films are 'very similar in style to the things we do in the UK – so they are the kind of projects that would never be done by an American company'.[56]

By and large, Handmade will attempt to keep the budgets of such films low and the same supervisory and creative rules would apply as do in this country. As Jones puts it:

> The kind of films you would see coming out of a Handmade stable in the United States would be films like *Track 29*: unusual films, not with an immediately identifiable large audience but hopefully which would fit into a niche.[57]

This is a trend affecting more and more British film companies with Zenith and Palace also making low-to-medium budget films in America. This strategy is significantly different from previous attempts on the part of British companies to make films in the United States. In the past this involved big budgets and so-called 'commercial' subjects. It invariably resulted in disaster: the examples of Lew Grade and EMI previously mentioned. The new breed of product is an American-based equivalent of the typical low-budget British model rather than an attempt by a British company to make a big-budget American film, and as a result, much less of a gamble for the companies involved.

## THE BFI PRODUCTION BOARD

The BFI Production Board has similar interests to Alan Fountain's department at Channel 4. The Board is able to invest in two to three very low-budget productions every year (courtesy of funding received from the government, a subvention from Channel Four and money from the Independent Television Companies Association and the British Film Fund Agency). It is able to do this by way of the 'Code of Practice' and the 'Workshop Agreement', negotiated with the ACTT which enables films to be made more cheaply and under more flexible conditions than elsewhere in the industry.[58] The origins of the Production Board lie in the Experimental Film Fund set up by Sir Michael Balcon in 1952. In 1969 the BFI assumed official administrative control of the fund. During the seventies the Board's policy towards film underwent a pronounced transition, involving a shift away from supporting rather insular traditions of avant-garde film-making towards more accessible cinematic forms. The first feature to be produced under this new policy was Chris Petit's *Radio On* and since then several important productions have been funded including Peter Greenaway's *The Draughtsman's Contract*, Edward Bennett's *Ascendancy*, Derek Jarman's *Caravaggio* and Terence Davies' *Distant Voices, Still Lives*. Like Channel 4, the Board is also able to fund workshop productions on a one-off basis.

Colin MacCabe, until recently the production head at the BFI Production Board, described his working practices thus:

We made a policy decision as long ago as 1979, that our major energies should go into making low-budget features . . . one, two or three major productions a year, rather than making the ten or twenty short films . . . which would be possible on my budget. For me a film isn't finished until it reaches an audience, and the patterns of distribution and exhibition in the 'commercial cinema' have changed so radically that it's now much easier to get our kind of stuff shown. There are, for example, ten cinemas in London which will accept work from outside the mainstream . . . . I certainly don't feel a conscious pressure which says I've got to make commercial product . . . . But I also think that I've got to make films which I think will reach an audience. I am really not under the tight commercial pressure that most producers are. Then there's the added advantage that if I succeed in getting an audience I also get money back which enables me to make more films.[59]

MacCabe was interested in scripts

> which capture, in some original way, some aspect of contemporary social experience . . . . Something that suddenly makes you see, or makes alive some part of the social and cultural reality of today.[60]

He was also particularly keen on initiating ideas with writers and then being involved in the process to find a suitable director for the project. In broad terms the film-makers were free to make the film they wanted. Nevertheless, they were not totally free from constraints or from pressure by MacCabe who attempted to give the director all the 'aggro and hard input' associated with a commercial producer with the difference that ultimately the director always had the final say.

In terms of their financial stability, the BFI Production Board has relied heavily on Channel 4. The Channel undertook to provide a subvention to the Board for three years of approximately £500 000 a year, on the understanding that the government would meet and equal that, which they did. In return Channel 4 has had the TV licence on all BFI product, most of which is broadcast on the 'Eleventh Hour' slot with features like *The Draughtsman's Contract* and *Caravaggio* included in the more prestigious 'Film on Four' seasons. Occasionally the Channel will make an equity investment in a BFI film. While this was welcomed by MacCabe he points out that his remit at the BFI stressed the importance of theatrical exhibition of BFI films:

> My job is to make films for the cinema, the fact that they have a UK television licence on them means I get some money for them, and the fact that they are going to get a TV audience means they are going to get some audience . . . . But my attention, interest and energy is concentrated on getting the films into cinemas.[61]

If the innovative and experimental underbelly of British cinema is to be maintained, the BFI Production Board must be allowed to continue its operations as an outlet for off-the-wall film-makers and ambitious newcomers who may or may not move subsequently into a more commercial arena.

PRODUCTION STRATEGIES: SUCCESSES AND FAILURES

What seems to unite the four companies dealt with in some depth, (with the exception of the BFI which is not subject to the same conditions as the others) is on the one hand, a determination to keep budgets low and to maximise returns by way of skilful and energetic marketing techniques (discussed in the next chapter) and on the other hand, by maintaining close involvement with film-makers at every stage of the process. In this way, these companies can be said to have a direct contribution to make at almost every stage of the film-making process. It is very interesting and informative to compare the strategies of the four, particularly Zenith and Handmade who are totally commercial enterprises with none of the protection afforded to Channel 4 or even British Screen, with other companies involved in production finance who have encountered severe problems in the course of their operations. Three companies who immediately spring to mind are Thorn-EMI, Goldcrest and Virgin Vision, all active in the equity financing of British production during the first half of the decade but now no longer so.

The problems began for Thorn-EMI Screen Entertainment (TESE) and Goldcrest in the summer of 1985. At TESE, Chief Executive Gary Dartnall decided not to renew Verity Lambert's contract as head of production. The reason behind this decision was the poor showing at the box office of a number of Lambert's productions. These included *Morons from Outer Space*, *Dream Child*, *Comfort and Joy*, *Slayground* and *Restless Natives*. Although the performance of these films was pretty bad, that was by no means the whole story. As James Park points out, TESE was a large conglomerate which required at least twenty films annually for its distribution machinery. Lambert's department was only one source for this product. Others included the acquisitions department, responsible for such big-budget flops as *The Holcroft Covenant* and *Wild Geese II*, and Dartnall himself, who made deals with US companies for the regular provision of their films. Each department felt it should have a key role in approving and determining what got made. Over and above this, the sales department were interested in films which were tried and tested and therefore not particularly original. This caused problems for Lambert: 'Almost every single film that I put money into so far has come back from the distribution people with a very low assessment.'[62]

Dartnall decided to set up a revolving fund of £1.5 million for the development of projects, with TESE having first option on taking any scripts developed under the scheme into full production. The finance for this production would come from a £160 million revolving credit facility which Dartnall was attempting to negotiate with twelve leading merchant banks. This fund, it was planned, would provide whole or partial finance for 15–25 medium-budget films a year. Initially, agreements were signed with various independent producers including Verity Lambert, John Bradbourne and Richard Goodwin – responsible for *A Passage to India*, which TESE had backed, Euan Lloyd of *Wild Geese II* fame, United British Artists, Jeremy Thomas and Simon Perry.

However, TESE was subsequently sold in 1986, first to Australian tycoon Alan Bond for £125 million, who one week later passed on his acquisition to the Cannon Corporation for £175 million. The outcome was not a particularly fortunate one for British independent production. As Julian Petley commented:

> Cannon have honoured the letter of the satellite producer deals, paying small development expenses where TESE had been contracted to do so, but certainly have not kept to the spirit of the thing. Not one project developed under the satellite scheme has been put into production, and all of the deals that have so far come up for renewal have been terminated on the first possible day – for example Euan Lloyd, United British Artists and Simon Perry.[63]

In fact Cannon have only really invested in two indigenous British productions: Harry Hook's *The Kitchen Toto* and Lezli-An Barrett's *Business as Usual*, a total investment on Cannon's part of £1.8 million. This is hardly a significant contribution from what was at the time the largest film company in Britain.

While Gary Dartnall was deciding not to renew Verity Lambert's contract at TESE, Goldcrest, the flagship of the British film 'renaissance', were having problems of their own. At Goldcrest the problem was not the disastrous performance of a group of films (although this was to come) but rather the realisation that the company, having embarked on an over-ambitious production programme, was going bankrupt. The basic precepts of the company's founding father Jake Eberts, who had left and been replaced by James Lee, seemed to have been forgotten in the pursuit of profits and prestige. Eberts had shown a great deal of prudence in building the company up from a £100 000 development outfit in 1977 to a £35 million production and marketing enterprise by 1984.[64] The films he had been involved with had all been covered by minimum guarantees and no single production had overstepped the $15 million budgetary limit he had set.

James Lee began with a similar policy – his initial portfolio seemed balanced and at least 60 per cent of investments were covered by presales. However, two of the major productions he had initiated, Hugh Hudson's *Revolution* and Julien Temple's *Absolute Beginners*, suffered from substantial cost over-runs. *Revolution* was a particularly expensive film which finally cost around £20 million. At the same time the company were involved in a third feature, David Puttnam and Roland Joffe's *The Mission*, which was budgeted at £17 million. The presale deals had been done on a basis of anticipated costs, so any over-run bit heavily into the profit potential of any film concerned. On top of this Goldcrest had put up its own completion guarantees on all three films – a policy initiated by Eberts with *The Killing Fields* which cost £11 million. This put the company in a particularly bad position. In the event none of the films did well enough at the box office to justify the amount of money spent on them. *Revolution* lost the company £10 million.

Lee's style of management also upset many people at the company. He was both inexperienced and something of an autocrat whose reputed egomania and controversial decision-making led to the resignation of sales manager Bill Gavin, managing director Donald Cruickshank and finally production chief Sandy Lieberson. One of Lee's most notorious decisions was to move the Goldcrest offices from its inexpensive base in Holland Park to a glass emporium in Wardour Street, adding significantly to the company's already high overheads. The board were finally forced to remove him and call back Eberts in an attempt to rescue the company. Production was immediately suspended for an indefinite period. Half the staff were dismissed and the company moved back to smaller and more affordable offices. By late 1986 Goldcrest had been reduced to little more than a sales and distribution company, handling films like *A Room With a View*, *Sid and Nancy* and *The Name of the Rose*.

James Park suggests that Goldcrest's problems were partly the result of departmental squabbling which meant that nobody could take an overall view on what was happening. Park writes:

A failure of the institutional structure is the only explanation of how a company with some of the most talented executives around could make such crucial errors of judgement. The fact that two major films were allowed to go over budget, with no provisions made for overcosts was an example.[65]

Park then attempts to draw comparisons between the problems at Goldcrest and those at TESE. Both affairs demonstrate for Park the problems large companies have in making creative decisions. He also points to the apparent lack of people equipped to run a major production department. Potential candidates like Puttnam and Jeremy Thomas prefer to keep a hands-on relation to production; or at least Puttnam did until his recent short stay at Columbia.

Park subsequently argues that smaller companies like Virgin and Zenith have a more integrated and intimate approach to productions, where there is little chance of inter-departmental wrangling and executives losing sight of what is going on. Also the risks are less in the low-budget sector in the sense that good marketing can help to ensure that a film costing £2 million or less stands a good chance of earning that money back in the long term. However, returns can often be slow due to the differential and complex distribution and exhibition patterns around the world and so the smaller the investment the less added expenses like interest rates are incurred. The company overheads of Zenith, British Screen and others are also relatively low, therefore cash flow does not create the same problems it did at a larger company like Goldcrest which had to keep turning over to pay its bills.

However, small companies can also overstretch themselves, as Virgin Vision have demonstrated. In October 1986 the company announced it was pulling out of the equity financing of feature films after only four years of producing films like *Secret Places*, *Electric Dreams*, *Nineteen Eighty Four*, *Loose Connections*, *Absolute Beginners*, *Captive*, *Aria* and *Gothic*. Their confidence had been shaken quite early on by *Nineteen Eighty Four* going well over budget, finally costing £5.5 million. Despite being popular in the North American market, by 1987 the film had not broken even. This was mainly due to the problem of interest charges. As former production chief Al Clark explained at the time:

> I'm sure if £5.5 million had just stayed at £5.5 million it would have been fine. But because we financed the whole thing, as you are

waiting to get your money back from distributors all over the world the money that you borrowed is inflating day by day.[66]

The events surrounding *Absolute Beginners*, which Virgin co-financed with Goldcrest, shattered what confidence the company had left. As Clark put it:

We were dealing with something that nobody in this country had ever attempted, which was a studio musical pitched on the kind of scale of a Hollywood musical . . . . We were all taking a rather big reckless plunge into the unknown and hoped that we were going to pull it off.[67]

They did not and Virgin paid the price, shifting focus from production to acquisition and distribution. In effect they moved from being a major player in the financing game to a supporting role, like other distributors such as Curzon and occasionally Rank. They are no longer in a position to initiate new projects but rather can only provide what is in effect 'top-up' money for productions which already have the bulk of their budgets in place.

The importance of companies like Channel 4, British Screen, Zenith and Handmade to the continuation and health of low-budget British production is vital. These are the only realistic sources of equity finance independent producers can turn to. They are augmented by a handful of production houses which, if not able themselves to fund a picture, are at least strong enough financially to develop a project and bring it to the attention of interested financiers. This group includes Palace and Working Title. As I have noted, Palace are primarily a distribution company, initially set up in 1980 as a video retail business by Nik Powell (a former partner of Richard Branson at Virgin) and Steve Woolley, who have been able to move into the field of production with films like *Company of Wolves*, *A Letter to Brezhnev*, *Mona Lisa*, *Absolute Beginners*, *The Dream Demon* and *The Courier*. They are constantly approached by people with new ideas, but as Steve Woolley explains, they are more likely to commission projects from writers the company know or have worked with in the past.

Woolley claims he is interested in

anything that's likely to upset someone, that's going to subvert their notion of what they think they are going to see . . . . For instance *Company of Wolves* was not really a horror film, it wasn't really a fantasy, it wasn't a film about an adolescent girl's coming of age – it was all of those things plus more . . . . So anything that's got an element of . . . trying to make people think a bit . . . to sit up and take notice.[68]

Like Zenith and Handmade, Palace have started to make films in North America with productions like *Siesta* and *Shag*. The major reason given by Woolley is the desire to crack the American market, enabling the company to make a range of products geared to different markets. In late 1988 he announced plans to make one low-budget film for the British, European and US 'classics' markets – *The Big Man*, a bigger-budget international film with an American star but still ostensibly a British film – *The Pope Must Die*, directed by Peter Richardson, and an American project – *A Rage in Harlem*. This mirrored the production programme for the previous year with *Scandal*, *High Spirits* and *Shag* roughly equivalent in size and projected market to the new slate. As Woolley explained, this programme crosses the board in terms of markets and audiences, minimising the risk to the company. Palace cannot afford to make only low-budget British films for a limited market.[69]

Working Title, on the other hand, have developed from being a producer of pop-promos (under the banner Aldabra) to a major production house responsible for films like *My Beautiful Laundrette, Personal Services, Sammy and Rosie Get Laid, Wish You Were Here, A World Apart, The Tall Guy, Paperhouse* and *Chicago Joe and the Show Girl*. Sarah Radclyffe claims to be interested in original ideas and about contemporary issues which concern people.

After *A World Apart* I'm looking for things that are more than just a flippant comedy or something. For me it's got to be something that I'm prepared to spend a minimum of a year of my life working on.[70]

Radclyffe seems to be true to her word in that *Laundrette*, *Sammy and Rosie* and *A World Apart* are probably three of the most politically-oriented commercial features released in this country over the last few years.

Both Palace and Working Title are very astute companies, alert to new possibilities and outlets. Both have recently set up television companies: Working Title have already produced a series 'Echoes' which was screened by Channel 4, while Palace's first TV project: *Lenny Live and Unleashed*, featured comedian Lenny Henry and was produced with backing from satellite television company BSB. Both Working Title and Palace are also successful producers of pop promos. Such a multi-media approach, already practised successfully by Zenith, is a response to the rapidly-changing media entertainment industry and is intended to give the companies the financial stability to continue producing innovative feature films.

It is companies like Channel 4, British Screen, Zenith, Handmade, Palace and Working Title who have created the space for film-making talent to develop and for some innovation to take place. These companies are run by people who share an enthusiasm for film as well as an astute awareness of the economic realities of film-making. By and large they have kept budgets to a minimum and while people are aware of the need to make a range of product, covering a range of markets, they also understand the dangers that over-budget productions can bring. David Rose, for one, is particularly enthusiastic about low-budget production and he invokes the example of *My Beautiful Laundrette*:

> We all felt it was a modest film for television . . . made on 16mm. We all got it wrong, happily, in that respect, but I think the atmosphere and the enthusiasm on that shoot derived from the fact that it was a small film . . . . Everyone believed in it . . . . There is a feeling within a crew you can sense very readily on a shoot, that they are behind it . . . . If it had gone to 35mm, people might have started to have greater aspirations and it might not have had that real tight team spirit about it . . . . I am in a way constrained to low-budget films and I'm very glad. If anyone offered me another £5 million to top up my budget I would still wish to make low budget films.[71]

The issue of budgets raises interesting questions with regard to ideas of film-making and creative freedom. Tom Priestley, an editor who has worked in the industry for many years makes the following observations:

> You think when you've got a bigger budget you can do more, but it's just as tight financially, often more so because there's an enormous pressure to get a certain something on the screen and then all these financiers have their ideas what it should look like.

So actually I think you are more free often with a low-budget film. There are a lot of other problems but I think you are freer to make the film you want to make.[72]

In a similar vein, a film-maker like Derek Jarman, who has worked in the extremely low-budget sector, argues that it is not financial resources which engender cinematic creativity but rather the felt necessity to make the film in the first place. On one hand Jarman finds no creativity in a big budget special-effects film like *Blade Runner*, describing it as 'a set designer's job. It's Fortnum and Mason's wrapping paper around a nothingness in the end.'[73] But on the other hand he does find a necessity in the work of certain film-makers like Peter Wollen, Ken Russell, Nicolas Roeg and others:

Kenneth Anger created some of the most marvellous cinema on absolute peanuts . . . *Scorpio Rising* is probably better than any other American feature in the year it was made . . . . So you don't need resources. It's an approach to life really.[74]

Other film-makers are more appreciative of what can be achieved with a substantial budget. As Julien Temple argues:

On one level there is an extraordinary freedom . . . I saw *Roger Rabbit* in America, which is formally a very important film . . . but you can in a sense do anything with $35 million. But then you do have the intense paranoia of the people who have put the money up and that's no joke. You feel a very heavy, almost mafia-like, pressure that if you fuck with their money your knees may be blown away – in a mental sense . . . . I'm sure this would be less on a three-million thing. I would like to do a small-budget film but I do have respect for the freedom money can buy: with the ideas you have by making them real.[75]

Bigger budgets may give a film-maker greater technical scope in the field of special effects but such levels of investment necessarily require a compromise in that the film must be seen to have potential mass appeal, which can require certain modifications at the level of narrative and plot. As Gareth Jones of Handmade puts it:

The bigger the budget is you've got to be able to say 'This has a mass appeal.' Therefore you cannot be so idiosyncratic in your taste, you have actually to get out there and say, 'Will this appeal to the great unwashed American public?' and by doing that you have to actually make compromises.[76]

In this sense lower budgets can actually give a film-maker greater freedom in terms of making the statements he or she wants to make. This is a fundamentally important consideration in terms of the question of the structuring of creativity in the context of cinema.

In conclusion, the companies examined in this chapter have been instrumental in the shaping of British cinema in the eighties. The close involvement these companies have at every stage of the production process has contributed significantly to the structuring of creativity in this context. What this chapter has done is to demonstrate the immense collective influence a small number of key decision-makers within the industry have in the context of low-budget indigenous production. Together, David Rose, Simon Relph, Margaret Matheson, Dennis O'Brien, Steve Woolley, Sarah Radclyffe and their close associates represent the 'gate-keepers' of the industry, effectively determining what British cinema is; what subjects are worth producing and even what the final product will look like. This state of affairs must, in turn, have some effect on film-makers: the writers, directors and producers directly responsible for creating 'British Cinema'. These individuals must initiate and develop their ideas in relation to existing patterns of funding and production. There is no point in approaching David Rose for example, if it is unlikely he will be interested in the idea in question. There is, I would contend, an underlying strain towards conformity in British film-making. This is probably more or less true for any national cinema at any time, but I believe it was particularly marked in the British cinema in the mid-to-late eighties.

# 5  The Film-Making Process: Sales, Distribution and Marketing

The movie business, for better or worse, has become primarily a marketing business.

Ned Tannen, ex-president of Universal,
interviewed in *Sight & Sound*,
Winter 1983/4

In spite of all its artistic and creative aspirations, practically all contemporary film-making, whatever the country or cultural climate, is subject to certain 'facts of life' which are primarily economic in nature. First of all, film production is an extremely expensive process: the average cost of a typical 'low-budget' British independent feature with domestic locations, no international stars or expensive post-production techniques, films like *Wish You Were Here*, *My Beautiful Laundrette* or *Distant Voices, Still Lives*, currently stands in the region of £1.5–2 million. More ambitious projects featuring special effects, large casts or international locations, films like *Brazil*, *Cry Freedom* or *High Spirits*, cost five to ten times more. Therefore, potential investors will only consider putting money into films which in their judgement stand a reasonable chance of making a profit at the box office. Their reasons for investing in film-making are, generally speaking, commercial rather than philanthropic. In order for a film to break even, let alone make a profit, in what is a highly competitive and volatile marketplace, it must be sold, distributed and marketed in a vigorous fashion, making full use of the most effective and up-to-date techniques. Considering that a feature must earn two-and-a-half times its production costs at the box office before any profit is realised, effective sales and marketing strategies are a crucial part of the film-making process.

At this point it is important to make some distinction between sales and marketing. As I have noted elsewhere,[1] British feature films are generally financed by means of a combination of presales and equity investments. Presales are usually to a major foreign (i.e. North American) distributor and will, in most cases, amount to a substantial percentage of the budget, being a reflection of a film's estimated market worth in a particular territory. This gives the distributors the rights to exploit that film as they see fit within their given territory and to appropriate any profits. Equity investors on the other hand will attempt to recoup their investment by way of sales to distributors in other territories (usually the rest of the world) which involves a fee for the rights, plus a share in the profits, if any. So basically films are sold or presold by the production company to various distributors (and broadcasters) around the world. It is then the task of these distributors to devise and implement marketing strategies. The primary interest distribution companies have in films is in their commercial viability: films are a commodity which must be commercially exploited to the full and brought to the attention of their potential audience in the most effective manner possible. The value of a film to its distributor lies entirely in its box-office appeal, being otherwise only a pile of cans of celluloid. It is therefore not unrealistic to argue that, in this context, the marketing strategy is more important than the film itself. As Marc Samuelson, an independent British producer, observes:

Nowadays people spend more on the marketing and promotion of a film than they do on the actual production which is amazing, but, if you think about it, not surprising. There are products like Coca-Cola where the actual product costs next to nothing. It's all in the packaging, the promotion, the marketing: that's where all the cost is. And in the USA films to some extent are the same. I think that in the UK the distributors don't do enough marketing. It's chicken and egg: 'The audience doesn't warrant it', they say, but you could say, 'The audience would increase if there was more marketing'. When a film gets a really good marketing push, like *Crocodile Dundee* it can do fantastically well.[2]

Some would dispute Samuelson's criticism of British distributors. While it is interesting to consider how much more is spent on marketing in the United States compared to the UK, we must be careful not to equate the British and American situations: the marketplaces are very different, particularly in terms of size. The emphases of many marketing campaigns are also different, with American distributors tending to favour a less subtle, more overtly exploitative, approach than some of their British counterparts. (In some ways this is a reflection of the kind of film each industry tends to produce.) In both industries the basic mechanisms and structures are similar, it is only their application in terms of scale and emphasis which differ.

It is vital to remember here that while film is very much a commodity this does not necessarily mean that it can be marketed as one would market any other commodity. The marketing of films involves the commercial exploitation of an 'expectation of a pleasurable experience', not a tangible object like toothpaste or a motor-car. Richard Kahn, the executive vice-president, motion picture distribution and marketing for MGM/UA, makes an important point that must be borne in mind:

> The marketing of movies is a unique phenomenon, as unique as the product it sells. It cannot be equated to selling homes, hardware or hairspray. Motion picture marketing deals with shadows on a screen, the merchandising of emotion.[3]

Before taking a closer look at the selling, distributing and marketing of feature films, from a British point of view, I want to argue that the culture/commerce division in film-making is a spurious one. All markets are an inseparable aspect of cultural production and cut right across the high culture/low culture distinction.

## THE MARKETING PROCESS AND CULTURAL PRODUCTION

Regardless of any commercial imperative, film remains a major cultural institution: at its most basic, the mass production of narratives within narrow pre-set guidelines; at its most sophisticated, a mature art form comparable to the best of modern drama, painting or literature. As such, film must be located within a wider cultural context. This helps to provide a solid grounding upon which more complex understanding of the nature of film production, sales, distribution and marketing can be built.

In his highly accessible essay *Culture*, Williams demonstrates the ways in which artists and other cultural producers have been linked historically to wider social institutions by means of economic criteria. He considers pre-capitalistic issues of patronage and sponsorship before moving on to the question of cultural production and the development of markets. Given the close relationship he identifies between cultural production and markets, Williams argues that it is legitimate to view cultural production as simultaneously commodity production, and cultural producers as a particular kind of commodity producer. He identifies a series of historically developmental stages of commodity production with respect to culture: artisanal, post-artisanal, market professional, corporate professional. The last stage is that which is currently dominant and involves the corporate organisation of cultural production in institutions like cinema, radio and television, and the rise of the salaried professional. As Williams explains:

> the effective . . . origin of cultural production is now centrally sited within the corporate market. The scale of capital involved, and the dependence on more complex and specialised means of production and distribution, have to an important extent blocked access to these media in older artisanal, post-artisanal and even market professional terms and imposed predominant conditions of corporate employment.[4]

Not only is access limited, but the dominance of planned marketing operations creates a situation where certain types of cultural production are positively promoted. Williams argues that this is most relevant to the highly capitalised forms of cultural production such as the commercial cinema. The buyer's choice, which is the original rationale of the market, is displaced to operate within a predetermined range. (In the case of film this would relate to the conception, on the part of big production companies, of 'what the public wants' or 'what is currently popular', which in turn helps to predetermine production strategies with certain types of film being promoted as 'commercially viable'.) This bestows a great deal of importance upon the role of the corporate agent with respect to the generation of cultural products. Williams describes this state of affairs in the following manner:

> In sophisticated market planning, a certain type of work can be selected at so early a stage, on the basis of a few examples or of

some calculated or projected demand, that production, from that stage, no longer originates with the primary producer but is commissioned from him . . . . This new form of innovation is at least primarily a marketing function, and this contrasts sharply with other kinds of innovation, which, governed by internal cultural purposes, often find themselves at the very margin of the market or outside it altogther.[5]

Williams goes on to suggest that even the contrast which he sets up between market-originated and producer-originated work is not absolute since cultural producers often internalise known or possible market relations in complex ways, involving different degrees of conscious and unconscious compromise. In other words, they internalise market trends and current fashions and tailor their work accordingly.

Williams's ideas have a great deal of relevance in the context of the present discussion of film-making. Most national film industries are highly capitalised, corporately constituted, commercial enterprises which tend to structure their products within sets of (in most cases) rather narrow guidelines. Issues of expectation and recognition, from the audience's or consumer's point of view, are important whether the film is a mass-market American genre movie or a specialised 'arthouse' production aimed at a minority audience. In this sense it could be argued that the effects of corporate planning referred to by Williams are an identifiable feature of contemporary film industries. These may be particularly so in the American context but even British production, which tends to be less mass-market oriented than the bulk of US production, is still structured by generic conventions and consequently most British films are readily identifiable as such. This is a complex issue but at the moment it will suffice to say that British films tend to deal with a particular range of subjects and to have a particular visual and narrative style.

It is important to note that the organisation of film production in both Britain and the US has undergone certain important structural changes over the past forty years. In some respects Williams's corporate model would seem to relate more closely to the old Hollywood studio system (and its British equivalent) where film production took place literally in 'film factories' owned by vertically-integrated companies who financed, produced, distributed and exhibited their own movies. These companies employed all personnel: creative, technical and administrative, on a permanent salaried basis.

Production programmes were decided on an annual basis and the studio heads retained the power to hire and fire, sanction projects and even to decide the final cut of a film. However, since the break-up of the studio system in the late forties and early fifties, the situation has been somewhat different in that film-making now tends to be structured more on a one-off individual film basis. Rather than an annual studio production programme of, for the sake of argument, twenty-five features, projects are now put together and funded as single 'packages'. This often involves the setting-up of a company for the sole purpose of making the film with that company being dissolved on the completion of the finished production. The film industry has become effectively 'casualised' in terms of employment with most personnel now operating on a freelance basis. Also, technical equipment and facilities (including studio space and post-production) are rented from hiring companies. This state of affairs has prompted some to argue that film-making has assumed the characteristics of 'craft production'.[6]

It is interesting to note that in recent years television has been subjected to a similar process: firstly with the introduction of Channel 4, which was set up to operate by commissioning programmes from independent producers, rather than making its own programmes in its own studios with its own creative and technical staff. This has proved so successful that the government subsequently forced the BBC and the ITV companies to commission 25 per cent of their programming from independent producers.

In spite of these changes, Williams's model still applies in the sense that financial control, and with it the power to commission work, has remained in a small group of corporate hands. According to Ned Tannen, in the US only five per cent of packages offered are actually realised as films.[7] More often than not these will be the packages which correspond with the financier's conceptions of a commercially viable product based on current trends and past experience. In Britain the percentage of successful 'deals' may be higher but there are so few sources of indigenous finance available that film-makers may be prepared to compromise significantly in order to get a project off the ground. In addition, companies like Channel 4, Zenith, Handmade and Palace will often commission work from writers in order to get the product they want.

## FILM SALES IN THE UK

As I have argued above, the major concern on the part of production companies is their ability to sell their product – particularly to the potentially highly profitable North American market. In most cases finance from an American distribution company will be in the form of a presale or 'negative pick-up' (a pledge guaranteeing the payment of a specified sum on delivery of the final negative which a producer can lodge with a bank). Given the relative size and importance of markets the North American deal is a fact of life. As Steve Woolley of Palace comments:

> No British film of almost any budget that I can think of can really go forward unless there is either a presale in place or incredibly good signs of getting a presale . . . . Your bank would have to be totally stupid to go ahead without an American presale.[8]

Selling a film to a foreign distributor effectively gives that distributor the right to exploit the film as they see fit. While this seems only fair given that the distributor will have paid a great deal of money for the film in question, it can also mean that the film-makers have effectively lost any say over how the film is to be distributed and marketed. In addition, certain distribution deals can create a situation whereby if a film proves to be highly profitable, little if any of this profit reaches the producers: it is all creamed off by the distributors. While the issue of the North American market is rather cut and dried, deals covering rights to the rest of the world can be more favourable from the producer's point of view if the production company can retain the right to sell the picture to foreign territories. Steve Woolley for one argues that his company Palace would rather

> take a bigger risk on the back end than on the front in terms of distribution because I would rather be distributing a film at the end of the day, that I'm making, in the UK and hopefully the world, than taking a big fee up-front. The future of the company is going to depend upon us having a flow of product.[9]

Gareth Jones of Handmade Films makes a similar point in commenting on the problems which may arise on a big-budget production with an American major involved:

the studio for instance might want world-wide distribution in exchange for giving you a producer's fee and we always want territories of our own to exploit because if you have a hit on your hands, that's where you are making the money.[10]

This is not always the case, as sometimes American companies will totally finance a British production in return for world-wide rights. Examples include *Brazil* and *Cry Freedom*. In the hardheaded world of film-production in the eighties, several British companies realised that in order to survive, certain alterations to existing business practices needed to be made.

In 1985 James Park suggested that:

most of Britain's major production finance companies have set up their own sales arms. It enables them to establish relationships with distributors for feedback about market conditions and discussions about future co-production deals. Self-distribution also ensures that the production company has direct access to revenues occurring from distribution and can charge a commission on sales.[11]

In the late eighties there were four major sales agents handling British product: Film Four International, who sold much of the work funded by the Channel; Gavin Film, headed by ex-Goldcrest sales manager Bill Gavin; and The Sales Company, which was set up in 1986 by Zenith, British Screen and Palace and has handled all the product of the founding partners and since 1987, Working Title productions. The other major British company, Handmade Films, have always sold and distributed their product 'in-house', although recently they used the services of Recorded Releasing to distribute their product in the UK. This is because Handmade's premises were too small to incorporate a major distribution office. But the relationship between Handmade and Recorded Releasing was somewhat different from the normal producer/distributor one as Gareth Jones explained:

We are putting up the distribution monies ourselves to cover costs. So it's not a true arms-length distribution deal. We obviously do deals with sub-distributors throughout the world but those deals are done by our own people. We don't use sales agents so distribution is something we very much want to keep under our own control. In the US we'd like to put together a distribution deal whereby we have control over distribution using the offices and some of the personnel of a studio distribution company. We would actually put our own films out and cover the P & A costs ourselves and get a bigger share of returns at the end of the day. Because distribution is where the money is made.[12]

The Sales Company, headed by Carole Myer, formerly of Film Four International, was set up in order to give the companies involved a more direct say over the question of how their products were to be sold, distributed and marketed in foreign territories. They also make a substantial saving on sales commission, paying in the region of 5–7.5 per cent to the Sales Company as opposed to the usual 15–20 per cent, effectively reducing the cost of recovering investments.[13] As John Durie, former Head of Marketing at the Sales Company puts it:

> There's very little point in making a picture . . . if you cannot really try to control the eventual audience, i.e. who is actually going to have an opportunity to see your film.[14]

The partners themselves know only too well the benefits setting up The Sales Company has brought. Steve Woolley, for example, is very enthusiastic:

> It's been really important because it has enabled us to keep the rights on pictures, raise money, hit targets in terms of foreign sales: which the banks are impressed by, thereby forging a closer relationship for future productions . . . . And it's also meant a good cementing of our ongoing relationship with Zenith and British Screen which is very important.[15]

Production companies in Britain are acutely aware of the importance of selling their product to distributors who will handle the distribution and marketing of a film intelligently and carefully. Given the importance of the American marketplace, it is crucial that British producers are able to secure deals with American companies who can do this as it will give their films a greater chance of success; a production company with such a deal can acquire a track record which will enable it to raise money for subsequent productions. Sarah Radclyffe of Working Title explained the situation in 1988:

There has grown up in the States a whole collection of smaller distribution companies, or 'mini-majors' as they are known, like Cinecom, Atlantic, Orion Classics . . . who know how to handle and place our sorts of films and know how to distribute them. Whereas if we'd just been left dealing with the majors there is a very large risk that if they don't angle it right, if they open it too wide . . . they will pull it after a couple of weeks. Just like that! Whereas if they get more personal attention . . . Atlantic did a great job with *Wish You Were Here* and so far they are doing a great job with *A World Apart* which is very political . . . . They could have easily said 'This is too political' and opened it in one cinema in Detroit or whatever . . . . If you are in with the big companies you don't have the personal relationship with people who are handling the project and I can't think of anything worse than spending a couple of years of my life doing something for some business executive in a major studio to say 'That's not going to work, it's too political!' It would be awful. I can't think of anything worse.[16]

The importance of The Sales Company to production houses like Working Title, Zenith or Palace lies not only in terms of selling or placing films, but also in the context of sensible budgeting practices: setting budgetary levels on the basis of the film's estimated market value provided by Sales Company forecasts rather than making a film for whatever it costs and then attempting to sell it as widely as possible. As Radclyffe argues, the value of The Sales Company is their ability to assess a script's worth in terms of foreign sales:

We can work it out roughly: the problems of a first-time director, unknown stars, the rest of it . . . . But they can work it out to a finite figure which is a great help.[17]

The Sales Company base forecasts on past selling experiences of similar features but, as John Durie explains, the most important elements in the process of forecasting are the script and the elements attached to the project: stars, director, writer, producer. From this information a calculated estimate of what the film is worth in foreign markets is made. Once a film has been sold to a particular territory The Sales Company offer the distributor advice regarding marketing by showing them examples of successful campaigns in other territories. But the final say lies with the distributor. As Durie puts it:

You have to sell to distributors who actually want your picture and are going to be enthusiastic about it. And if they say 'That's a great campaign in Britain but it's just not going to work in Germany or Australia', then you have to trust what they are going to do. Also, they have paid a lot of money for the picture and they should have the right to market the picture as they see fit in their territory. That's why we independent sales agents are much different from the majors because what the majors do is . . . from Hammersmith UIP [United International Pictures, the largest film distributor registered in this country which handles, among other things, films made by Paramount, Universal and MGM/UA] say what the postering in South America or the Far East is going to be. It's a very different approach.[18]

Film sales agents tend to conduct their business at a series of annual international film markets. The three major 'must attend' markets, as Durie puts it, are the American Film Market, held in Los Angeles at the end of February, the Cannes Film Festival, which takes place in May and MIFED, which is based in Milan during the last week of October/first week in November. Durie explains that these three events are the main commercial forums for assisting and selling a film. The major difference between them is that the Cannes Film Festival tends to cross the perceived divide between the cultural and commercial sides of the industry: i.e. minority-audience 'art-house' films and mass-market commercial productions, while both the AFM and MIFED are purely commercial markets with very little cultural glamour attached. In addition to the 'big three' there are a handful of other important festivals: most notably Berlin and Venice which, like Cannes, are both guided by a cultural and critical imperative and again like Cannes are used to launch particular films: giving them a certain profile which will hopefully generate a favourable critical response. At MIFED and the AFM business is described by Durie as 'straight selling' with films being advertised, distributors discussing projects with agents, viewing the film and then deciding whether to buy it or not.

One consequence of the commerce/culture distinction drawn by Durie is that particular films are targeted at particular markets depending on their form and content. As Durie puts it, an 'avant garde' film like Derek Jarman's *The Last of England*, which The Sales Company handled, would play well at Berlin but would definitely not go down well at MIFED or the AFM which are only interested in mass-market commercial films. Cannes, on the other hand, has the ability to span the whole spectrum. Durie explains that the appropriate placing of a film is vitally important. To present an 'art' film at Milan would be to do it a disservice as the buyers who would be interested in it would not be in attendance and its all-important 'profile' would be lost.

The idea of the 'profile' means that The Sales Company treats every film it handles as a distinct entity and sells it as such, within the parameters of the selling process: festivals, markets, trade publications and so on. The company attempt to stress the particular individuality of a film by way of an artwork 'image' used in the form of a promotional poster or incorporated in a glossy sales brochure which includes a plot synopsis and biographical information on those involved with the project – director, producer, stars, etc. More often than not, this work will be done at the presale stage of the process. As Durie explains, creating an image for the film before it is made is important because it plants in the minds of potential buyers some image or idea about the project and hopefully stimulates interest:

> although there is an eighteen-month lead time from when a picture is actually given the go-ahead to when it's actually finished, everything happens in those eighteen months in terms of marketing it, selling it, getting contracts and actually creating a distribution marketing campaign. So when it goes out, people are very well aware of it. It's a very important ingredient in the whole film business because if you don't sell it, you don't get the money, and if you don't get the money, producers can't make their next picture.[19]

So far The Sales Company have been successful in their task. Their business acumen and enthusiasm for the films they are handling has ensured this and is a reflection of the will to survive on the part of the indigenous British film industry. These attributes are also shared by the more successful independent production and distribution companies currently active in the UK.

## DISTRIBUTION AND MARKETING

In the UK the key marketing agents are the distribution companies. As Archie Tait points out in his article on distribution included in *British Cinema Now*, there were 110 registered film distributors in

Britain in 1983.[20] Of this figure three large companies handled the films made by the American majors: the staple product of the two major cinema circuits in this country – Rank's Odeon chain and Cannon cinemas. These 'big three' are UIP, Twentieth Century-Fox and Columbia-Cannon-Warners (formerly Columbia-EMI-Warners). These companies have handled the distribution of quite a few British productions in the eighties including *The Killing Fields*, *A Passage to India*, *Revolution*, *Highlander*, *The Mission*, *Castaway*, *A Month in the Country* (C-C-W, who handle less product than they formerly did when Thorn-EMI were a major producer), *Brazil*, *Dance with a Stranger* (Fox), and *Personal Services*, *Cry Freedom*, *A Fish Called Wanda* and the James Bond series (UIP).

Below the 'big three' there are Rank Distributors, who have handled some British product like *Defence of the Realm*, and a group of small independent British companies who have successfully handled much of the independently produced features in the UK. Examples include Palace Pictures, who have distributed *Company of Wolves*, *Mona Lisa*, *No Surrender*, *The Hit*, *Insignificance*, *Sid and Nancy*, *Absolute Beginners*, *Wish You Were Here*, *Sammy and Rosie Get Laid* and *A World Apart*; Recorded Releasing, an offshoot of producer Jeremy Thomas's Recorded Picture Company (*Heavenly Pursuits*, *Eat the Rich*, *Withnail and I*, *Track 29* and *Drowning by Numbers*); Curzon (*A Room With a View*, *Nanou*, *Comrades*, *Little Dorrit*, *Prick Up Your Ears*); Virgin (*Gothic*, *Empire State*, *Aria*); and a few others like BFI distribution, Blue Dolphin, Mainline and Enterprise Pictures. Some of these companies rely on their own independent cinemas for releasing films and most of the British product handled by them tends to be exhibited either in dependent cinemas or the BFI-subsidised Regional Film Theatres.

The value of these companies is recognised by producers. As Patrick Cassavetti, the producer of *Brazil*, *Mona Lisa* and *Paris by Night*, argued in 1987:

> Palace are brilliant because they will take a film and they will push it. They will invest a tremendous amount of enthusiasm into the marketing and selling. Sometimes it works, sometimes it doesn't. But I think, on the whole, the thing about Palace and others is that they are great film enthusiasts so they will enjoy the whole business of promoting a film. They believe in film in general and they will spend a lot of time encouraging people, encouraging exhibitors

And I think that's what you need to do. For so long people have just churned films out.[21]

The issue of marketing movies is a relatively recent phenomenon, catching on in the US, as B. J. Franklin suggests, in the sixties.[22] In the days of the studio system, the Hollywood majors tended to rely on their publicity departments to generate interest in film productions. However, once the industry had undergone major structural change, competition became much fiercer in what was a shrinking marketplace. Finding the most effective way to sell your film to the public became a vital consideration. As Al Clark, former head of production at Virgin, puts it:

> Good marketing is absolutely indispensable . . . . I would defy anyone to name a film that was a success without good marketing. Word of mouth has some effect obviously, once a film has opened, but the opening of a film is linked directly to the effectiveness of its marketing . . . . To distinguish the film from anything else that's opening in that week, to give it an aura of 'must see', to create a sense of occasion around it without lapsing into empty hyperbole.[23]

Other producers currently active in British cinema agree with Clark. Margaret Matheson makes the following comments regarding the issue of marketing:

> I think it's very important, and I think it's something you need to learn, coming out of television where you just make it and bang it on the box with promotion which follows very similar patterns. Learning how to promote cinema has been interesting. Knowing what you've got to sell . . . . And then careful consideration of the best form of advertising depending on a particular audience you think will go for it.[24]

The unique nature of each film means that each must be marketed as a discrete commodity in much the same way as The Sales Company creates a 'profile' for a film to attract potential buyers. This involves the creation of a 'narrative image' (again similar to the selling process) capturing the essence of the film which must be communicated to the cinema-going public. The idea of the 'narrative image' can be applied both in a literal sense: a poster design or logo, or in a broader sense encompassing the key marketable features of a project which will be concentrated on during the campaign and hopefully implanted in the mind of the potential audience. In terms of the literal definition, the basic idea is, in the words of Richard Kahn, to

> seize upon the factors (or preferably a single all-powerful one) that stand out as the dominant reasons people have for wanting to see the movie and to communicate the resulting theme via the words and images in the ad.[25]

Paul Webster, the former Managing director of Palace Pictures, is unequivocal about the importance of the poster design to those who made the film and those who will release it:

> It becomes for the movie the single image that attempts the impossible: to capture the essence of the film and transform it into an image of seduction.[26]

Palace made their name as a film distributor on the back of their phenomenal success with films like *Diva*, *The Evil Dead* and *Merry Christmas, Mr Lawrence*. Steve Woolley, who along with Nik Powell is the driving force behind the company, explains how he came up with the 'narrative image' for *Diva*:

> I sat in front of a video screen and just kept watching images of the film thinking 'What can you take?' and eventually came up with that helmet, which was a beautiful blue image and represented to me . . . the kid and the woman, the blue light behind. But then it didn't have everything, so we thought 'Let's rip the corner off and put that guy with the earphone coming through that'. So you get the murder/romance line that we came up with . . . . And Jean Jaques Beineix (the director) thinks that is the best image he's seen for the film . . . . It takes a lot of work and a lot of time to get a campaign right . . . . I think it's really a case of not asking a director what he thinks of an image, but asking him why he made the film or understanding the notion of why it was worth doing it in the first place . . . getting under the skin of the person . . . and making that your campaign.[27]

The creation of a poster design can be a hit-or-miss situation and sometimes film-makers are not at all happy with the poster design created for their film by the distributors concerned. An interesting example of this is *Empire State*, whose director Ron Peck was far from happy about the poster produced by Virgin for the film:

> I don't think it was very interesting. It wasn't very arresting. It didn't give you any information. There were no credits on it. It just looked to me like something that was thrown out quickly.[28]

Peck contrasts this with the design created by stills photographer Mike Laye which was subsequently used by the sales agents Overview in selling the film overseas. 'They sold the film widely on the strength of it, which was interesting . . . . It drew people's attention.'[29] As a consequence of his experiences with *Empire State*, Peck is determined to have more control over the marketing of his subsequent films. This may prove a difficult thing to achieve given the rights of companies who have paid a lot of money for the film to market it as they see fit.

Turning to the broader application of the idea of the 'narrative image', this can include information presented in the poster in the form of credits or a photograph of the leading actors. But it also goes beyond the poster design in that the idea behind it is to create an impression in the audience's mind as to why the film is worth paying money to see. The naming of stars is a popular device and dates back to the earliest days of the Hollywood studio system. The importance of stars may have diminished slightly from the days of Humphrey Bogart, James Cagney, Bette Davis and Joan Crawford but the inclusion of a big star like Clint Eastwood, Sylvester Stallone or Meryl Streep in a film can still give it a vital boost at the box office. The British cinema boasts few international stars so production companies will often hire an American actor or actress to give them a better chance of attracting US finance. Recent examples include the casting of Barbara Hershey in *A World Apart*, Denzil Washington and Kevin Kline in *Cry Freedom* and Steve Guttenberg and Daryl Hannah in *High Spirits*.

A film can also be marketed on the basis of its subject matter or genre. In this way it can be identified with the success of other productions which are similar in some way: the phenomenon of spin-offs and sequels, or simply being categorised as belonging to a genre which is currently fashionable, be it horror, action adventure, comedy or whatever. While spin-offs and sequels tend to be more a feature of American cinema (*Rocky, Police Academy, Nightmare on*

*Elm Street* have all generated several sequels), British cinema in the past has also relied on series such as the Bond films, Hammer Horrors and the Carry On films, although, with the exception of the James Bond series, this is unusual in the current context. However, the question of genre is still important on both sides of the Atlantic. In the US several sub-genres have been created, reflecting the youthful composition of the audience: gung-ho adventure films, adolescent sex comedies, the 'Brat Pack' movies, etc. British cinema, while by and large tending not to use genre as a major marketing device, is broadly structured on generic lines. The major popular British genres include eccentric comedies (often with serious social themes like *Letter to Brezhnev*, *My Beautiful Laundrette* and others), thrillers (*Defence of the Realm*, *Mona Lisa*), biopics (*Sid and Nancy*, *Personal Services*, *Prick Up Your Ears*) and the odd big-budget 'liberal epic' like *A Passage to India*, *The Killing Fields* or *Cry Freedom*.

Staying with the question of subject matter, a film can also be marketed on the basis of its association with other popular forms; the classic example being an adaptation of a bestselling novel or a popular play. Such literary adaptations have been particularly significant in terms of British cinema which has constantly looked to this country's strong literary tradition for ideas, often to the detriment of cinematic innovation and experiment. Recent examples include *A Room With a View*, *Maurice*, *Little Dorrit*, *A Month in the Country* and *A Handful of Dust*.

A third category which can be manipulated as a marketing device is the reputation of the director of the film, or in a few cases its producer: for example David Puttnam. Directors are arguably more marketable than they once were given the general rise in interest in directors as 'authors' of the films they make. This idea originated with the critics writing for the French journal *Cahiers du Cinéma* in the fifties and is reflected in the bulk of film reviews in the 'quality' press and on television. In the US the latest film by Steven Spielberg, George Lucas, Martin Scorsese or Francis Coppola are marketed on the strength of their directors' reputation, while in Britain productions by John Boorman, Richard Attenborough, Bill Forsyth, Nicolas Roeg, and one or two others can be given a similar push.

However, as John Ellis notes,[30] the utilisation of a film-maker's reputation as a major marketing device has its pitfalls for those concerned. The set of expectations which the marketing campaign utilises can serve to constrain a film-maker by locking him or her in a particular image which they may be unable to break. Like actors and actresses they can become 'typecast' as a maker of comedies or action-adventure movies, and investors will only back projects which relate closely to their previous successes. The creativity to which they owe their reputations can become progressively stifled in the drive to retain their popularity with audiences and backers alike. This is an example of a totally negative constraint relating to the worst excesses of commercial cinema.

In this way we can begin to see how the categories explored above can interrelate: particular directors and stars can become strongly associated with particular kinds of film. The task of the executives assigned to devise and implement a marketing campaign for a film must attempt to combine these elements in the most effective way possible, highlighting the strengths and downplaying any weaknesses: for example concentrating on star performers to cover up what may be a mediocre plot. In addition, while there is a tendency to standardise, to cash in on past successes by employing similar techniques, some innovation is required if formulas are not to become too overworked and repetitive, leading to a drop in box-office popularity. In addition, there is no such thing as a dead certainty in the film business: the inclusion of stars, a name director, or a popular subject may give a production a greater chance of commercial success but this success will certainly not be ensured. The marketable elements of a project must be combined and packaged in particular ways using a range of marketing techniques which are sensitive to the complexities and characteristics of what is a volatile and highly elusive market.

## THE MARKETING STRATEGY

As I have indicated above, marketing campaigns are as individual and idiosyncratic as the films they are designed to promote. However, there is a common set of parameters and techniques within which campaigns must operate and which they must make use of in the most effective manner possible. Richard Kahn identifies four distinct categories within the concept of 'movie marketing': market research, advertising, publicity and promotion. He describes the first of these – 'market research' – in terms of a currently evolving pheno-menon which is designed to increase the effectiveness of decision-making with regard, not only to questions of sales and advertising, but also to 'the very judgements that determine what movies will be made'.[31] This appears to bear out the observations made by Williams regarding market-originated cultural production. However, Kahn preaches some caution on the issue in that market research does not, in his opinion, provide some set of objective guidelines for commercial success, however important it may be:

> Trained judgements, intuitive leaps, good guesses and common sense must remain the hallmarks of motion picture marketing; if we veer away from these criteria, we're going to be in a great deal of trouble.[32]

Market research has three different applications in terms of the film-making process. Firstly, it can be used to target an audience: who will be interested in your film and is this market substantial enough to justify the amount of money you intend to spend on the production? In Britain decisions regarding target audience tend to be based on past experience; knowing what it is you have to sell and looking at how similar products have sold in the past, talents for which The Sales Company, for example, are widely noted.

Secondly, market research can be used to test a finished film by way of organising previews screened to an invited audience whose reactions are observed throughout the screening and who are subsequently asked to comment and make suggestions as to how the film could be improved. This can result in changes to the final cut of the film; sequences which played well can be highlighted, those which didn't can be shortened, the whole film can be tightened up. Decisions can also be made regarding target audience at this stage, on the basis of who the film seemed to appeal to the most on a basis of age, sex and social class. From this information the most effective ways of marketing the film to its target audience can be worked out.

A third and final application of market research is to use it to construct a 'formula picture': bringing together certain elements which research has shown to be popular to the public. This would seem to be an application of market research which ignores Kahn's warning in that it sets out to make the ultimate audience-oriented picture regardless of other issues of form and content. As a result it has never been used in Britain and only occasionally in America. However, as John Durie points out, a company called Pacific

International, which was involved with films like *The Wilderness Family* in the seventies, used this form of market research:

> It was almost like making a picture out of multiple choice elements: taking on the right elements and making the picture. And they were actually very good at that.[33]

Widespread use of such techniques could only lead to creative paralysis in the long run as it gives up the whole question of initiation in favour of some vague and dubious notion of 'what the public wants'.

Kahn describes advertising as the marketing tool with the highest profile. It is also the most expensive: in 1978 $500 000 000 was spent on movie advertising in North America.[34] Advertising is conducted through the channels of newspapers ('the bulwark of the motion picture ad campaign'), magazines, radio, television and outdoor posting. The all-important print ad 'image' represents the major foundation of a successful advertising campaign for all the reasons discussed above. In addition, the placing of ads in appropriate (in relation to target audience) publications and at appropriate times in broadcast schedules is vital. The advertising campaign carried out by Palace, through PSA, their publicists, for Nicolas Roeg's film *Insignificance* is described by Shelly Bancroft in an issue of *AIP & Co.* magazine.[35] The film was aimed at a young (mid-twenties), fashion-conscious, educated audience and consequently particular attention was paid to coverage in magazines identified as having this kind of readership: *The Face*, *Blitz* and *I.D.* These ads put a strong emphasis on Roeg's directorial style and also stressed the strong fifties glamour image of the film (reflecting the current vogue for fifties icons and fashions). A more mainstream release would have been advertised rather differently, probably making more use of popular newspapers and prime-time television advertising.

Relating it back to the idea of market research, an advertising campaign may be subject to testing in much the same way as the completed film is at a preview. This is justified by John Durie on grounds of cost:

> The film industry is terribly expensive. It's very costly to make prints and take advertising and to sustain a campaign, let alone just the making of the picture. So it's a question of, are you actually

doing the right campaign for the right picture, releasing it at the right time to the right audiences in the right cities?'[36]

The issue of publicity in Kahn's model refers to all direct public attention brought to a product by means of the same media used by advertising, but in this instance using time and space that has not been directly purchased. This is the crucial difference between the two. Ongoing publicity is an important aspect of a marketing strategy from the moment the project is approved to when it reaches the cinemas. It embraces things like news and feature stories concerning the project and those involved in it, interviews with such individuals and documentaries on the making of the film. Continuing with the example of *Insignificance*, publicity for this project included a *Time Out* feature on actor Tony Curtis, chatshow appearances by him on 'Wogan' and 'Breakfast Time', and a fashion spread in a major woman's magazine featuring Theresa Russell who also stars in the film. In addition, a documentary on the making of *Insignificance* was shot by Nicolas Roeg's son Luke.

Kahn points out that a qualified unit publicist is usually assigned to a production at a very early stage and it is his, or her, job to generate a flow of press material that will continue to call attention to the film throughout the course of its production. The unit publicist is responsible for organising and supervising visits to the set by media representatives and also has the task of assembling the final 'press-kit' which will be handed out at press screenings for review purposes and at festivals. The kit is made up of notes on the production and those involved with it, feature stories and production stills. Glinwood, the sales agents for *Insignificance*, produced an electronic press kit – a video consisting of clips from the film and soundtrack and sections of Luke Roeg's documentary – which was handed out at the Cannes film festival. Kahn also includes the making of a trailer to be shown at the cinema where the film is due to be exhibited at the promotional stage.

The final stage of the marketing process according to Kahn is promotion. This involves the use of a variety of subsidiary devices to call attention to the film. These devices include paperback novelisations of the screenplay or, if the film is an adaptation, a new edition of the original novel featuring artwork from the film on the cover – usually the poster design. Soundtrack records are also common promotional devices. Steve Woolley of Palace is particularly emphatic about the importance of a soundtrack album as a promotional device:

> On *Scandal* we have an original score by Carl Davis, we have 20 different songs from Peter Sellers to the Shadows to Nat King Cole and Frank Sinatra . . . . And The Pet Shop Boys have done a track with Dusty Springfield which they are releasing in February and that will be at least a top ten hit. We release our film in March . . . . People say you are bastardising the film because you've got The Pet Shop Boys on the credits at the end. To me if I can get The Pet Shop Boys audience – expecially the older ones, to take the picture semi-seriously then I've got an enormous market there.[37]

It is interesting to note that stars like David Bowie, Mick Jagger, Sting and Phil Collins, from the pop music world often appear in films. This is in itself a marketing function to a certain extent. In the case of big blockbuster films like *Star Wars* or *E.T.* the promotional net is thrown much wider to include toys, games, mugs, T-shirts and other novelties.

A final promotional device which is not mentioned by Kahn but which B. J. Franklin picks up on, is 'word of mouth'. This can be a very effective, and cheap, way of drawing attention to a film. As Franklin suggests, 'If a film catches on by word of mouth the only thing that people need to know is where it's playing.'[38]

All the hard work done at the marketing stage can be thrown away if a film's distribution is botched. In fact, in some cases a film's ultimate success or failure can rest on how and when it is released into cinemas. Franklin points out that in North America there are two peak releasing periods during the year: Summer and Christmas. While these are popular periods this also means that competition is at its highest and selling a particular film to the public will be all the more difficult. The onus is on the distributor to handle the film carefully and intelligently in order to ensure the most favourable outcome. There are two typical release patterns – fast, where the market is saturated quickly and a film is screened simultaneously in cinemas all over the country, and slow, where a film is opened in one or two cinemas in selected areas and interest in the form of reviews and word of mouth is allowed to build up before it is released any wider. Franklin gives a detailed account of the releasing strategy employed by Columbia on Robert Benton's film *Kramer versus Kramer*. The movie was originally targeted at a sophisticated 'adult' audience since it was to be released during the Christmas period and in direct competition with a host of 'family'-oriented blockbusters. When it came round to actual release, *Kramer versus Kramer* was given limited as opposed to blanket exposure: a slow rather than a fast release. This was to give the impression of the film being available, but not too available and was probably a self-conscious decision by Columbia to avoid any overt feeling of the film being in competition with the more high-profile blockbusters. In any case the film proved to be both a commercial and a critical success.

While good placing can help a film's success, a releasing strategy which is inappropriate, or badly thought-out, can wreck a film. This is exactly what Ron Peck claims happened to his film *Empire State* which, as is pointed out above, was distributed in this country by Virgin. As Peck puts it:

> Virgin ended up doing a deal with Cannon, therefore it went into Cannon cinemas and it seems to me it shouldn't have played in those cinemas. It was the wrong place. I went up to Newcastle to see it. It opened there and played for one week, which was interesting because even the cinema manager said the film would do much better at the local regional film theatre . . . . Virgin opened the film in something like thirty cinemas on the first day which again was a big mistake. It should have opened in one cinema and allowed to hopefully generate interest, which is a tried and tested way of opening films like *Mona Lisa* and *My Beautiful Laundrette*. These films opened in a place where there was a focus.[39]

In addition to the insensitive release pattern, thirty prints of the film must have been struck. At £1000 a print this seems an unnecessary expense for a film which could have earned more at the box office with a slower releasing pattern using six to ten prints. The larger companies, who are used to dealing with mass-market American product, seem to be unable at times to treat more 'difficult'products with the care they require. As Steve Woolley observes:

> I see all the time companies like Rank and Cannon, who have so much on their plate they don't know what they're doing; they don't know when they've got a good film or a bad film, so they throw

them all out . . . . And they throw the baby out with the bath water every time.[40]

There is occasionally a problem of access to particular cinemas which can hinder the distribution process. Simon Relph explains that in the case of *Comrades* the plan was to release the film into the Curzon cinema as its pre-general release showcase (Curzon being the film's UK distributors). However, the film was delayed slightly due to problems with the editing process and as a result it missed its turn in the queue at the Curzon, losing out to *Prick Up Your Ears*.

These then are the major components of the marketing process. To conclude this discussion, I shall describe in some depth the marketing campaigns which were designed for the release of two British films into UK cinemas in the mid-eighties.

## THE MARKETING OF *THE KILLING FIELDS* AND *COMPANY OF WOLVES*

Most home-produced films are marketed in this country by British distribution companies. There are some which have been substantially funded from North America and as a consequence the right to distribute these films, even in the home market, remains with the American distributor. This is the case with Roland Joffe and David Puttnam's film *The Killing Fields* which was marketed in this country by Warner Brothers European Advertising and Publicity department and distributed through Columbia-EMI-Warner.[41] The film was initially previewed at selected venues, enabling the makers to assess feedback and make any alterations if necessary. The response at these previews was generally positive, particularly from females and young males. The advertising strategy was to play-safe by aligning the film with both *Chariots of Fire* (by virtue of David Puttnam being the producer of both) and *Gandhi* (by virtue of the production company Goldcrest), both multiple Oscar winners, serving to boost *The Killing Fields* by association and give it a particular profile as a 'quality' film.

The decision was made to open the film exclusively in one cinema. This was the pre-Christmas period and if the film had been given a general release at this stage it would have found itself in direct competition with American blockbusters like *Ghostbusters* and *Gremlins* and probably would have suffered accordingly. The strategy generated much interest: both word of mouth, and critical in the form of published reviews. Favourable quotes from critics were used in subsequent poster and ad campaigns. *The Killing Fields* was then released into three other London cinemas in order to build up the momentum gradually. Finally, a general release was planned for February 1985. This was good timing as the Christmas films had come to the end of their runs and *The Killing Fields* was tipped to clean up at the BAFTA ceremonies (the British Oscars). Around sixty prints were made for maximum nationwide exhibition. (In the US an equivalent general release would involve over one thousand prints: a stark indication of the difference in market size.)

*The Killing Fields* enjoyed the benefits of having a powerful and established marketing organisation. *Company of Wolves*, on the other hand, was the first film produced by Palace, only two years after they had begun to distribute films.[42] *Company of Wolves* was perceived as an 'art' film and consequently posed certain problems as to the most effective way to market it. It had no direct structure and did not fit into any existing generic category, there were no big stars appearing in the film, and the director Neil Jordan was, at that point, virtually unknown. Therefore, the decision was made to market the film as an 'enigma', as Paul Webster, the man responsible for the campaign, puts it. The marketing campaign was to be limited by financial considerations: only £200 000 was available (minus the cost of prints), which is extremely modest compared to the average five to six million dollars spent on an American film at home. So the initial steps were to make selective placements of ads in certain quality publications including the *Guardian*, *The Sunday Times* and *Time Out* and on local London radio. Palace found that the tabloid press was of little help because no popular personalities were attached to the project.

The advertising campaign utilised five key sentences, each beginning 'Once upon a time'. These were designed to puzzle and fascinate, but not to inform as such: to give the impression of 'something stirring in the undergowth' as Paul Webster puts it. The film was previewed at the 1984 Edinburgh Film Festival, 'to a very confused audience', as Neil Jordan remembers,[43] and subsequently was given its London premiere at the prestigious Odeon, Leicester Square. As Webster points out, the Rank circuit had a great deal of faith in the film, making wide distribution relatively painless. The premiere was followed by a party held in a marquee by the Thames, which was appropriate since the film features a grotesque banquet in a marquee where all the guests are turned into wolves! The film was then given a general release and it proved to be popular, particularly with metropolitan audiences.

Palace expressed some disappointment at the film being given an '18' certificate by the British Board of Film Censors as it had been particularly enjoyed by children at a special showing in Dublin. An American distribution deal was arranged with Cannon who marketed the film in a similar fashion stateside, although the delicate balance between exploitation/intelligent film which had been achieved in the UK campaign tended to be upset with a gravitation towards the exploitative elements. Steve Woolley was dissatisfied with the job done by Cannon, feeling the film had been 'thrown away'.[44]

Both *Company of Wolves* and *The Killing Fields* were subsequently released on video cassette. Paul Webster argues that a video release is absolutely vital to a film of limited appeal like *Company of Wolves*. The theatrical release is used to set the tone and video is a primary follow-up. Seventeen thousand video cassettes of the film were released by Palace compared to sixty prints for theatrical distribution. This is very much a reflection of the pattern of film consumption in the UK today and it makes simple economic sense to treat the film in such a way. The same justification is given for the high concentration on the London area as far as the advertising campaign for *Company of Wolves* was concerned. Cinemagoing is much higher in the capital compared to the provinces, justifying the considerably higher profile. This is all part of effective targeting and utilisation of resources within the marketing campaign.

These are only two examples of thoughtful and successful marketing campaigns, demonstrating an awareness of product, of potential audience, and of the most effective means to bring the film to the attention of that audience. At the end of the day this is vital, for the simple reason that unless films can reach an audience of a sufficient size to justify the amount of money spent on them, production companies would go out of business and film-makers would be unable to work. Therefore in practically all cases potential projects will only secure funding if the investors are convinced the film can perform in the marketplace. These are the economic imperatives informing the industrial structures within which the creative process of film production necessarily takes place.

# 6 Genre, Aesthetics and Criticism

There are other factors which contribute to the structuring of the film-making process which are also worth examining. These include aesthetic and cultural factors which are less tangible than issues of finance and technology but are just as significant nonetheless. The aesthetic domain embraces those resources constituted by the techniques of cinema – modes of narration, *mise-en-scène*, montage and so on – which any film-maker can draw upon in the course of their work. It is through the utilisation of such aesthetic resources that film-makers establish an active communication, in Williams's sense,[1] with their audience. These resources are related to technological resources such as cameras, lenses, film stock, lighting, editing and dubbing facilities. Consequently, the individual film-maker is afforded a wide range of aesthetic and technical possibilities from which to draw upon.

While subjective elements such as individual aesthetic preferences and techniques (elements of style) do play a part in this process, choices are always made in accordance with external considerations and determinants. These range from the readily identifiable – size of budget, demands of investors, availability of technology and so on, to the less tangible – the social and cultural context within which creative activity occurs. Factors such as normative and value systems, history and politics also contribute to the social context within which film-making, as well as writing, theatre and painting (all of which in turn have influenced the development of cinema), take place. Contrary to the claims of idealist philosophy, aesthetics cannot transcend the material and social world of which they are a part. With these remarks in mind I shall now consider the cultural context of British cinema, in both an historical and a contemporary sense, in the attempt to identify the characteristics and parameters of the 'aesthetic space' within which film-making occurs.

## GENRE AND BRITISH CINEMA

All national cinemas can be described as more or less heterogeneous with regard to the range of films they produce. The British cinema is no exception to this in that each film possesses its own unique characteristics and narrative. Unlike American cinema, there are very few sequels – which often contain all the elements of the original plot in a slightly different order or combination – produced in British cinema. It is consequently very difficult to say anything meaningful about 'the British cinema', as opposed to the particular film. For this reason we must impose some system of classification, however inadequate, on to the heterogeneity of product in order to identify underlying patterns and possible categories into which individual films can be placed.

The most common system of film classification is genre, developed in relation to American cinema from the earliest days of Hollywood and persisting in a modified form to the present day. Its institutional function is described by Gledhill:

In cinema . . . generic forms were one of the earliest means used by the industry to organise the production and marketing of films, and by reviewers and the popular audience to guide their viewing. In this respect genres . . . emerged from the studio system's dual need for standardisation and product differentiation. The genres, each with its recognisable repertoire of conventions running across visual imagery, plot, character, setting, modes of narrative development, music and stars, enbled the industry to predict audience expectation. Differences between genres meant different audiences could be catered to. All this made it easier to standardise and stabilise production.[2]

Generic forms therefore developed in relation to the commercial imperative which has underpinned Hollywood film-making since the days of the pioneers. In addition, certain genres were the construction of critics as opposed to being consciously-developed marketing devices by studios. *Film noir* is perhaps the classic example, the term being coined by French critics to refer to a range of private detective films and other thrillers, made in Hollywood during the forties and fifties, characterised by their innovative use of particular thematic and stylistic devices.[3] Genres tend to possess a distinctive iconography and stock characterisations and narratives which are readily recognisable to an audience.

But genre is also subject to historical determination and change. The original generic forms adopted by Hollywood often originated in popular literature: the hard-boiled detective, the western, the horror film. Other genres have emerged as responses to particular social and political events. Science-fiction films, inspired by sci-fi literature, also emerged as a response to the existence of nuclear weapons and the possibility of space travel (in conjunction with the development of sophisticated special-effects techniques). Other genres have been popularised by certain technological developments within the institution of cinema itself. For example the epic, despite several early examples, really came into its own with the introduction of Cinema-Scope. The first film to be shot in this widescreen format was *The Robe* in the early fifties. In recent years there have emerged sub-genres aimed at the youth market which forms a substantial part of current cinema audiences. Examples include 'slasher' horror films: the *Nightmare on Elm Street*, *Halloween* and *Friday the Thirteenth* series, and the 'Brat Pack' movies. Numerous sequels and spin-offs are a particularly strong feature of this kind of film-making.

Generic forms have provided film-makers with an aesthetic 'context' within which they could develop their own cinematic vision by self-consciously relating it to marketable conventions and iconography. Leo Braudy describes genre film-making as:

> the equivalent of conscious reference to tradition in the other arts – the invocation of past works that has been so important a part of the history of literature, drama and painting.[4]

However, working within a set of generic constraints need not be at the expense of self-expression: a film-maker can use the conventions in a creative manner to explore particular social, political or psychological issues within an ostensibly commercial and recognisable format.

Edward Buscombe, in an article which attempts to demonstrate that genre and auteur analysis are not necessarily mutually exclusive frameworks, argues that working within the convention of genre can allow good film-makers to be better. It equips them better, he contends, to deal with popular art and forms of expression:

The artist brings to the genre his own concerns, techniques and capacities – in the widest sense, his style – but receives from the genre a formal pattern which directs and disciplines his work. In a sense this imposes limitations . . . certain themes and treatments are, if not ruled out, unlikely to be successful if they work too hard against the genre. But the benefits are considerable. Constant exposure to a previous succession of films has led the audience to recognise certain formal elements as charged with an accretion of meaning.[5]

These formal elements comprise the iconography of the genre. Familiarity with such elements enables an individual film-maker to make personal films by working within the structures of the genre in original ways. An example given by Buscombe is Sam Peckinpah's western *Guns in the Afternoon* which constantly works against the conventions of the genre. Such originality is also detectable by audiences who are similarly aware of generic conventions and construct their expectations of films in accordance with this awareness. The internal subversion of conventions can be argued to constitute a process of generic transformation.

In recent years generic transformation has also embraced a combination of genres in one film, the classic example being burlesque or parody – the introduction of self-reflexive comic elements into an established 'serious' genre. Examples include the films of Mel Brooks including *Blazing Saddles*, *Young Frankenstein* and *High Anxiety*. Much of the film and television work associated with 'The Comic Strip', and to a lesser extent *Monty Python*, is structured in terms of generic parody. Other examples of genre combination include two films directed by Ridley Scott: the combination of the suspense thriller and science fiction in *Alien* and the futuristic *film noir* of *Blade Runner*. Genre film-making need not therefore be characterised by bland repetition and formula. It can allow film-makers to be creative and to self-consciously relate their own cinematic concerns to convention and established forms.

The British cinema, like its American counterpart, has relied on generic forms throughout its history although these have not been so strongly defined. There is no ideological British equivalent of the myth of the American dream which in different ways informed the classic American genres including the western. Britain does not have such a pervasive cultural myth to build upon; the closest equivalent in

British cinema has been the tendency to fall back on a cultivation of nostalgia. Tom Ryall argues that while the prevailing industrial conditions in the twenties and thirties (size of the industry, quality and popularity of output, competition with American product in home and international markets, etc.) tended to work against the development of a sharply-defined and varied generic profile of the kind that developed in Hollywood during the same period the British film industry did produce 'a small number of broadly defined genres with a certain degree of internal diversity'.[6] Ryall points out that the three major genres which emerged during the thirties were the crime film, the comedy and the musical. In addition to these big three there were minor genres such as romantic dramas, adventure films and the historical costume picture, as exemplified by the productions of Alexander Korda.

Generic forms have been historically specific in the sense that certain genres have emerged at certain periods, have enjoyed commercial appeal and then have declined only to be replaced by others. For example, films about the Second World War were popular from the war years through to the sixties and in some cases beyond. However, there are very few war films made in Britain today, including a significant absence of films dealing with the role of the British army in Northern Ireland. In addition, certain studios or production companies became identified with particular genres in much the same way as some of the Hollywood studios did during the thirties and forties: Warners with gangster films, Universal with horror, MGM with musicals. In Britain the major examples are Ealing studios with comedy, Hammer Films with horror, Gainsborough with historical romance and Woodfall films with naturalistic social drama: the 'kitchen-sink' or new-wave films of the early sixties.

Such close correlations between companies and genre is not so significant in the present context due partly to the different organisation of production on a one-off rather than a continual studio basis. However, until recently Handmade films tended to concentrate on comedy, partly because of their close connection with the various members of the *Monty Python* team. Goldcrest films, until their severe financial problems in the mid-eighties, produced a series of low-budget 'rites of passage' films under the 'First Love' banner, made primarily for television although some did have theatrical releases. This particular genre remains popular in British television drama as the first 'Screen Two' season broadcast in 1988 on BBC2 demonstrates.

The major genres which have contributed to the structuring of the British film industry's output in recent years include the ever popular comedy, which is actually more encompassing and flexible than a genre and is not tied to iconography in the same way. Comedy can more usefully be thought of as a mode, which in British cinema permeates a broad range of films and embraces a range of attendant categories such as the grotesque and the eccentric. I shall consider the significance of the comic mode in British cinema in some depth below.

Concentrating on the identification of more definable genres in British cinema, the thriller has been the prominent generic form with regard to recent production. British thrillers often revolve around the criminal activities of an urban underworld (often based in the East End of London). But some have attempted to be more sophisticated, weaving current political issues, such as Northern Ireland, the abuse of state power and corruption, into the narrative. Manipulation and revenge are often key themes in British thrillers. Recent examples of the genre betray a diversity of subject matter and stylistic influence with some productions such as *The Long Good Friday*, *The Hit*, *Parker*, *Sour Sweet* and *Bellman and True* coming out of the naturalist TV drama tradition of *Z Cars* and *The Sweeney*. Some demonstrate European influences: *Angel*, *Captive* and *Melancholia*, while others are more American in style: *Defence of the Realm*, *Empire State*, *Mona Lisa*, *A Prayer for the Dying* and *Stormy Monday*.

The thriller can be seen as a highly-structured (in line with genre conventions) variant of the social drama which dominates British cinema and which can be traced from the 'social problem' films of the fifties (which were concerned with issues such as juvenile delinquency, prostitution, homosexuality and race), the 'kitchen-sink' dramas of the early sixties,[7] and subsequently the 'Play for Today' tradition in television drama. What acts as a backdrop in the thriller is foregrounded in the social drama: the current nature of British society and its social, economic and political problems. In this way important issues such as unemployment, racial and gender inequality, and questions of state repression can be highlighted. The social drama, like the thriller, is marked by a heterogeneity of style and subject matter. The following examples examine a broad range of social issues and problems: *Giro City*, *Looks and Smiles*, *The Ploughman's Lunch*, *Wetherby*, *My Beautiful Laundrette*, *The Good Father*, *Blood Red Roses*, *Boy Soldier*, *Business as Usual*, *Hidden*

*City, Distant Voices, Still Lives, For Queen and Country, Sammy and Rosie Get Laid* and *High Hopes*.

Significantly, many of these films were backed by David Rose at Channel 4. Rose had previously been Head of Drama at BBC Pebble Mill where he commissioned several notable TV plays during the seventies. This is exactly the tradition of small-screen social drama which feeds directly into much of the current output of British cinema. It is also interesting to consider that in general these films are less cinematic than some of the thrillers mentioned, such as *Defence of the Realm, Empire State* and *Stormy Monday*, which draw more heavily on particular stylistic conventions.

The historical costume drama is still a popular genre with a current emphasis on the late Victorian and Edwardian periods. Unlike earlier examples of British costume drama, in particular Gainsborough melodrama, recent films have stressed social issues (in line with the contemporary social drama) and stylistically, they have placed a great emphasis on accuracy of naturalistic detail. Current costume dramas are frequently adaptations of writers such as E. M. Forster and Evelyn Waugh and tend to deal with upper and middle-class subjects, occasionally critically. The Merchant/Ivory production company have been responsible for several of these films. The cycle was sparked off in part by the huge success of television's *Brideshead Revisited*. Examples include *The Shooting Party, Heat and Dust, A Room With a View, Maurice, A Month in the Country, A Handful of Dust* and *The Rainbow*.

Despite the attempt to incorporate previously unexplored issues such as colonial oppression and repressed homosexuality, this cycle of films can ultimately be related to an evocation of nostalgia which has been a feature of much British cinema in the eighties. This nostalgia is very class-specific; it could be described in terms of a 'country-house' nostalgia, which deals only with the upper classes and is ultimately a yearning for a lost world where life was less compli-cated than it is in the modern world. For all its critique of the aristocracy, a film like *A Handful of Dust* still attempts to stimulate audience curiosity with the upper classes, unfortunately aligning it with the aims of the ultra-nostalgic Heritage Industry in this country.

The evocation of nostalgia is important in relation to the idea of renaissance which was espoused in the early part of the decade following the Oscar success of *Chariots of Fire* and *Gandhi* in successive years. Both these films can be seen as part of the international (both in terms of location and commercial appeal) liberal epic tradition in British cinema which dates back to the films of David Lean from *Bridge on the River Kwai* through *Lawrence of Arabia* and *Dr Zhivago* to *A Passage to India*, from Forster's novel. The three film-makers most associated with this kind of film-making are Lean, producer David Puttnam (*Chariots of Fire*, *The Killing Fields*, *The Mission*) and Richard Attenborough (*Gandhi*, *Cry Freedom*).

Politically, these films tend to demonstrate broadly liberal sentiments. Some are concerned with a reassessment of Britain and the Empire while others deal with international issues both historical and contemporary. While some films – for instance, Attenborough's *Cry Freedom* – can be seen as mildly progressive, others such as *Chariots of Fire* are open to question for their uncritical patriotic sentiment. Lean's *A Passage to India* attempts to criticise the Raj but cannot resist portraying India in terms of an 'exotic other' which at times borders on the patronising. Lean's adaptation does not have the ambiguity of Forster's novel regarding the relationships between the Indians and the colonials. The casting of Alec Guinness as an Indian is also extremely clumsy given the ideological intentions of the film. In any case, the terms of such film-making – big budget, usually provided by an American backer keen to see a return – dictate that commercial viability must not be compromised by political sentiments. Even with the best intentions these films will never be too challenging or radical in approach. Such films are also trumpeted as the standard-bearers of the British film industry and are the most likely to receive American Academy Award nominations.

One genre which has enjoyed a high profile in recent years is the 'biopic': an examination of rather more controversial episodes of recent British history, focusing on the lives of particular 'deviant' characters who represent a challenge to prevailing social mores and standards, often still with some resonance today. These films all contain some, often rather mild, social critique worked out through the relationship of the central characters to the wider society. The 'deviance' of the characters is often rather eccentric, giving many of the films a comic twist in that the exploits and actions of the major protagonists are often highly amusing. The commercial potential of such films is apparently great as they can be marketed in relation to newspaper gossip columns and the British obsession with sexual scandal. Examples of this kind of film include *Wish You Were Here* and *Personal Services*, both based on the life of Streatham madam Cynthia Payne; *Dance With a Stranger*, the story of Ruth Ellis, the last woman to be hanged for murder in Britain; *Sid and Nancy*, the tale of Sex Pistol Sid Vicious and Nancy Spungen; *Prick Up Your Ears*, the story of Joe Orton; *Buster*, the life of Great Train Robber Buster Edwards; *White Mischief*, concentrating on the mystery surrounding the murder of Josslyn Hay the Earl of Errol, the leader of the Happy Valley set in Kenya during the Second World War; *Scandal*, an examination of the Profumo affair of 1963 which focuses on the relationship between Stephen Ward and Christine Keeler; and *The Krays*.

The fantasy/horror film, particularly prevalent in the sixties and early seventies, is still strongly represented in British cinema although in style and content these films are very different from the rather narrow tradition of Hammer Horror. Once again we are dealing with a rather diverse bunch of films, some of which are essentially comic-book fantasy relying heavily on special effects technology and substantial budgets: *Brazil*, *High Spirits* and *Baron Munchhausen*; others betray various influences including the gothic literary tradition, modern horror writers such as Stephen King and cult films such as *Nightmare on Elm Street*. Examples of British fantasy/horror films include *Company of Wolves*, *Gothic*, *Hellraiser*, *The Magic Toyshop*, *The Lair of the White Worm*, *Dream Demon* and *Paperhouse*.

Basically, these are the major broad generic categories which operate in relation to contemporary British cinema. (There have been occasional musicals – *Absolute Beginners*, *Billy the Kid and the Green Baize Vampire* and *It Can't Happen Here* featuring The Pet Shop Boys – but these films were all box-office flops and unlikely to instigate a revival in this genre.) While unable to accommodate the work of such individualistic film-makers as Derek Jarman and Peter Greenaway, these identifiable patterns nevertheless help to impose some sort of structure on British film-making at least with regard to subject matter.

In a sense genre fulfils the function of fusing the eccentric and the iconoclastic with the idea of cinema as communication. Generic conventions are familiar to cinema audiences and enable film-makers to develop their eccentricities within a recognisable framework. It is significant that the non-generic films of Greenaway and Jarman are more difficult and place greater demands on their audiences precisely because of their unfamiliar narrative structure and aesthetic affinities with less readily recognisable cultural forms and cinematic conventions. The same is true of European Modernist cinema in general which either avoids genre or attempts to radically interrogate and deconstruct it as do the early films of Godard.

I shall now extend this discussion to consider broader aesthetic and critical concepts which help to make up the particular cultural context within which British cinema is produced.

## THE WIDER AESTHETIC AND CULTURAL CONTEXT

Within the current British context, I wish to identify certain factors which have contributed to the determination of the particular cultural and aesthetic configuration which has shaped the development of British cinema in aesthetic terms and which exerts a strong influence on current production. These factors, which can be seen in terms of 'modes' or aesthetic tendencies, transcend the barriers of genre and contribute to the determination of a cinema which can be appropriately, if rather tentatively, identified as 'British' as opposed to 'German', 'French' or 'American'.

Obviously any 'national cinema' is open to influence from abroad. American cinema was influenced by German Expressionism and British cinema has always borne the mark of its close relationship with Hollywood. But at the same time, internal traditions are very robust and strongly determine the ways in which external influences are absorbed to conventional practices. For example, Hollywood absorbed Expressionist techniques, which were developed in relation to Modernist narrative forms in Weimar Germany, to its dominant melodramatic tradition. In Britain's case there was, during and immediately after the Second World War, an appropriation by feature film-makers of the strong tradition of documentary realism, pioneered by film-makers such as John Grierson and Humphrey Jennings, instigating a dominant aesthetic trend which can be traced through the history of British cinema to the present day. The British documentary tradition was aesthetically diverse, ranging from the informative style of the GPO documentaries to the poetic approach of Jennings. The realist aesthetic generated by this tradition was lauded by critics who called for a determined effort on the part of British film-makers to build a national cinema distinct from that of Hollywood in terms of style and ethos.

In addition to a consideration of the realist mode in British cinema, I shall also examine two other aesthetic developments which have contributed to the structuring of formal tendencies in British cinema from the days of the pioneers to the present. Firstly, there is predominance of the comic mode in British cinema, noted above, which can be related to a tradition rooted in British popular culture and identifiable in other forms – in particular the novels of Dickens and the music-hall tradition which, as Andy Medhurst points out, was as much of an influence on the development of cinema in Britain as the rich literary and theatrical traditions.[8] This tendency is still extremely relevant in the current context. Secondly, the influence of these other forms (and later of television) contributed to the develop-ment of a cinema noted for its verbal primacy: the over-reliance on words, as opposed to images, to convey information and narrative development. This aesthetic tendency has been the focus of much criticism of British cinema in general over the years and I shall consider its implications in relation to current film-making.

## REALISM AND BRITISH CINEMA

British cinema has been historically dominated, in critical terms, by a 'realist' ethic favouring the depiction of 'real' or recognisable people in 'real' or recognisable situations. The dominance of realism as the favoured mode of cinematic representation can be traced back to the prestigious documentary tradition, referred to by one commentator as 'Britain's outstanding contribution to the film',[9] and associated with the work produced by Grierson, the GPO, Crown and Group 3 documentary, in particular, the work of Grierson and Jennings, is perhaps be better referred to as poetic realism as much British documentary; in particular, the work of Grierson and Jennings is characterised by dynamic and lyrical editing. It was during the war years that documentary and fiction began to fuse. On one hand, documentaries, such as Jennings' *Fires Were Started*, began to appropriate narrative techniques, while on the other, feature film-makers strove to make films as realistic as possible by utilising the aesthetics of documentary and shooting on location if possible. In addition, several notable documentarists, including Harry Watt and Alberto Cavalcanti, began to move into feature production.

The fusion of documentary realism and fictional narrative, which was derived both from the British theatre and Hollywood cinema, was extremely important in the formation and development of a national cinema distinct from the Hollywood product which contin-ued to dominate the British exhibition circuits. As Andrew Higson points out, the documentary idea involved a cinematic–political discourse which made a powerful differentiation between 'realism' and 'escapism' (or 'tinsel' as Michael Balcon put it), the latter being particularly associated with Hollywood cinema and certain traits within British cinema. Realism on the other hand was deemed to be the true vocation of a socially responsible national cinema. This ideal was subscribed to by Michael Balcon, among others, who was the mastermind behind the output of Ealing studios in the postwar period.[10]

John Ellis argues that the moral desirability of the development of a national cinema guided by the realist imperative was reinforced by the construction of a critical discourse which posited realist cinema as essentially quality cinema. He attempts to demonstrate the pervasive-ness of the ethos of realism/quality by way of a close and detailed examination of the writings of film critics published in the 'quality' press and film journals of the period: the work of C. A. Lejeune, Richard Winnington, Roger Manvell and others.[11] Ellis argues that these critics tended to regard good film-making technique as synony-mous with unobtrusive service – the use of narrative devices which did not draw attention to themselves, such as invisible editing and relatively static camera-work – which were the hallmarks of the British realist tradition. However, what Ellis neglects to consider is how much of an influence Italian Neo-Realism was on these critics. The realist discourse he identifies probably owes as much to this Italian influence as to the moral imperative of an indigenous British tradition of documentary realism.

But there are numerous instances of sustained critical attacks directed at films and film-makers who somehow defied the categories of realism and consequently those of 'quality' and 'good taste'. Ian Christie examines the critical savaging of Michael Powell's film *Peeping Tom* in the context of tension between 'Powell's "deviant" cinema and the prevailing norms of British "quality" cinema'.[12] The result of this almost unanimous condemnation was the effective demise of Powell's British career, which is interesting given that earlier critical attacks did not affect production strategies. Powell was something of an exception; for example, the output of Gainsborough during the forties, and Hammer Films from the late fifties to the early seventies, attracted similar critical flak or were simply ignored. Alexander Walker, for example, makes no reference to Hammer Films in his survey of British Cinema in the sixties.[13] Nevertheless they remained immensely popular with domestic audiences. Care must be taken not to equate the material object British cinema with the critical construction 'British cinema'.

Alongside the development of documentary realism, which concerned itself with contemporary subjects, is a tradition of historical cinema which has also adopted a broadly realist approach to its subject matter. This tradition includes big budget 'prestige' productions, praised by the critics as 'quality' British cinema aimed at the international market. This tradition includes historical epics like *Bridge on the River Kwai*, *Lawrence of Arabia*, *The Battle of Britain*, and more recently, *Gandhi* and *A Passage to India*, and the Edwardian costume dramas discussed above. The realist emphasis is generally placed on accurate recreation of period detail: a broadly realistic portrayal of time and place.

But what exactly were the strengths and weaknesses of the realist project in British cinema? Andrew Higson sums up the social project of the realist tradition in the following way:

> each successive realist movement in British cinema and television has been celebrated both for its commitment to the exploration of contemporary social problems and for its working out of these problems in relation to 'realist' landscapes and characters. In particular, since the 1930s, these films and television programmes have consistently been proclaimed as politically progressive because they extend the conventional social discourse, because they deal with working people.[14]

Like Ellis, Higson ignores the possibility of external influences. There was a significant turning-point in the sixties with the 'kitchen-sink' films such as *Saturday Night and Sunday Morning*, *A Kind of Loving* and *This Sporting Life* being far more 'realistic' in terms of character and environment than anything previously. This shift was influenced in part by the French 'New Wave', providing the aesthetic underpinning, and the literature from which many of these films were adapted.

The question of class generated particular problems in the British cinema, particularly during the forties and fifties, with middle-class actors unconvincing in their efforts to portray working-class characters. This began to change with the arrival on the scene of actors from lower-class environments, like Albert Finney and Tom Courtenay. A comparison between Finney in *Saturday Night and Sunday Morning* and a more classical actor like Richard Burton in *Look Back in Anger* effectively illustrates the point I am trying to make. Alexander Walker writes:

> Had it been filmed eighteen months later, much about *Look Back in Anger* might have been different and probably better. The new wave of working-class or lower-middle-class actors might have conferred a more class-conscious sharpness on Jimmy Porter . . . .[15]

In comparison, Walker describes Albert Finney's success in the part of Arthur Seaton in *Saturday Night and Sunday Morning* as 'total'. It certainly represented a move towards a greater realism of character portrayal in British cinema at the time.

These developments continued in the television and cinema work of film-makers such as Ken Loach and Tony Garnett (*Cathy Come Home, Kes, The Big Flame, Looks and Smiles*), Barney Platts-Mills (*Bronco Bullfrog, Private Road*) and Peter Watkins (*The War Game*), and the 'Play for Today' tradition of TV drama which has embraced the work of politically progressive playwrights such as Trevor Griffiths, Jim Allen, Dennis Potter, John McGrath, G. F. Newman and David Leland. Raymond Williams praises British TV drama for its portrayal of the working class in that it represented 'a conscious extension of dramatic material to areas of life which had evidently been excluded even from majority drama'.[16] This represented a logical extension of the process of cinematic enfranchisement begun by Ealing in the forties.

This tradition feeds directly into the kind of TV/cinema hybrid associated particularly with Channel 4 and which forms the backbone of current British production. Marty Auty explains that television drama has an ability to specifically address domestic social and political issues because a TV producer does not have to have one eye on the international marketplace and can afford to tackle subjects which might be criticised as too parochial for an international audience.[17] Given the close relationship between large and small screen product since the emergence of Channel 4 this is a criticism which is frequently directed at British cinema. Tony Lawson for one suggests that British cinema is 'fairly inward-looking':

> Parochial is perhaps not the right word. It explores things of an intellectual and national nature . . . certainly American films, although they do concern themselves with national issues, [are] not

quite so concerned that they let [them] take over the entire film. They tend to take a wider view.[18]

Lawson's criticisms are specifically addressed to the vision and ambition of a type of film-making which is closely related to television – the typical cinema/TV hybrid. But the general thrust of British realist cinema has also been criticised as limited, unadventurous and conservative.

John Ellis describes in detail the elements of the naturalistic, but largely studio-based, aesthetic utilised by Ealing studios: the use of locations and realistic settings, flat natural lighting and so on. Ealing's depiction of lower middle-class characters and social environments was innovatory to a certain extent, particularly with regard to the attempt to show social groups as opposed to heroic and exceptional individuals.[19] However, the Ealing approach to film-making was ultimately compromised partly due to ideological reasons: the sentimental 'little England' view of the world adopted by the majority of the Ealing film-makers (Alexander Mackendrick and Robert Hamer being the exceptions) which worked against realism, and partly to economic reasons: low budgets and tight schedules which worked against aesthetic innovation. Ellis explains that film-makers at Ealing never used expressionistic light, camera effects or subjective inserts such as dream sequences. Editing tended to be strictly functional and music was used to heighten the linear progress of images by denoting discontinuities of time and place. While such aesthetic techniques are not directly translatable to all instances of realist film-making in British cinema, they do provide the basic elements of what is effectively the general orthodoxy with which most realist film-makers have complied.

Consequently it can be argued that British cinema has failed to be in the vanguard of more 'objective' developments in realism, particularly during the postwar years, in spite of the strength of the documentary tradition. As Roy Armes explains, films which were praised for their realistic approach to contemporary social problems, for example Robert Hamer's *It Always Rains on Sunday* and Carol Reed's *Odd Man Out*, 'relate far more closely to the prewar French cinema of Carné and Duvivier than to contemporary developments in Italy or the USA'.[20] There is, for example, no British equivalent of Italian Neo-Realism, of the deep-focus experiments of Gregg Toland, Orson Welles and William Wyler, or even, in a more recent context, of the kind of low-budget improvised cinema associated with film-makers like Eric Rohmer. In comparison, the British cinema seems formally and stylistically unadventurous, caught between an essentially neo-realist impulse on one hand and the pervasive influence of theatricality on the other. In many British films – Ealing, some of the 'kitchen-sink' films – there is noticeable stylistic discontinuity between the naturalistic treatment of exterior locations and rather stagey interior studio sets.

The heart of the problem revolves around the question of realism and what it actually means. Realism is not a reflection of an unproblematic 'reality' but rather a mode of constructing reality. There have been several 'realisms' in the history of cinema, and indeed other forms, including Italian Neo-Realism, the deep-focus realism of Wyler and Welles, documentary realism, psychic realism, epic realism, magic realism and so on. John Hill explains that the plurality of uses of realism relates to the problem of defining 'reality' itself. As he puts it: 'What has counted as a valid or satisfactory approximation to reality has depended on the epistemology of the real which has been assumed in the first place.'[21] Hill then refers to Raymond Williams's assertion that there are two types of 'revolt' against previous conventions constituting a 'break towards realism' in the arts. On one hand there is an injection of new content: new people, new problems, new ideas. On the other, there is the invention of new forms which undermine habitual versions of dramatic reality and thus communicate new and more fundamental underlying realities.

Hill argues that the realist project in British cinema, with particular reference to the social problem and 'kitchen-sink' films, was of the first type identified by Williams. These films did inject new content in the shape of new characters (the working class, juvenile delinquents), new settings (the factory, the housing estate) and new problems (race, homosexuality). But he also contends: 'Although this was accompanied by a certain degree of stylistic novelty (location shooting for example), it did not, in any major sense, entail the "invention of new dramatic forms".'[22] Hence it can be argued that the British cinema was informed by a 'naturalist' rather than a 'realist' aesthetic. Williams makes a rather tentative distinction between the two arguing that in a twentieth-century context 'naturalism' has come to be regarded in terms of a representation of surface, while 'realism' is concerned with depth and the hidden dynamics of reality.[23]

Consequently, British cinema never really produced any Modernist experiments in the manner of the French, Italian or German cinemas in the sixties and seventies. In many ways Modernism represented a vigorous examination of questions of realism and cinema. Some Modernist film-makers can be said to have extended the domain of realism from the objective world to the subjective domain: the psychic realism of Antonioni and Bergman. Others such as Godard profoundly called into question the idea of realism by drawing attention to the artifice of the medium of cinema and its codes of representation. This contrasts strongly with British 'naturalism' which tended to remain broadly functional in approach with an emphasis on the objective and rather one-dimensional 'reality' of characters, motivations, situations and locations. There were no attempts to question reality or to view it as ambiguous and shifting. In this way both contemporary and historical realism in British cinema can be seen as limiting forms of realism, concerned with the verisimilitude of surface detail rather than with the complex and often contradictory realities of the world.

British cinema has also relied heavily on melodrama (largely derived from the theatrical tradition) as a narrative form. Robert Philip Kolker contrasts melodrama and Modernism in the following way:

> Melodrama demands a great emotional response from its audience, an identification with the central characters of a film (whose personal problems are foregrounded without being linked to a defined social context that may determine them), and insists that conventional attitudes and gestures be accepted as unique components of a character's psychology. Melodrama is a form of assurance and security; . . . it all but guarantees that what is experienced in one film will not be very different from what has been experienced in most others. Just such forms of repetition, emotional safety and reinforcement are what the modernists oppose with forms of question and surprise.[24]

Kolker discusses melodrama as the dominant narrative form in American cinema but given the close relationship between Hollywood and British cinema it is unsurprising that the latter should adopt a similar mode. Even the films of the British new wave, which represented a determined effort to construct a new cinema dealing with the realities of contemporary working-class existence, are ultimately, in Kolker's view, undermined by melodramatic elements: the foregrounding of 'exceptional' characters with whom the audience is expected to identify and conventional narrative patterns of resistance and defiance ultimately culminating in resignation and defeat.

But the question of melodrama and its relationship to British cinema is rather more complex and ambiguous than Kolker suggests. Christine Gledhill notes that melodrama was generally a pejorative evaluation until the sixties when it was revalued in a more positive light: for example, the Hollywood melodramas of Douglas Sirk were re-read as a critique of the American bourgeoisie.[25] Most of the cinema attacked by the champions of realism and quality was extremely melodramatic: the films of Powell and Pressburger, Gainsborough costume melodramas and Hammer horror. This 'repressed underlife' of British cinema has similarly undergone something of a reappraisal in recent years and recast in a positive light. Julian Petley argues that the melodramatic mode worked against the 'stiff upper-lip' conception of the British character and explored taboo areas such as sexuality and exoticism. Many of these films are also distinguished by their stylistic flamboyance (in strong contrast to the flat naturalism of Ealing and Woodfall). In this way such films have come to be seen as a subversive, and therefore progressive, tendency within British cinema.

The obsession with authenticity and accuracy has also been stylistically detrimental to historical projects. This can be demonstrated by way of an example which stands out as an exception to the rule. Derek Jarman's *Caravaggio* is deliberately non-realist in design, being shot entirely in a warehouse and featuring anachronistic 'modern' props like a typewriter and a pocket calculator. The effect is initially quite shocking: an indication of how strong realist expectations are. Christopher Hobbs, Jarman's production designer on *Caravaggio*, is particularly critical of the naturalistic tradition he is deliberately attempting to avoid:

There's a great fashion at the moment for what I call archaeological designing. It can be very good, like *A Room With a View*, where the design was immaculate, it was done with such a light touch that you were actually not aware of it being a period movie in many ways. But then you get other movies like *Little Dorrit*, it was such a bore, everything was right. You could see they had reams of researchers checking up on how to roll up cigars in the nineteenth century. And it's unnecessary because in the first place such little details are only what we know from records and you can be pretty certain that there are dozens of other ways of rolling cigars which we don't happen to know about because no one's remembered or nobody's made a note of it. So when I'm doing a period film I invent the past half the time because nobody knows what it is really.[26]

The approach Hobbs is criticising necessarily works against stylisation which is often what makes cinema interesting. It also mitigates against experiment in the area of design which mirrors the disinclination of British cinema in general to experiment with formal strategies.

Despite the continuing dominance of the realist tradition in British cinema through much of 'Film on Four', it is interesting to consider that film-makers currently working within the British industry tend to be aware of the strengths, and more importantly the weaknesses of that tradition. James Park tends to overstate the case when he argues that 'British film-makers have finally learned to dream',[27] but it is interesting that directors in this country are frequently working in film-making traditions other than social realism. The shift away from the realist tradition occurred in part because the current generation of film-makers have benefited from the internationalisation of Modernist techniques, beginning with the appropriation of such techniques by American film-makers like Arthur Penn in the late sixties, which have broken down old forms of cinema narration. The influence of the Italian Modernists and French New Wave is now extremely widespread. This aesthetic shift is related to more general cultural trends: the growth of consumer capitalism, the relaxation of censorship and moral constraints, amounting to a general process of liberalisation. Expansion in educational opportunities helped to create a more sophisticated audience which could cope with the Modernist infringement on traditional cinema narrative.

Amongst the beneficiaries of this general process of cultural and aesthetic liberalisation are experienced film-makers such as Nicolas Roeg and Ken Russell (who both made their debut features in the sixties) and a variety of 'newcomers' including Neil Jordan, Derek Jarman, Terry Gilliam, Peter Greenaway and Terence Davies. This is not to construct a new auteurist 'pantheon' – the above-mentioned are just as open to criticism as those who are more traditionally 'British' in approach. What is important is that their work demonstrates, in different ways, that British cinema can be something more than naturalistic in intent and execution and can draw upon diverse traditions and aesthetic influences. I would argue that a healthy national cinema is nourished by and thrives on stylistic and formal diversity and experimentation.

This development is also being encouraged by the current critical reappraisal of British cinema history by writers such as John Ellis, Charles Barr, Christine Gledhill, Ian Christie, David Pirie and Julian Petley.[28] This represents an attempt to resurrect certain anti-naturalistic traditions such as the work of Michael Powell, who has been cited as an influence by Jarman, Jordan and Julien Temple, and the output of Gainsborough and Hammer films. These writers share the desire to identify and explore critically neglected traditions of British film-making which will enhance British cinema culture.

The question of quality, which was related to the realist project by certain critics, is still pertinent to any discussion of British cinema although its meaning has shifted somewhat. Current definitions of quality cinema utilise the concept not as a critical evaluation but rather as appraisal of technical skill and standards of practical competence, particularly within low-to-medium budget film-making. Film-makers are expected to aspire to the highest possible standards in their work: to produce the best results possible with the resources available. Producer Patrick Cassavetti argues that creativity in film-making

> lies in making the best of what you've got. That is the art. It's about having a small amount of money or a large amount of money and doing the best you can while wasting as little as possible.[29]

Quality becomes related to issues of resource utilisation in an industry characterised by its relative lack of resources. As Marc Samuelson puts it, 'the thing to try and do is to make a film that looks and feels like it's a much bigger budget than it actually is.'[30] There is a strong sense of a self-conscious promotion of British cinema as aspiring to particularly high standards of technique and performance and 'value for money', and this is where the idea of quality has been relocated.

British technicians have become accustomed to working with very tight budgets and have consequently become very resourceful, as Christopher Hobbs points out with specific reference to production design:

> I think we have an advantage over the Americans for two reasons. One, we are used to working with very small budgets and therefore

have learned to make things look good without having to spend vast amounts of money. The other thing is the theatrical background of a lot of designers. If you've had a theatrical background where there is usually no budget at all, then you have to be able to make anything out of anything, with no money and in no time. It's a very good training and it's certainly the training I had. On something like *Caravaggio*, where there really was no money, we just had to invent and be crafty.[31]

The resourcefulness of Hobbs and the rest of the production team, a demonstration of the importance of creative collaboration in British cinema, on *Caravaggio* combined to produce a visually imaginative quality (in the new sense) film. This notion of quality as high production value is a characteristic of current British cinema in general and something which the industry has attempted to build a reputation on both to sell British films abroad and to encourage American producers to continue making films in British studios with British technicians.


## THE COMIC MODE

Another identifiable aesthetic tradition or tendency in British cinema is the predominance of a comic mode. This embraces a wide range of films from straightforward comedy, to the rich assortment of oddball, grotesque and eccentric humour which crops up in predominantly serious films. This phenomenon is partly a reflection of the considerable influence the music-hall tradition has had on British cinema, but it is also an aspect of a tradition identifiable in other 'popular' forms: a classic example being the novels of Charles Dickens.

George Orwell argues that Dickens developed the notion of eccentricity, with regard to the development of character in his work, which he took from earlier novelists. Eccentric characterisation also looms large in British cinema history. Eccentricities also help to foreground and 'individualise' characters, rendering predicaments personal rather than social and conforming to the requirements of melodrama. However, what makes Dickens unique, according to Orwell, is his fertility of invention with regard to turns of phrase and details. As Orwell puts it: 'The outstanding, unmistakable mark of Dickens' writing is the *unnecessary detail*.'[32] In other words, touches which do not advance the story but which create that special Dickens atmosphere and the idiosyncrasies of his characters.

A variant of the unnecessary detail is identifiable in British cinema. Screen comedy is often heavily dialogue-based: the exchanges between the characters, superfluous 'gags' and catchphrases, which were also trademarks of music-hall comedy, give many British films, and comic actors, their eccentric character. But occasionally the effect can also be visual. Much of the humour generated in the *Monty Python* films, for example, comes from the incongruous juxtaposition of ridiculous characters and situations within 'realistic' historical landscapes such as the filth and squalor of medieval England in *Monty Python and the Holy Grail* and *Jabberwocky*.

Orwell also argued that Dickens's popularity stemmed from his ability 'to express in a comic, simplified and therefore memorable form the native decency of the common man.'[33] This informs much of the British comic traditions discussed below including the music-hall and slapstick strain, Ealing comedy and much current British comedy including the work of Bill Forsyth. It is also consistent with the liberal humanistic stance informing British cinema in general. Eccentricity is also a method of dealing with the tension between naturalism and theatricality. In British cinema it can be argued that the cult of the eccentric is what makes naturalism acceptable and popular, by foregrounding character and humour against a naturalistic, often highly depressing, background. The same could be said of Dickens's novels which on one level dealt with the horrors of urban squalor in Victorian London.

The thirties were a major comic period in British cinema with several stars of the music-hall, including Gracie Fields, George Formby and Will Hay, moving into feature films. The late forties saw the development of the Ealing comedy, which began with *Passport to Pimlico*, *Whiskey Galore* and *Kind Hearts and Coronets*, all released in 1949. In general terms, Ealing comedy concerned itself with the idealisation of community, a nostalgia for the war years in a period of postwar austerity. This quickly solidified into a 'little England' obsession with the archaic, a reaction to postwar change and progress, although there are some exception, including the rather black humour of *The Ladykillers*. Ealing spawned many imitators and its influence can still be detected today in films such as *Local Hero*.

The fifties witnessed a series of cycles ranging from the big-budget prestige post-Ealing humour of the *Doctor* films to the slapstick of

Norman Wisdom and the anarchy of the *St Trinian's* films. Then came the inauguration of the *Carry On* cycle (twenty-seven films in all) with *Carry On Sergeant*, released in 1958. In the case of each of these series, the first film was the most interesting with very little development taking place in subsequent productions, merely repetition of successful elements.

The 'swinging sixties' gave rise to the zaniness of *Tom Jones* and the increasingly surreal films of Richard Lester including *A Hard Day's Night*, *Help!* (both featuring the Beatles), *The Knack*, *How I Won the War* and *The Bed Sitting-Room*, while the seventies witnessed the production of various features based on popular television comedy series such as *On the Buses*, *The Alf Garnett Saga* and *Steptoe and Son*. Television comedy was a major influence on British cinema from the sixties onwards, as Andy Medhurst points out.[34] TV comedians such as Tony Hancock relied heavily on language, rich characterisation and the humour of the unnecessary detail (relating back to my points about Dickens) and this has fed directly into cinema comedy. The seventies also saw the emergence of the grotesque humour of *Monty Python* which is still very much part of present-day British cinema comedy as I shall demonstrate below.

Examples of ostensibly 'straight' films with quirky elements include the numerous adaptations of Dickens which, like the Hammer horror films, constantly feature a range of lower-class 'grotesques' and eccentrics. This type of caricatured portrayal of working-class people by middle-class film-makers can also be found in films like *It Always Rains on Sunday* (an example of a 'serious' Ealing production) with its slightly ridiculous East End criminals. It is interesting to note that the most ridiculed characters in many British films, particularly in the thirties and forties, tended to be either working-class or upper class – social strata other than that from which most of the creative personnel working in the industry were drawn. This began to change as class boundaries became less rigid in British society in the fifties and sixties. The humour of lower-class characters was subsequently generated in relation to their fantasies to escape their humdrum existence in films like *Billy Liar*, which avoided being patronising, or in terms of their 'sharp' talk and sexual conquests in *Alfie*.

There are numerous other examples of comic and off-beat film-making in the present context, including some of the most commercially successful British films of recent years. One reason for the persistent high profile of comedies is that humour is international and consequently it may be easier to sell such films around the world. This was as true in the past as it is today. As director Ken Annakin noted in 1958:

> it is safer to make comedies, because they are the only pictures which, in Britain bring back any profit at all to the people who put up the money.[35]

Recent examples of commercially successful British comedies include *Gregory's Girl, Time Bandits, Educating Rita, A Letter to Brezhnev, Brazil, Personal Services, Wish You Were Here, A Fish Called Wanda, The Tall Guy* and *Withnail and I*. Eighties British humour is more socially observant than its predecessors, drawing on the developing social consciousness of British cinema in general. The comic mode also enables film-makers to address problematic issues while still being accessible to a large audience. *My Beautiful Laundrette* tackles questions of race, homosexuality and urban deprivation but its quirky style prevents it from becoming didactic or ponderous. Consequently, comedy can be described as a highly communicative mode.

Two of the films noted above – *Time Bandits* and *Withnail and I* – were financed by Handmade Films, a company closely associated with comedy since becoming involved in film-making with Monty Python's *The Life of Brian*. They subsequently made a series of films involving various members of Python in a range of capacities from directing and writing to acting. These include *Time Bandits, The Missionary, Privates on Parade* and *A Private Function*. The Pythons have since set up their own production company, Prominent Features, but Handmade continue to make comedies, although not exclusively so, believing they have a 'surer touch' (and an all-important track-record) in this area of film-making.

If Handmade are the company most associated with comedy in the context of current British cinema then the film-maker who has achieved a similar association is Bill Forsyth. Forsyth has been responsible for five features to date: *That Sinking Feeling, Gregory's Girl, Local Hero, Comfort and Joy* and *Housekeeping*, all of which use humour as a way of exploring the predicaments in which the protagonists find themselves. Forsyth's films are a celebration of the human spirit with all its foibles and are therefore very much in the British tradition of gentle humanistic comedy, although his wry wit and attention to detail, both visual and verbal, gives his work an edge lacking in much British cinema comedy.

Forsyth explains that the reason why he chose comedy as his medium of expression in the first place had to do with a severe lack of financial resources (both *That Sinking Feeling* and *Gregory's Girl* were made on shoestring budgets). Comedy was considered to be the most appropriate approach in the circumstances, particularly in the case of *That Sinking Feeling*, which relied on actors giving their services for no payment. To ensure their interest Forsyth had to make the process as much fun as possible: he regarded comedy as the most appropriate approach. Forsyth's former partner Charlie Gormley, who has written and directed two, broadly comic, films to date, *Living Apart Together* and *Heavenly Pursuits*, explains the philosophy:

> Bill and I decided on comedy for a very simple reason – because it was cheap. People always say 'Don't do comedy, it's too dangerous, you can't make them laugh, it's too hard.' But it's a cheaper way of getting production value than any other. Also if you can think up a good gag then the audience will forgive you a multitude of sins. And I think you can always make them laugh in any circumstance.[36]

Comedy is perhaps an apt mode for a cinema characterised by low-budget production and a general lack of production finance.

Particular comic elements, including the eccentric and the grotesque, continue to be found in a broad range of British films: the parody of eccentric upper-class mannerisms in *A Room With a View*, the bizarre social situations and locale within which the protagonists of *My Beautiful Laundrette* find themselves, the savage political and social critique of *How to Get Ahead in Advertising*, and the hyperparodic suburbia of *High Hopes*. In the work of a film-maker like Peter Greenaway we find the marks of an English eccentric with his interest in intellectual game-playing, the ridiculous obsessions of his characters and the situations they create for themselves. Greenaway's films combine abstract formalism and social eccentricity. He uses comic eccentricity without being a director of comedies. A good example of the eruption of quirkiness into a non-comic form is provided by the substantial physical presence of Robbie Coltrane in a wide range of comic roles in serious films such as Derek Jarman's *Caravaggio*, Neil Jordan's *Mona Lisa* and Chris Petit's *Chinese*

*Boxes*. Coltrane is closely associated with the television 'Comic Strip' team, whose anarchic and satirical approach to humour is very much in the *Monty Python* tradition and they have recently ventured into features with *The Supergrass* and *Eat the Rich*. Subsequently his appearance in more serious films is experienced as a disruption or parody even when his portrayal of a character is more or less straight. In this way prior association can generate particular expectations and condition audience response.

## VERBAL PRIMACY IN BRITISH CINEMA

This factor can be seen more in terms of an aesthetic tendency than a mode, a largely unintended consequence of the particular cultural influences on British cinema rather than the conscious appropriation of a highly valued or popular aesthetic tradition. What I want to turn my attention to is the issue of the relationship between words and images in the context of British cinema. Several arguments have been made to the effect that throughout the history of British cinema the strength of the writing has tended to be detrimental to visual experimentation. Film-makers have often solved narrative problems with the use of dialogue rather than images. Some arguments have been made which relate this to aspects of Britain's cultural heritage. Tom Priestley, for example, argues that 'traditionally we are not a very visual country'.[37] Derek Jarman contrasts the British with the Italians whom he regards as having a supremely visual culture. On the production of *Caravaggio* he noted the difference between Italian and British extras in terms of their body language:

> When the extras who were Italian relaxed they relaxed into classic poses. They never relax into the formlessness of the British. The visual language is absolutely in the body of the Italians so it is natural for it to come out in the film.[38]

Roger Deakins recalls the condescending attitude he experienced at art college when he expressed an interest in photography as a form of expression. The prevailing attitude was one which regarded photography as primarily a recording medium. Charlie Gormley also comments on the prevailing attitude to cinema in British society, with an emphasis on education:

This is a country which is by and large literate and almost supremely proud that it's not cine-literate. You just couldn't say to your English teacher, 'I went to the movies last night'. You could say, 'I read a bad book'; that would be fine. But if you went to the cinema it was regarded as too easy or silly.[39]

This state of affairs is directly related to the literary and theatrical influences on British cinema. Tony Lawson explains that a British film-maker would handle a dialogue scene in a very different way to an American, French or Italian director would and this, he explains, is partly because: 'the English love language and they like to use it.'[40] It is therefore not surprising that film-makers have consistently turned to this country's literary and theatrical heritage for ideas and inspiration. This tendency also places special emphasis on the role of the writer in the film-making process. Petley claims that

the British Cinema, even in its early days, became increasingly dominated by literary and theatrical conceptions. The writer, though badly paid by Hollywood standards, tended to be regarded as the major creative force in film-making and most screenplay writers tended to be men of theatre or literature.[41]

This created particular problems. Original screenplays and adaptations alike tended to be conceived not in specifically cinematic terms but rather as translations from theatrical and literary conventions.

On the question of the literary influence, the problem isn't so much one of adaptation *per se* – the American cinema has been similarly indebted to the novel in particular, as Brian McFarlane has pointed out.[42] It is the manner of adaptation particular to British cinema which is the issue. McFarlane suggests there is no *a priori* reason why adaptations should not be original and innovative, but that this has been the exception rather than the rule in the British cinema:

More often, British adaptations have exhibited a decorous, dogged fidelity to their sources, content to render through careful attention to their *mise-en-scène* the social values and emotional insight of those sources rather than subjecting them to critical scrutiny or, indeed, to robust exploitation.[43]

Petley argues that most British adaptations fail to rework the material from within, ' to create cinema', as Hitchcock put it. In other words nothing is added to the original source, resulting more often than not in a pale imitation. The desire to adapt dense literary texts is questioned by Roger Deakins, one of the top cinematographers currently working in Britain and a supporter of visually-oriented cinema. Deakins remarks:

> The independent producers in this country slave away for years to make the film they always wanted to make. In America that would be the Coen brothers making *Blood Simple*. But in this country when that sort of thing happens it's *Little Dorrit*. I'm sure it's wonderful but it's not cinema, whereas *Blood Simple* is.[44]

His argument rests on the fact that *Blood Simple* is a genre piece – a modern B-movie which relies on visual style and narrative tension associated with Hitchcockian thrillers, while *Little Dorrit*'s reference is the literary world of Charles Dickens.

Even the British new-wave films which were highly innovative in some respects were almost exclusively adaptations. Many failed to transcend their original source material. Roy Armes regards the new wave as representing a slight improvement within the literary tradition in British cinema. Many adaptations, for example, were contemporary rather than historical: the original authors including John Osborne, Alan Sillitoe, Shelagh Delaney, David Storey, Keith Waterhouse and Willis Hall who were all involved in translating their own material into screenplays. However, it is significant, Armes continues, that only one of these writers, Shelagh Delaney, ever made the transition to writing an original screenplay with *Charlie Bubbles*, directed in 1966 by Albert Finney.[45]

As I suggested, the theatrical influence on British cinema has also contributed to the verbosity of British cinema because much British theatre has similarly relied on dialogue rather than physical action. This point was made as early as 1931 by Norman Marshall in an article examining contemporary British cinema. Marshall writes:

> The weakness of English directors for the pedestrian production of stage plays on the screen is a symptom of their inability to realise that the film, even with the addition of sound, is essentially a visual art and must express itself in movement. Here again there is the temperamental handicap, reflected in the methods of the English theatre. English stage producers, players and playwrights are at their happiest when they can settle down for the whole three acts in

the same set (a typical English drawing room for preference), confining movement to a few steps from one piece of furniture to another. English actors, devoting themselves to the faithful reproduction of English character, rely almost entirely on the voice, using the bare minimum of movement and gesture as a means of expression.[46]

As Petley points out, in the formative years of the British cinema many producers and directors came out of the theatre with the result that many films were little more than 'celluloid records, of very varying adequacy, of whole stage productions, with stage directions very little changed by the directors'.[47]

The British cinema continued to look to the theatre for both source material (adaptations of Shakespeare, Coward, Osborne, and Pinter), actors and directors.[48] While contemporary British theatre has improved since the days of Norman Marshall, adaptations such as *Look Back in Anger* and more recently *The Dresser*, certainly owe more to the theatre than the cinema in terms of formal construction. Such films still rely on dialogue and characterisation to the detriment of cinematic devices such as *mise-en-scène* and montage.

The influence of television on cinema in Britain has also played its part, and this is tied in many ways to the theatrical tradition, with early TV drama being staged as plays, performed as such without breaks and covered by several cameras. According to Ellis, television drama has always been informed by words rather than images:

> Broadcast TV offers a small image of low definition, to which sound is crucial in holding the spectator's attention. [While cinema on the other hand] offers a large-scale highly detailed and photographic image to a spectator who is engaged in an activity of intense and relatively sustained attention.[49]

As a result, the words are more important in the case of television drama, with the images tending to add little in themselves to narrative development. The close ties which have developed between television and cinema in Britain – television companies like Channel 4 financing films, film-makers moving over to cinema from mostly television work – has helped to reinforce the problem of the importance of the word in British cinema. Charles Barr comments:

the average up-market British film/TV hybrid comes across as straightforwardly functional in style, serving the script, which is both its strength and its weakness . . . . There are sources of cinematic and cultural energy which the standard TV/movie hybrid does not tap, partly because of the tendency of its production strategies to put it 'in the script'.[50]

Barr's argument is supported by individuals active in film production. Al Clark contends that British television has enjoyed great international distinction while there has been little in British cinema to attain that accolade. In television the writer became the dominant figure (following on from the theatrical tradition) and the emphasis was placed on filming a good script rather than having a great idea and writing a script around that. This in turn influenced cinema with similar priorities being adopted. Mike Radford, whose debut feature *Another Time, Another Place* ranks among the most 'cinematic' of the early films backed by Channel 4, argues that the strong influence of television and its attendant techniques has resulted in the production of films which amount to little more than the 'photographing of dialogue'. Cinema, he argues, should rely on *mise-en-scène*, as opposed to 'close-ups of people talking', in order to communicate to an audience. This in turn can affect the commercial viability of a film in the world market. As Sarah Radclyffe puts it: 'If you solve things entirely by words they tend to be smaller in a way.'[51] Many of the films made for Channel 4 are criticised for being too small in Radclyffe's sense. Even film-makers involved in such productions will acknowledge the problem. Cinematographer Michael Coulter, for example, refers to *The Good Father*, directed by Mike Newell as:

a modern story, an important story. But yet it was also a bit wordy in that it was what the characters were saying to each other which told the story. It wasn't really the images.[52]

This then is the detrimental side of television's considerable influence on British cinema over the last two decades. However, as Ron Peck argues, it needn't have taken the form it did. Television drama needn't have clung to the naturalistic aesthetic I have described in this chapter. As he puts it:

I don't think television has to be that way. It's just got stuck in certain conventions which should be challenged, especially in terms of drama.[53]

These conventions have been challenged recently by productions like Dennis Potter's *The Singing Detective*, which was extremely innovatory for a television drama serial, adapting editing and narrative techniques from cinema, creating a non-naturalistic narrative which examined memory, sexuality and the intermingling of fact and fiction. As such it was a radical departure from the usual linear social drama.

British cinema is often contrasted rather unfavourably with American film-making. Peck argues that American cinema is exciting because the script is of no more importance than the lighting, the soundtrack, the camera or the movements of the characters within the frame. This is something he rarely sees in British cinema:

I'm not interested in a film in which it's all in the script, then it becomes pointless going to the cinema for me. I found *Sammy and Rosie* a very unrewarding film as I found *My Beautiful Laundrette* to be. Whereas I will see a Minnelli film – *The Cobweb* – hundreds of times because I think it's astonishing visually.[54]

Like Peck, Julien Temple is a great enthusiast of American cinema, particularly musicals, which for him:

get closer to the idea of total cinema, with the music and the movement and the colour, which are, in an almost abstract sense, as important as the dialogue.[55]

Bill Forsyth makes some very interesting comments regarding the dominance of the writing in British cinema. He regards this state of affairs as having bred a certain kind of 'lazy film director', as he puts it:

someone who came upon a film when it was finished . . . when the script was written. Because in large measure, it is the most creative period when you are script-writing: it's then you are actually making the film. You're not just putting words on a page, you are actually creating the feelings, the pace, the images almost. All you are doing is transcribing these onto paper so you don't forget them . . . . And I think that just by getting the procedure wrong the British cinema got the whole thing wrong: by having this compartmentalised thing where someone wrote or adapted something or created a script and then handed it on to another technician called a director. The actual creative process was lost somewhere in the middle. I don't think writers actually knew they were supposed to be film-makers. I think they thought they were just writers. So no one thought they were a film-maker: there was no such thing as a film-maker in the whole organisation. I think that's why British cinema suffered.[56]

Obviously Forsyth believes strongly in the importance of an integrated sense of purpose with regard to writing and directing, and this is consequently identifiable in his own work.

The predominance of the word over the image in British cinema which I have been describing primarily in an aesthetic context also relates to the industrial and economic structures of the British film industry. Part of the problem is the lack of finance available. As Julien Temple explains, when budgets are meagre, words are easier to film than spectacular images. James Mackay, who has worked for many years in the ultra-low-budget sector, making films with directors such as Derek Jarman and Ron Peck on Super-8 and video explains the rationale behind this kind of production and sheds some light on the predicament of the industry in general:

The alternative to working in Super-8 or video seems to be writing a script and spending an awful long time peddling it around trying to get money. I've seen this happen to a few people who haven't made films before and have spent a lot of time trying to get those scripts produced but have rarely got beyond the development stage. I think it's important to make films continually, otherwise you never develop as a film-maker, you just become a writer.[57]

This is an extremely important point. While a good script is obviously important, the main elements of film-making are images and sounds. Words are only the starting point.

However, not everyone working in the British film industry takes a pessimistic viewpoint. Neil Jordan believes that in the past five years things have begun to change with the emergence of 'visual' film-makers like Peter Greenaway. Tom Priestley and Julien Temple argue that exposure to television and pop promos, respectively, have helped create a generation who are extremely visually literate. There has also been a reappraisal of British cinema history which has attempted to identify a vibrant 'submerged' tradition of non-naturalistic and primarily visually-oriented British cinema on which contemporary film-makers can draw. Julien Temple describes Michael Powell as 'one of the most visually-oriented directors there ever was'. Such developments may help to change the situation and provide film-makers with more fruitful indigenous aesthetic reference-points which can benefit their own work.

Taken together, the various factors I have been discussing – the various trans-generic modes of realism, melodrama and comedy, and the aesthetic tendency characterised by verbal primacy – serve to constitute the dominant aesthetic context within which most British film-making has, and still does take place. A film like *Wish You Were Here* incorporates aspects of all of these tendencies, being 'realistic' in surface detail, melodramatic, humorous and talky. Rarely does a film avoid all of the dominant tendencies – an argument could be made for a profoundly visual, non-realist film like *Company of Wolves*, but such exceptions are rare. Obviously the dominant aesthetic/cultural context contributes significantly to the structuring of creativity in British cinema. It provides guidance to film-makers in the form of a 'tradition'. The 'recognition' this implies is particularly important to a creative process in which issues of commercial viability and expense are vital considerations. Consequently, any innovation within this context tends to assume the form of 'variation on a theme' and generic transformation rather than radical breaks as these may represent too much of a risk in commercial terms. The most vulgar form of this process is the phenomenon of the 'sequel', which, as I explained above, is more a characteristic of American film-making than British cinema.

The strain towards tradition is not simply bound by economic considerations, however: film-makers being forced to comply with the wishes of their financial backers in terms of 'playing safe' with form and content. Writers and directors themselves often look to the substance of tradition for ideas and possible solutions to problems. They effectively absorb elements of that tradition and their work can consequently be located in relation to the general constitution of the cultural tradition in which they operate. This process may be largely unconscious or alternatively, film-makers may be very self-conscious about the ways in which their work relates to that which has gone before. All are subject to the context in which they work and that context can be seen in terms of the cultural space generated by the aesthetic concepts I have been discussing. This cultural space provides certain aesthetic resources – as important as financial and technological resources – which film-makers draw upon in the process of their work. The creative activity implied in this process is therefore fundamentally structured in terms of the availability of these resources: they effectively set the parameters within which the activity can take place and creative decisions can be made.

# 7 Creative Collaboration and the Production Process

In addition to the technological, financial and aesthetic contexts already discussed, the structuring of creativity is also affected by the nature of interpersonal relationships within the process of film-making itself. As I indicated in Chapter 1, Coates asserts the existence of a necessary conflict between a film director's individuality on one hand and 'opposing material', including key collaborators, on the other.[1] Film-makers require this confrontation to refine and direct their own vision and creative energies. This raises the question of whether film-making should be considered as a collaborative undertaking. Certainly the logistics of making a film requires the involvement of a considerable number of people from start to finish and these people must be able to work together towards the same end – the production of the best possible film given the resources available. As producer Steve Woolley remarks:

> Films are an absolute collaboration right from the word go. You are collaborating all the time: with writers, with agents, with financiers.[2]

Collaborative relationships are crucial in such a context and are therefore not entered into lightly.

While the general question of the organisation and coordination of the contributions of the various people who are involved with any particular project at different stages in the process is an interesting one, the primary focus of this chapter will be collaboration in relation to creativity. Therefore the relationships between film-makers and their key 'creative collaborators' will be explored in some depth in the attempt to shed some light on the creative dynamic at the heart of the film-making process. This will be done by emphasising three specific areas of collaboration: the working relationship between directors and screenwriters; that between directors and producers; and a consideration of the contributions of the key technical personnel, including cinematographers, editors and designers, and actors to the creative process.

## CREATIVE COLLABORATION

All film-making, beyond the most basic 'home movie'production, is essentially a highly collaborative process, regardless of period or cultural climate. The production of feature films involves the integration of various specialised skills: screenwriting, acting, design, cinematography, editing, direction, and so on. It is therefore small wonder that the history of cinema is marked by enduring working relationships between teams of creative personnel collaborating over a range of different projects.

The British cinema is no exception. Some of its most outstanding films have been produced in circumstances where creative collaboration has been explicitly acknowledged. Examples include the films of Michael Powell and Emeric Pressburger ('The Archers') with both men sharing the writer, director and producer credit on more than fifteen features during the forties and fifties, among them *The Life and Death of Colonel Blimp*, *A Matter of Life and Death*, *Black Narcissus* and *The Red Shoes*. Powell and Pressburger also worked with the same creative collaborators whenever possible. At their critical height they benefited enormously from the contributions of key individuals including cinematographer Jack Cardiff, designers Alfred Junge and Hein Heckroth, editor Reginald Mills and composer Brian Easdale. Working alongside The Archers as an independent production unit, under the umbrella of the Rank Organisation, were the Cineguild team of David Lean, Ronald Neame and Anthony Havelock-Allan and the enduring partnership of Frank Launder and Sidney Gilliat.

Moving into the 1960s, the films made by the Woodfall Company, including *The Loneliness of the Long-Distance Runner*, *A Taste of Honey* (classic examples of the British new wave or kitchen-sink drama) and *Tom Jones*, involved the same creative 'core' of director Tony Richardson, writer John Osborne (both partners in the company) and cinematographer Walter Lassally. This team developed an innovative realist aesthetic borrowing the techniques of the French

New Wave and applying them to contemporary working-class subjects.

But perhaps the most critically acclaimed creative collaboration in
the history of British cinema is that between director Joseph Losey
and the dramatist Harold Pinter, which resulted in three features
produced between 1963 and 1970: *The Servant*, *Accident* and *The
Go-Between*. The collaboration proved to be a fruitful one for both,
especially Losey. As Alexander Walker explains, with particular
reference to *The Servant*:

> Losey had never before had to work so tightly within the disciplin-
> ing limits of another man's 'frame'. Yet instead of confinement *The
> Servant* signals his breakthrough to a freedom of expression that,
> just because it is controlled by underlying rhythms, as a sea is by its
> tides, never lets the unity of vision slip out of focus.[3]

Walker suggests that Pinter curbed Losey's tendencies to baroque
Romanticism while Losey amplified Pinter's economy with visual
suggestiveness. Certainly it is arguable that neither man was able to
match the quality of the collaborations in their other productions.
Pinter and Losey provide a classic example of a working relationship
where the constraints placed on one by the other served to focus and
direct their respective creative energies more effectively than would
otherwise have been the case.

## CREATIVE COLLABORATION AND CURRENT BRITISH CINEMA

### I: Writers and directors

The Powell/Pressburger and Losey/Pinter collaborations are
examples of screenwriting and direction meshing together in the
production of visually inventive cinema. In general, British cinema
has been characterised by the strength of its writing which has
overshadowed visual realisation. While cinema is usually regarded by
critics and theorists (in the wake of the 'auteur theory') as a director's
medium, the British cinema, due largely to its close relationship since
the late sixties with television drama, has frequently privileged
writers over directors. Hence it is Alan Bennett's *A Private Function*
rather than Malcolm Mowbray's which we hear about. Similarly films

such as *No Surrender* and *Letter to Brezhnev* are more often attributed to Alan Bleasdale and Frank Clark respectively than directors Peter Smith and Chris Bernard. In each case the writer is popularly held to be the creative force behind the film, as is the norm in television. This serves to neglect an appreciation of what is often notable directing.

The tendency to privilege writers in British cinema and television drama is partly justified. The screenplay always constrains film-makers to the telling of a particular story with particular characters, locations and events, but unfortunately many British film-makers do little to build upon the concepts and ideas contained in the screenplay. They tend to translate words into images in a broadly functional manner, relying on dialogue to convey much of the narrative information in the process, rather than reworking the basic structures of the script in fundamentally cinematic ways, as a film-maker like Hitchcock was able to do.

There is, however, a great awareness of this problem within the film-making community at large and consequently, many film-makers have attempted to combine the arts of writing and directing in the effort to create screenplays which are a mere blueprint for profoundly visual ideas rather than great literate works full of dialogue. The strain has been towards a more integrated process rather than what Bill Forsyth describes as 'the compartmentalisation of scriptwriting and directing'.[4] Mike Radford, for example, argues that film, in the sense of writing and directing, 'is an unseparated-out totality'.[5] Ron Peck is enthusiastic about the benefits of a director writing his or her own scripts, from a cinematic point of view:

> I think that as you are writing the dialogue you are to some extent imagining the camera movements, and movement may replace a line of dialogue, or a shock of colour may indicate something you are aiming at – all the dramaturgy of the film is related to how you're orchestrating everything.[6]

Bill Forsyth on the other hand has a different point of view of the process:

> What really happens when you are writing is the movie unwinds in your head. If you had to stop and see every shot you would forget what you are feeling or what the sense of it was. It's the spirit of the film that unwinds in your head as you are writing and that's the

most important thing. How that's realised visually either in one shot or how the design works or whatever, is part of the conversations that come afterwards.[7]

One major transition in British cinema from the seventies to the eighties has been the emergence of the writer/director. This phenomenon is partly the result of the training programmes carried out at the major British film schools, in particular the National Film School at Beaconsfield and the London International Film School. These establishments teach students a broad range of skills and most of these who train ultimately to be directors also tend to be interested in writing their own screenplays. As Tom Priestley, an experienced editor who has worked in the British film industry for more than thirty years, comments:

> I think we now have a new generation of film-makers rather on the European line: people who want to make films to express their ideas and feelings about life today.[8]

Consequently British cinema currently abounds with writer/directors, some primarily interested in original material, others favouring adaptations. Their numbers include Forsyth, Radford, Peck, Neil Jordan, Bill Douglas, Derek Jarman, Terry Gilliam, David Hare, Terence Davies, Peter Greenaway, Karl Francis, Ken McMullen, Alex Cox, Lezli-An Barrett, Harry Hook, Connie Templeman, Mike Leigh, Charley Gormley, Mike Figgis and Peter Wollen. There are also recent examples of screenwriters directing their own scripts: Paul Mayersberg, Martin Stellman, David Leland, Stephen Poliakoff and Bruce Robinson. This may signify an integration of the creative elements of writing and directing but on the other hand it could be an affirmation of the ascendancy of the writer in British cinema. In any case it would appear to provide the justification for taking an essentially auteurist approach to British cinema. This is something I wish to avoid for reasons I shall attempt to elaborate below.

Not everyone in the film industry necessarily believes in the idea that combining writing and direction is a recipe for success. Colin MacCabe, the former head of the BFI Production Board, which has funded the work of several of the writer/directors referred to above, makes the following comments:

as a result, largely I think, of the auteur theory . . . there has been a great emphasis on the writer/director. And without in any way trying to suggest that there should be no such beasts, many good directors can't write. And I am concerned with trying to get more writers involved who are not directors.[9]

James Brabazon, in an article published in *A.I.P. & Co.* magazine, champions the cause of the writer in British cinema. He argues that without a script you can't construct a schedule or a budget and without a good script you can't attract finance in the first place. Brabazon makes the case for the importance of good storytelling, citing *My Beautiful Laundrette* as a perfect example of a film whose popularity lies in the story rather than production values or visual imagery. However, he does accept that there is a problem with British screenwriting which he attributes to an apparent disinclination on the part of writers who have been trained in television (or the theatre) to learn the discipline of film. Brabazon writes:

> unfortunately many writers in Britain are not keen to admit that they have anything much to learn. A vague impression has grown up amongst them (fostered originally at the Royal Court Theatre) that their lightest word is good enough for production and should never be altered. This is the writers' counterpart to the directors' auteur theory, and is equally fallacious and damaging. But this attitude is often reinforced by the crass way writers are treated by producers, directors and story editors – people who ought to know how to get the best out of them. What should be fertile cooperation becomes a dog-fight.[10]

Although many would argue that film is, in the last analysis, a director's medium, there is a general consensus which admits to the crucial importance of scripts, and by extension screenwriters. As Brabazon points out, it is scripts which attract finance. A good script is also often an important incentive for collaborators to get involved – particularly such important figures as the director of photography, the production designer, the editor and the actors. Sometimes an experienced technician will be attracted to an inexperienced film-maker's project on the basis of the script, an example being cinematographer Roger Deakins' decision to work on Harry Hook's debut film *The Kitchen Toto*.

Brabazon's idea of a fertile cooperation is an important one. However, as he indicates, conflict and tension may arise between the writer, who is the originator of ideas in a sense, and others whose task it is to translate these ideas into images. Writer Hanif Kureishi makes some interesting comments in his diary of the making of the film *Sammy and Rosie Get Laid*. He displays a certain ambivalence towards the necessity of collaboration. At first he felt a great sense of relief when director Stephen Frears and producer Tim Bevan became involved with the project. As Kureishi puts it:

> Getting a film going is like pushing a huge rock up the side of a mountain and, until now, writing the script I've been doing this alone. Now other people can take the weight.[11]

However, Kureishi found the moment he had to relinquish control, to let go of the script and allow Frears to make the film, a particularly difficult one. This is hardly surprising given that a writer may have worked on a script for a long time only to watch it being changed beyond recognition by the director. It may be one reason why more and more screenwriters are starting to direct their own scripts. As Kureishi puts it:

> the film-writer always has to give way to the director, who is the controlling intelligence of the film, the invisible tyrant behind everything. The only way for a writer to influence a film is through his relationship with the director. If this is good then the film will be a successful collaboration; if not, the writer has had it. And most writers are lucky if directors even allow them on the set.[12]

Kureishi, who had collaborated successfully with Frears on *My Beautiful Laundrette* prior to the production of *Sammy and Rosie*, was fortunate in that he was able to make a considerable contribution throughout the production.

There are numerous other examples of fruitful collaborations between directors and screenwriters in British cinema. Neil Jordan, who has written his own scripts, enjoyed the benefits of such a collaboration with novelist Angela Carter on *The Company of Wolves*. As Jordan explains:

> Angela's got a vision all of her own. It's wonderful to work with her because I want to share her vision and I want to explore it. She's

got so much to contribute because she's created such a unique
world. There's a certain normal level of what people call a
scriptwriter; in other words somebody who moulds material for the
screen, who makes it suitable for the screen. I wouldn't be
interested in working with somebody like that at all.[13]

Jordan is much more interested in imagination than technique when
it comes to scriptwriting. He found Carter's approach to writing
particularly cinematic:

There were very strong visual metaphors running through the
whole thing. It wasn't only that she'd described it in visual terms, it
was that things like the colour red, the wolf with the silver bullet in
its foot and all that sort of stuff, which propels the story from
beginning to end.[14]

The end-result was an imaginative and visually inventive film,
something rare in a cinema not often noted for its visual qualities.
Jordan shared the writing credit on *The Company of Wolves* with
Carter and his next project *Mona Lisa* was also co-scripted, this time
with David Leland.

Mike Radford is another film-maker who has written his own
scripts alone: adaptations of Jessie Kesson's novels *The White Bird
Passes* for the BBC, and *Another Time, Another Place* which was his
first theatrical feature film, and with others such as Jonathan Gems
who contributed to the *Nineteen Eighty Four* and *White Mischief*
screenplays. On adapting Kesson for the screen Radford found that
she tended to write in such a visual way that he was able to imagine
how he would shoot the film and subsequently found the writing
process rather easy. With regard to his working relationship with
Gems, Radford comments:

He is a theatre writer and he's very used to solving his problems in
dialogue. But he writes wonderful dialogue and he's influenced me
in the way I think about dialogue. He is also very good at the basic
structure of human motivations. In terms of actually refining how
the film could use the language of cinema, that I do almost entirely.
But he's probably much better than I am at constructing a dramatic
scene, he has that training.[15]

Other directors who obviously are heavily involved with the project at the scripting stage are less inclined to take a credit. Julien Temple makes some interesting comments in this context. He explains that he was quite heavily involved in the writing of *Absolute Beginners* but wasn't credited as such. The reason for this according to Temple is that directors are closely involved at every stage of the process from the writing through photography to editing and no director would ask for an editing credit, for example. Therefore, he concludes, unless a director has actually written the screenplay he or she should not take a credit for it.

There is apparently no single formula which is demonstrably the most productive approach to writing and directing feature films. What is important is that writers, directors or writer/directors understand cinema as a medium distinct from television, theatre and literature and consequently make greater use of the unique language of cinema rather than relying on narrative techniques borrowed from other forms.

The writing stage is also in many respects the least constrained part of the process, where a writer is free from the various problems of budgets, schedules, technology and working relationships and can let his or her imagination take over. However, even the screenwriting stage is highly structured in certain ways. Most screenplays tend to conform to the received idea of what a screenplay should be, in terms of narrative structure. The screenplay will also feature a particular small group of well-drawn characters – the leading roles – and a host of rather two-dimensional supplementary characters. Finally it will tend to be a particular length: between one hundred and one hundred and twenty pages, with one page roughly corresponding to one minute of screen time. This is related to the expectations of financiers who are notoriously conservative given the high-risk nature of the film business. It is interesting to consider that Ron Peck had problems raising the finance for *Empire State* partly because of the multi-character nature of the script which did not conform to the – two or three major characters – norm. Unsurprisingly, the vast majority of screenplays conform to the structural norm. The major exceptions to the rule in British cinema are a handful of maverick film-makers such as Derek Jarman, who filmed *The Last of England* without writing a screenplay.

## II: Producers and directors

MacCabe's comments above were part of an account of his developing role as an initiator of projects. Initiation is obviously a very important part of any creative process and in terms of current British cinema it has been argued that producers have become more and more involved in the creative aspects of film-making in general and during the pre-production stage in particular. As James Park argues:

> Most of the producers associated with the new directors do much more than just raise money for projects. To a greater or less degree they all play a role in steering films through the development and production process to their marketable form. Throughout they both represent the interests of financiers and assist the director to ensure that the best film is made with the resources available.[16]

The latter part of Park's argument is supported by producer Patrick Cassavetti, who suggests that:

> the role of the producer is really to create a financial structure that allows the director as much freedom as possible with as little interference as possible, provided they abide by the rules as well. There is a moral obligation to try to bring the film in as close to budget as possible.[17]

Cassavetti himself had a difficult time keeping director Terry Gilliam within budget on the production of *Brazil*. Many of Gilliam's ideas simply had to be rejected on the grounds of cost and Cassavetti had to be on hand to keep him in check. It is in such a way that the relationship between producer and director serves to constrain creativity, which is often a positive constraint in that it restricts directorial excess. Certain film-makers such as Alex Cox would arguably benefit from a curtailing of certain self-indulgent elements in their work.

The importance of the producer in British cinema is reflected in Alexander Walker's book *National Heroes: British Cinema in the Seventies and Eighties*. Walker dedicates two chapters (out of a total of ten) to David Puttnam, perhaps the one name synonymous with 'British cinema', at least in the popular mind, in the eighties.[18] Puttnam is cited by James Park as a classic example of a 'creative producer', being active at every stage of the film-making process from initiating projects, developing screenplays, and casting, through the production stage to the editing, dubbing and final distribution of the finished film.[19] In fact Puttnam is so involved with the creative aspects of the process that there are strong thematic and aesthetic continuities running through his work regardless of the different directors and writers involved. In this sense a case could be made for Puttnam as a producer-auteur, given the classical formulation of the auteur theory.

There are other producers currently active in British cinema who like to get creatively involved in every stage of the project but who do not seem to dominate the proceedings in the manner of David Puttnam. As Sarah Radclyffe puts it:

> I'm more interested in the creative side than the financial side . . . . I can only work on one film at a time and get totally involved in it. I get involved from the script, all the way through pre-production. I'm there every single day at the shoot and all the way through post-production.[20]

Steve Woolley has demonstrated the creative involvement of the producer with regard to *Scandal*. The project was initially conceived as a mini-series for television but no TV company was interested in commissioning it, so Woolley and director Michael Caton-Jones together stripped down the script to make it into a feature film. Woolley asserts:

> I always find I have a very strong creative influence over the screenplay. I also have a very strong hand on casting and I feel I need to have a strong hand for me to be there and follow it through to the end. It's really on the shooting that there's very little a producer can actually do and I think that's really when you've got to get your director straight, or be straight with him, and have a relationship that allows a lot of trust to pass between you. Because on the shooting of a film you can't walk off the set. You can on the script or casting: you can go off and have a screaming match. But on the day, the shoot, if you've scheduled the film properly then the director should simply go out there and direct the film. All you can say is, 'You are going too slow' or 'You've gone so slow you've lost a day so you've got to cut this'.[21]

He also admits to heavy involvement in the post-production stage, helping to choose the soundtrack music and spending a lot of time with the editor, particularly during the shooting period when the rushes are being assembled but the director's concentration is still on the actual filming. But Woolley claims he would never recut a film without a director. For him, it is up to the director, in conjunction with the editor, to make the final decisions regarding all aspects of post-production.

Mark Shivas, presently the Head of Drama at the BBC and a producer of great experience both in television and cinema where his credits include *Moonlighting*, *A Private Function* and *The Witches*, explains that producers working in television haven't had quite the same hassles regarding money in the sense that the finance is either there or it isn't. So the producer automatically is involved in choosing the director, as generally the script is completed before a director is appointed to a project, casting, shooting and post-production. When such a producer moves into theatrical film-making he or she expects to have the same level of involvement.

Obviously the working relationship between director and producer is a crucial one, as Steve Woolley's remarks above suggest. The producer must be able to assist the director without imposing upon him or her in such a way as to restrict their vision. As Woolley acknowledges, the director is ultimately the person standing behind the project: it is the director's film first and foremost. James Mackay, who has produced several of Derek Jarman's projects, describes the relationship between producer and director in the following manner:

The director looks after the inner content of the film, the direction in fact. So they are aptly named. The producer looks after the production, looks after the contributors, making sure they are all in time with each other and they are all doing it right. And having an overview to the production: to see it's ending up where it's supposed to end up and it's not getting side-tracked. When directors are very close to a production they can get side-tracked very easily, so you have to have someone who isn't there looking at it every minute of the day but who can step in for a short time and say, 'Well, you know that wasn't quite where it was going. Why has it gone that way?', and that usually works alright. I think the producer is more distant from the minutiae of the production while the director deals specifically in that.[22]

This view is supported by Steve Woolley. He suggests that it is a producer's job to have an overview of the production, to have some clear sense of what the overall effect should be, and not to be swamped by every minute detail:

> you've got to help him or her with what you can see that they can't. You can see behind the kerbs, they can't do that because they are on the bend all the time.[23]

This idea of closeness and distance from a project, either being totally involved in the minute details of a project or having an overview, is a crucially important aspect of successful collaboration as a good film must have both an attention to detail and strong overall direction.

It is not surprising that some film-makers, having found a producer they can work well with, prefer to maintain that relationship on subsequent projects. A good example of this is the Mike Radford/ Simon Perry team responsible for *Another Time, Another Place*, *Nineteen Eighty Four* and *White Mischief*. Marc Samuelson, Perry's former colleague at Umbrella Films, argues that the collaboration between Perry and Radford goes 'right across the board' with Perry involved heavily at every stage: 'Ultimately Mike's the director, so he's in charge, but he consults, and works very closely on creative issues, with Simon.'[24] Radford himself describes Perry's contribution in terms of much needed 'support':

> he can stand back and take a critical eye at what I'm doing. He's not a 'director manqué': he's already directed a feature film so he hasn't got that urge and desire to take you over. So he stands back very much, trusts me, and keeps the flak off my shoulders. But he also acts as a critic.[25]

Similarly, Steve Woolley has produced all of Neil Jordan's films to date with the exception of his debut feature *Angel*. Woolley is very positive about their working relationship, describing it as the strongest collaboration he has experienced as a producer:

> We've always developed things from a story, an idea (usually Neil's) found in a newspaper – like *Mona Lisa*. I tend to be able to get in quite closely with him on that early stage.[26]

In each case the films produced reflect very much the vision of the director in question rather than the producer, as is arguably the case with David Puttnam.

Al Clark, who agrees very much with the argument that producers have taken a very active role on productions, is also cautious with regard to the possibility of over-involvement. He describes his own involvement in projects as:

> considerable, but not smothering in the sense that I know there's a point at which films do not benefit from interference. You have to be able to judge when what you are contributing is really a contribution and when it's just an attempt to impose yourself on circumstances that just don't need you.[27]

The term 'producer' is rather ambiguous in that it covers a range of very different tasks and responsibilities. The three most common formulations of the title 'producer' which appear in film credits are producer, associate producer and executive producer. In general terms, the producer is the person who has been responsible for developing a project and approaching potential investors for a financial commitment. This is the kind of person we have been discussing so far. An associate producer (or line producer) is essentially, a glorified production manager, hired to supervise the day-to-day running of the production. Finally the executive producer is usually someone connected with the company which has put up the money – for example most films backed by Handmade Films give George Harrison and Dennis O'Brien executive producer credit, Colin MacCabe enjoyed a similar accreditation with regard to the BFI-backed films he was involved with. Some executive producers do little more than keep tabs on the production from afar. Others are much more involved, often in creative decision-making. Sometimes production credits can be misleading. On Terry Gilliam's *Brazil* Arnon Milchan and Patrick Cassavetti were both credited as producers. Cassavetti explains that Milchan was actually the executive producer, having been instrumental in setting up the deal with Universal and Twentieth Century-Fox but subsequently spending very little time on the project. Cassavetti, on the other hand, was involved in the day-to-day running of the production, communicating with Milchan by phone (the latter remained in America while the film was shot in London) every couple of days.

Al Clark, former Head of Production at Virgin Vision, encountered a broad range of experiences in his (usual) capacity as executive producer. In the case of *Secret Places*, the only one of their films not distributed by Virgin, Clark was involved in setting up the film from a financial point of view by raising money from the National Film Finance Corporation, Rediffusion and Rank. With *Secret Places* Clark also went through each draft of the script and suggested ways of re-doing particular scenes. On *Nineteen Eighty Four*, because Virgin were bankrolling the whole thing, it was much more intense and on-the-spot. Regarding *Captive*, Paul Mayersberg approached Clark with an idea and the two discussed ways in which it could be turned into a screenplay. In addition, Clark monitored the project and made suggestions at every stage of the process. *Absolute Beginners* involved a process of keeping the project buoyant for a year until it could be financed and produced. On *Gothic*, the project arrived as a final screenplay and Clark appointed director Ken Russell, helped with casting and supervised the project from Virgin's side. As Clark puts it:

> The term 'executive producer' covers everything from, in America, sometimes an honorary title just for staying with something during a long period of time . . . to a very active involvement which is sometimes more considerable than that of producer.[28]

It has been suggested by one writer that the role of producer has always been particularly significant in the context of a national cinema which has never enjoyed the luxury of a stable, financially secure environment within which film-making, and perhaps more importantly, film-making careers, could flourish. John Caughie suggests that the idea of independence has been central to British film-making since the days of John Grierson.[29] The desire for independence should be seen in the context of the British cinema's relationship with Hollywood and it is also related to the notions of realism and quality discussed earlier. What film-makers wanted was to develop a cinema distinct from the American product which dominated British screens. The aesthetic and critical standards to which an indigenous British cinema could aspire were those of realism and quality. But such a cinema required its own funding structure distinct from the Hollywood model which informed the British duopoly of Rank and the Associated British Picture Corporation. The result was the pitifully inadequate National Film Finance Corporation.

Caughie argues that the desire for independence was formative for British cinema in the same way television had been guided by a conception of public service. This desire created the necessity for the organisation of independence given the historical lack of a stable source of indigenous film finance in Britain, a task which could only be fulfilled by individuals who were passionate enough about the art of cinema to expend the energy required to raise the necessary finance. In this way, Caughie argues, the history of British cinema is one of producers:

> Grierson . . . Balcon, Dean, Korda, Powell and Pressburger, Lean, Richardson, Reisz, Anderson, Attenborough, Puttnam: none of them are purely directors, many of them are not directors at all. Outside of a studio system or a national corporation, art is too precious a business to be left to artists: it needs organisers. The importance of the producer–artist seems to be a specific feature of British cinema, an effect of the need continually to start again in the organisation of independence.[30]

In terms of current British cinema, the extreme difficulties associated with raising production finance place a great deal of importance on the contribution of producers, whose role in most cases includes getting the project off the ground in the first place. It is little wonder that many subsequently wish to get involved in creative decision-making. Mark Shivas contends that: 'the least interesting part for the producer is the deal and finding the money. Making the film is much more fun.'[31] Simon Relph, a producer whose experience of film-making has been vital in the realisation of projects by first-time directors, in particular Richard Eyre and David Hare, with regard to the production of *The Ploughman's Lunch* and *Wetherby* respectively. He has stated that he would not do the job if it did not allow him to be creative. There must be some kind of compensation for doing what is otherwise often a rather thankless task.

British cinema is still dominated by the producer. Both David Puttnam, since returning from his ill-fated spell at Columbia, and Jeremy Thomas (producer of *Eureka, Merry Christmas, Mr Lawrence, Insignificance, The Hit* and *The Last Emperor*) have recently each secured substantial deals to finance a portfolio of films to be directed by major international film-makers. These films will be produced under the banner of each producer's company: Puttnam's Enigma company and Thomas's The Recorded Picture Company. Given the difficulties of raising finance for even a low-budget production, this is a major achievement for both of them. It must be stressed, however, that the films will be very much 'international' rather than indigenous productions, perhaps based in British studios using Britich technical expertise in very much the same way as many American productions, including the recent blockbusters *Indiana Jones and the Last Crusade* and *Batman*, continue to do.

### III: The contributions of key technicians

The relationship between a director and key technical colla-borators – director of photography, editor, production designer and so on – is extremely important. It is only through discussion and the mutual suggestion of ideas, within the parameters set by budget, schedule and location that creative decisions can be made. In terms of pre-production planning, the director will often get together with the cinematographer and perhaps the production designer to hammer out a shooting plan or storyboard from the information contained in the screenplay. During the pre-production of *Caravaggio* Derek Jarman, along with cinematographer Gabriel Beristain and designer Chris-topher Hobbs, spent three months prior to the shoot constructing a shooting plan for every sequence of the film. The sets had already been designed so they knew the dimensions of the spaces they would be working in. As Jarman recalls:

> There was a lot of freedom within this tight structure. By the time we actually got on to the set we really had a clear knowledge of it, we'd worked it out so precisely it was actually possible to jettison it.[32]

The time spent on constructing the shooting plan helped to cement the relationships between the key creative collaborators, ensuring that all were working towards the same objective.

Shooting plans are vitally important in heavily art-directed or special effects films. Neil Jordan, for example, used storyboards extensively on his two studio-based films *Company of Wolves* and *High Spirits* in order to work out the action in relation to the sets and special effects. Bill Forsyth encountered a similar necessity with his film *Housekeeping*:

> Storyboarding for me is a technical tool. For instance when we were doing the floods, I would have preferred it if we had been able to flood the whole town and then wander round with a camera filming things. But we couldn't flood any of it so we had to create flooded images one by one and I was forced into storyboarding that because we only had money for say six flood shots. I was forced into actually trying to imagine each single shot.[33]

Storyboarding or shooting plans also give a film-maker an anchor which, as Julien Temple points out, allows him or her to take risks that they otherwise wouldn't be able, or have the confidence, to do:

> It forces you to think things through. If you end up with one scene from the storyboards you've done, you've also thought through five or six others and the storyboards refresh your memory of those other ways so when you shoot you have other options.[34]

Ron Peck agrees:

> I think storyboarding is a very good way of evaluating the entire film and trying to foresee problems. I've storyboarded everything. It's a kind of security as well to go into your first day's filming knowing that you have thought through the entire thing – every moment of the film as an image or possible camera movement. And then possibly to jettison it when you are actually doing it for something better.[35]

The major benefit of this thorough planning to the collaborative relationships on set is that the director has a clear view of objectives, enabling collaborators to direct their energies into finding the most suitable and effective ways of realising them.

Not all directors work with storyboards, however. Mike Radford for one argues that he works out of the atmosphere and feel of the locations in which he is working. He likes to have the freedom to change things on the day, and explains it is only within very broad parameters that he knows what he wants to do. The compensation, from a planning point of view, is that Radford spends a long time on his scripts, so he is confident that they will work and it is the confidence of knowing he has a good script behind him, of 'feeling the structure of the screenplay' as he puts it, that enables him to improvise on the set.

The specialised technical knowledge of key collaborators is a vital resource for many film-makers. Derek Jarman, for example, relies heavily on the knowledge of his directors of photography during the production of his films:

> I don't know anything about lenses, I wouldn't even know how they are calibrated . . . . It never seemed to me to be the main concern because there's always people like Chris Hughes or Gabriel Beristain who are absolute experts in this field. If you can describe to them more or less the sort of atmosphere you want to generate they are really good at doing it. What it does, if you work that way, is it gives these people confidence to join in. They are not simply being dictated to.[36]

Experienced technicians can also prove invaluable to neophyte directors either beginning their career or moving into larger-scale production. This was the case with Ron Peck on *Empire State*, his previous experience having been in the workshop sector. The lighting cameraman on the film was replaced, at the insistence of the investors, after shooting had commenced because he was too slow and the production was falling behind schedule. He was replaced by Tony Imi, a cinematographer whom Peck did not know:

> Our first day together was pretty tough because it was a certain testing out of each other and each other's authority. He was a much more experienced industry cameraman and he came in with a problem because the crew had to respond to him too. But in the end he worked very fast so we were able to do a lot of things we wouldn't otherwise have been able to do. And I think that had the investors not imposed the change the film might well have run into incredible trouble.[37]

Cinematographers are particularly important collaborators as they can do much to determine the 'look' of a film. It has been suggested by some that the visual style of a particular director of photography can be traced through a body of work involving several different directors. The distinguished cinematographer Nestor Almendros argues that the house-styles of the Hollywood studios owed much to their resident cameramen and gives numerous examples of a consistency of visual style attributable to cinematographers like Gregg Toland, William Daniels and Rudolph Maté, regardless of the directors involved.[38]

The role of the cinematographer is defined at some length by Dennis Schaefer and Larry Salvato in the introduction to their series of interviews with contemporary cameramen. They argue that a successful cinematographer must be familiar not only with the technicalities of lighting and photography but also with the history of the visual arts. The cinematographer:

> must help and support the director in getting exactly what he wants even when the director is not fully able to articulate it himself. He must deal on a daily basis with art, set property and costume departments to ensure that their contributions are consistent with the overall tone and style of the film . . . outside of the director he is normally the single most important force on the set.[39]

Michael Coulter, whose credits include *No Surrender*, *The Good Father*, *Heavenly Pursuits*, *Housekeeping*, *The Dressmaker* and *Diamond Skulls*, describes the role of the director of photography in the following manner:

> People say you are the head technician. One of the most, if not the most, important technician because you are responsible for the 'look' of the film. But basically it's to interpret what the director wants and try to give him it – get out of him what's in his head and between you put that on the screen.[40]

Coulter makes a distinction between 'the role' and 'the job' done by a cinematographer. For him, the job represents the technical side of things and involves collaboration with the director and various other technicians including the rest of the camera crew: operator and focus-puller and the gaffer or chief electrician:

> you'll find that most guys work with one gaffer if they can, because you are already up and running if you are working with a guy you already know and who understands your style – you don't have to explain everything. Then you can go on to start talking about

working with the art department and all that stuff. Then you are getting back to talking about the 'look' of the film.[41]

A cinematographer must be able to work with his crew as well as collaborate with the director. Coulter had some problems on the production of Bill Forsyth's *Housekeeping*, shot on location in Canada. Coulter used incredibly low lighting in some of the sequences while his crew on the production were used to working in American television where everything is very brightly lit.

Roger Deakins, one of the top cinematographers working in Britain, with credits such as *Another Time, Another Place, Nineteen Eighty Four, Sid and Nancy, Defence of the Realm, White Mischief* and *Stormy Monday*, makes the following observation on the actual construction of the film and his contribution to this process:

On one picture it could be totally how a film is shot: everything from the lighting to the angles, to the way you break down a sequence. You can find yourself doing all of that. On something else it can be very much just the light, and discussing the shots with the director, but less the breakdown of scenes. An experienced director will know exactly how he wants a scene covered. I always operate so I like to have considerable control and involvement in the way a scene is shot, not only the framing and the lighting but also in the way something is broken down – the overall style of the picture. Whether you play scenes in fairly static compositions – shots that take long sections – or with lots of little cuts. I like to be involved as much as possible on that whole side of things.[42]

Despite this desire for a high level of involvement in a production, Deakins likes to have direction, a solid set of guidelines within which to work, claiming that there is nothing more frustrating than a director who just leaves the cinematographer to get on with things:

Hopefully the ideal relationship is where you know what the director wants, you've discussed it enough, you know the style, you know what he wants and it's also what you want, and you don't really have to communicate much while you're shooting. Discussion then comes down on the set to quite often performance or how to cover a scene, depending on what the actors want to do.[43]

This relates back to the previous discussion of storyboarding and shooting plans and the need for a director to have a strong idea of his or her objectives.

Of all the films Deakins has worked on, he is particularly pleased with his contribution to *Sid and Nancy*, directed by Alex Cox. Deakins explains that he did not always get along with Cox during the production but this tension ended up being fruitful rather than destructive:

> I find conflict is a good thing. I have strong ideas and hopefully they have and you kind of rub up against each other.[44]

This sounds very much like a specific practical example of the process theorised by Coates when he talks about authorship being a clash between a director's individuality and counteracting forces including the contributions of the key collaborators. Ideas can be more sharply focused by confrontation, forcing individuals to put more effort into the production process. Providing of course this confrontation does not develop into hostility or animosity.

The cinematographer is also the link between the creative 'core' of a production (director and immediate collaborators) and the laboratory which is an important stage of the process, though a rather ignored one. The final 'look' of the film depends on the skill of the laboratory technicians and carefully planned and executed lighting designs can be totally destroyed if the lab is not fully in tune with the production. Roger Deakins explains that he will visit the labs frequently to ensure that they are developing and printing the film in accordance with his and the director's wishes. For Deakins the lab work is crucial and it is his responsibility to oversee this particular contribution to the overall process.

There are several notable cinematographers working in the British film industry at the present time. Besides Deakins and Coulter there are Chris Menges, arguably the top cinematographer in Britain today with over twenty years' experience and credits such as *Angel*, *Local Hero*, *Comfort and Joy*, *The Killing Fields*, *The Mission* and *Fatherland* to his name, veterans such as Douglas Slocombe, Freddie Francis and Billy Williams, and relative newcomers such as Alex Thomson, Oliver Stapleton, Peter Hannan, Peter Biziou, Gabriel Beristain, Thaddeus O'Sullivan, Mike Southon and Roger Pratt. Many of these individuals have distinguished themselves in the international area, having worked on prestige American films both in Hollywood and in British studios.

The production designer is also a key figure with regard to the 'look' of a film. This role is described by Rita McGurn, who designed Charlie Gormley's two feature films to date: *Living Apart Together* and *Heavenly Pursuits*, in the following way:

> The role of the production designer is to design and be responsible for everything that appears visually in front of the camera. In theory you should have design decisions about the lighting but in actual fact that's pretty much the lighting cameraman's problem. But very often you decide on the practical lights to be used on a set. They certainly oversee the wardrobe, make sure that the colours they have chosen for the sets are going to be seen in conjunction with the costumes the actors are wearing.[45]

McGurn's area of design has been largely naturalistic and contemporary. On the other hand there are production designers who have specialised in projects where imagination coupled with a strong sense of period detail is called for. One such designer is Christopher Hobbs who has worked on *Caravaggio*, *Gothic*, *The Wolves of Willoughby Chase*, and *Loser Takes All*. Hobbs likes to get involved on a project at an early stage and to spend a lot of time talking to the director in order to decide what approach to design would best suit the script. The film he is most proud of is *Caravaggio* which he worked on for a very long time and on which he was given a considerable degree of autonomy by the director, Derek Jarman. The film was also made in a studio setting which Hobbs, like most production designers, prefers:

> It was a studio but as a studio it was a scruffy old warehouse. It meant that there were no studio constraints either because a proper big studio has all sorts of built-in constraints, partly to do with unit set-ups and the way studios work in rather quite rigid ways. Literally in that empty warehouse we could have done anything. There was almost nothing to stop us apart from money and time.[46]

Like everyone else involved on a film, the production designer must be able to work with a range of people, particularly the director and the cinematographer. With regard to the latter, Rita McGurn explains that you have to work closely with him because a cinematographer can make a designer's work look terrible if he can't tell what the designer is getting at or if things have not been planned properly. Christopher Hobbs has had a range of different experiences working with cinematographers, as he explains with reference to three specific productions:

> On *Caravaggio* Gabriel Beristain was there reasonably early and wanted to talk a lot about designs and how they should work with the lighting. Because you can't separate them really. On *Gothic* Mike Southon and Ken Russell didn't agree on the way it should be lit, and all of the lighting had to be behind the camera because there was nowhere to hide lights. It made it very difficult for Mike. And so I hardly spoke to him at all throughout the film. On *The Wolves of Willoughby Chase* we had Paul Beeson who's old and very experienced. I didn't know how he was going to light it. There certainly wasn't much time to talk about it because he arrived the day before we started shooting. However, after I saw the first rushes I realised he knew precisely what he was doing and wherever possible I talked to him about it. He gave it a sort of big classical look, it was good quality, solid, well-founded lighting with lots of atmosphere, rather gloomy and dark, which I liked. I was very worried we'd get some bright young spark who would light it up like a television set. He didn't do that, and he understood about big sets.[47]

Rita McGurn makes some interesting observations regarding the relationship between a designer and actors. She argues that actors and designers should discuss the sets. The sets represent the physical milieu of the characters in the film and the actors must feel comfortable with their surroundings.

Finally there is the collaboration between the production designer and the art director. Christopher Hobbs explains that the latter is the designer's assistant. While the production designer does the actual designs and concentrates on the visual aspects in relation to the budget available, the art director's job is to organise the construction managers and such people to make sure that what is on paper actually ends up on the set in the manner intended. In other words the art director takes care of the nuts and bolts and helps with working out the details of the financing.

Included within the design concept of a film is costume design. While this is generally not as important as production design to the overall effect of the film, occasionally costumes can be crucial: such as in period pieces or in the case of a film like *Housekeeping* where the costumes, designed by Mary Jane Reyner, a Bill Forsyth regular, helped to signify aspects of the characters in the film and ultimately to chart the growing differences between the two girls in the film and their relationship to the wider society of Fingerbone, the town in which the drama is set.

Another key technical collaborator in the process is the editor. Along with photography, editing represents the creative essence of film-making in the sense that cinema relies on two processes: the construction and recording of images and the assembly of these images. It is through editing that narrative tension can be built and paced. Bad editing can ruin a film no matter how well the production is directed, photographed, designed and acted. Tony Lawson, an experienced British editor whose credits include *Bad Timing*, *Eureka*, *Insignificance*, *Castaway* and *Track 29*, explains the editor's role in the following manner:

He should bring what the piece demands, in a sense. If it's a slow-paced, lyrical subject then you have to think in those terms. Bearing in mind that you can alter things drastically and change storylines and everything, you really have to try to understand what the director's after or what the director's style is and work within that and hopefully build upon it to increase the particulars of the script.[48]

Lawson stresses the importance of an editor having a sense of the rhythm of the piece, whether to extend the tension or suspense of a sequence by drawing things out, or whether to force the pace along to generate excitement. He explains that more subtle things such as dialogue scenes are less obvious and he tends to rely on intuition in such circumstances in working the sequence up to some dramatic point.

Tom Priestley, a vastly experienced editor, concentrates on the relationship between the editor and the director in his elucidation of the editor's role. First of all he stresses that 'in order for an editor to work creatively, the material has to be shot in a way that allows him a certain flexibility'.[49] Priestley goes on to explain how the film 'emerges' from the collaborative efforts of editor and director:

All work in films is a kind of experiment because you are never remaking the same film, so that you are having to guess how it's going to work. What people don't really understand about editing is that it is very much a process so, just as a film doesn't emerge fully-made out of the camera, neither is it the first cut that the editor makes. The first cut is a very strange sort of personal moment between the editor and the director because in fact it's neither of their versions of the film. It isn't the director's version because the director, up to that time, has merely looked at the rushes and made some choices if he's had room to do so. But how it goes together for the first cut is really totally up to the editor. But equally, because he's dealing with a mass of material, the editor is not saying, 'This is how the finished film should look.' Because it isn't the finished film, it's a stage in the process. The equivalent would be a painting where you block in where the shapes are going to be and maybe indicate a bit of colour. But it's not a finished picture.[50]

The crucial difference between this first cut (or rough cut) and the finished film is explained by Priestley in terms of the distinction he makes between 'cutting' and 'editing':

Cutting to me is putting it all together, and editing is then the process of refinement. It's where the editor is the first member of the public because generally speaking he's not party to the shooting of it. And equally then he and the director have to be the first two critics.[51]

Staying with the rough cut for a moment, sometimes editors may be faced with a tremendous amount of material, given that some directors have a tendency to shoot as much footage as they can, covering scenes from a multitude of angles. Cinematographer Nestor Almendros argues that Americans tend to shoot far more material, and consequently rely on fragmented editing techniques, than their European counterparts.[52] Often this is because they lack a clarity of vision and purpose with the end-result being a film which is devoid of personality and style. Tony Lawson suggests that this may not always be the case:

I think that if there's a lot of film because the director likes a scene or likes what is going on then it's easy to handle. If there's a lot of film because he didn't know what do so he just shot a lot of film in order to sort it out later then it's not so easy.[53]

Lawson has worked on several films with director Nicolas Roeg and he explains that sometimes Roeg has shot a lot of footage while other times he has been more sparing but in each case he had a clear vision of what he was trying to do.

The relationship between editor and director has some affinities with that between producer and director as explored above. This is particularly true with regard to the sense of closeness to and distance from the minutiae of a film and how this relates to the general sense of 'direction'. In the case of director and producer it was the latter's role to be able to 'stand back'. With respect to director and editor the process is reversed, as Tom Priestley explains:

> In shooting, the director is obviously very close to his material. The editor starts at a distance and as he gets closer ideally the director moves further away. So that is why I don't like directors who insist on sitting in the cutting room day after day, looking over your shoulder. Because then I think you become totally obsessed with detail and no one has a proper overview.[54]

He cites an example of this with reference to *Nineteen Eighty Four*, directed by Mike Radford:

> What was interesting about *Nineteen Eighty Four* was because of the circumstances it had to be done in a rush. We really had a tight schedule and we tried to cut corners. One of the corners we tried to cut was to start editing – to actually start moving things about – before we'd got the whole film together. And what Mike [Radford] wasn't able to do was to stand back, so that for the first few weeks of post-production we were marking time because we soon realised that until he could get some objectivity we couldn't advance with the editing.[55]

The situation was eventually remedied and Radford did get some distance from the film but it is a good example of how the process of closeness and distance is crucial if a film is to develop and grow.

A film-maker must also be able to work successfully with actors. Some directors are particularly dictatorial in their relationship with actors, as Hitchcock was, or they may attempt to use them as ciphers or plot devices rather than people as such. The obvious example in the current British context is Peter Greenaway. While others, such as Mike Leigh, take the opposite approach and allow characters to emerge through a process of improvisation, giving the actors a very substantial input. However, in most cases the relationship will be more one of mutual cooperation but with the director ultimately in the driving seat, in other words supplying 'direction'.

Current British cinema does not have a 'star system' as such: there are no British equivalents of big American stars such as Redford, Newman, Eastwood, Streep or Stallone. British films are seldom sold on the strength of who the leading performers are. As John Ellis points out, the star system was essentially developed in Hollywood as a marketing strategy with stars performing a similar function as the creation of a 'narrative image'; that is, to say they 'provide a foreknowledge of the fiction, an invitation to cinema'.[56] There are some performers such as Michael Caine and Sean Connery who come close to serving this function in the British context but both are coming to the end of their acting careers. Arguably the biggest indigenous stars in British cinema are borrowed from the world of rock music: Sting, David Bowie, Phil Collins and Bob Geldof have all appeared in British films over the past few years.

British cinema is much more characterised by solid performers rather than by stars. Individuals such as Ray McAnally, John Hurt, Vanessa Redgrave, Gary Oldman, Miranda Richardson, Daniel Day Lewis, Tilda Swinton and others. These actors, some of whom are extremely experienced and could arguably be regarded as minor stars (for example Redgrave), are also heavily involved in television and theatre which tends to work against star-status in the sense that neither form has the 'larger than life' status, and effect, of cinema. In the theatre, stars are demystified to an extent, they are witnessed 'in the flesh' as living, breathing, sweating individuals rather than screen 'idols'. Television, on the other hand, as John Ellis points out, tends to foster 'personalities' rather than stars. Television does not produce the same kinetic effects as cinema and consequently one's emotional attachment (which includes the recognition and idolisation of star personas within the fiction) is generally less intense. The lack of home-grown stars has helped create a situation where, in order to make a project commercially viable in North America, British film-makers are importing American stars (usually minor, because major league performers demand huge fees which effectively price them out of a typical low-budget British film) such as Kevin Kline

(*Cry Freedom, A Fish Called Wanda*), Denzil Washington (*Cry Freedom, For Queen and Country*), Jeff Goldblum (*The Tall Guy*), Darryl Hannah (*High Spirits*), Melanie Daniels (*Stormy Monday*) and Brigit Fonda (*Scandal*), among others.

Despite the absence of stars, British cinema in general is characterised by strong acting. There are numerous examples of recent British films which, in spite of any technical merits they might have, are carried by the performances of the leading players. This often relates to the rather limited scope of such films. A classic example is *My Left Foot*, which is dominated by the central performance of Daniel Day Lewis as the handicapped Irish writer Christy Brown. Similarly, *Wish You Were Here* is driven along almost singlehandedly by actress Emily Lloyd. The ascendancy of the actor parallels the dominance of the writer in British cinema and can similarly be related to the strong theatrical influence on British cinema.

Actors are often cast according to type so that their physical characteristics determine what kind of roles they will be asked to play. In this respect the casting director is an important member of the production team. Steve Woolley has worked on several occasions with casting director Suzy Figgis and is full of praise for her ability to help a producer and a director with precise advice over casting. Charlie Gormley also acknowledges the benefits of a good casting director. Being secure in the knowledge that casting is done by someone with effective expertise gives the director confidence in much the same way as a good script represents a solid foundation on which a director can build.

The casting of Bill Douglas's film *Comrades* was interesting in that he deliberately chose relatively unknown actors to play the roles of the Tolpuddle Martyrs and their families, while the actors chosen to play the establishment figures were by and large more familiar faces. As Douglas explains:

> I chose unknowns for the Tolpuddle men because I was interested in George Loveless and his men and I didn't want anything to interfere too much with that. So I didn't want a Robert Redford standing for George Loveless because the audience will see Robert Redford and they won't see the glory of this man, and I think he is worth remembering in his own right. When I came to the aristocrats it wasn't a terribly difficult decision because I decided it didn't really matter too much if the audience felt a kind of division between the character and the actor. In fact it was a conscious

decision to cast well-known actors – the 'aristrocrats' of their profession – to emphasise the class distinction.[57]

However, sometimes in the process of casting particular actors who do not correspond to the director's original conceptions of the part can make such an impression that the character is subsequently modified to fit the particular actor. Mike Radford explains that this happened on both *Another Time, Another Place* – with one of the three Italian POWs, and on *White Mischief* when 75-year old Trevor Howard was cast in a part originally created for a 50-year-old. In each case the actor cast was able to bring something fresh to the part.

Another problem that can arise in relation to actors is the different approach of British and American actors to their craft in a film industry where, as I pointed out, Americans are often cast to help the project's commercial potential in the United States. Patrick Cassavetti recalls that on the production of *Brazil* there were great differences between the way Robert De Niro and Jonathan Pryce would approach a scene. De Niro, being a Method actor, required several 'takes' to warm up and get into the part while Pryce required only two or three attempts. Such a state-of-affairs could create problems in that the actor who is used to a minimal amount of takes could possibly burn out if the scene had to be played over and over again.

There are other creative collaborators who deserve a mention, particularly in the often-neglected sound department. The sound-track composer is important and the British cinema has relied heavily on the input of two composers: George Fenton and Michael Kamen, along with a variety of rock musicians, over the past few years. The sound editor is also an important contributor, particularly on an experimental film like Derek Jarman's *The Last of England*, which was shot silent; the sound, including a full footsteps track, was added later. Ron Peck is one film-maker who is particularly aware of the importance of a strong soundtrack to supplement the images and both his features *Nighthawks* and *Empire State* are distinguished by their use of strong driving dance music.

In these ways then, the contribution of such experts is crucial to the film-making process. At the end of the day, however, the director is usually still in the position of final arbiter. As Bill Forsyth suggests: 'everyone is free to make suggestions but the director is in the luxurious position of being able to say yes or no'.[58] Similarly, Bill Douglas argues:

> If I have a strong idea that something is going to work there's no point in diverting me over to another way of thinking. I've really worked it out and convinced myself.[59]

It is the director who must reconcile the various creative contributions and preserve some overall sense of purpose and vision, or the result will probably be chaotic. There is a two-way process in operation: the director can crystallise his or her ideas by drawing upon the technical knowledge and suggestions made by the cinematographer, the editor, production designer or actors, but on the other hand, such ideas and suggestions must be considered in relation to the requirements of the production in hand.

Forsyth believes he has found a very satisfactory way of working with his collaborators on a production:

> When you crew up – when you're in pre-production for two or three months before you start filming – that period is just one long conversation between the director and the five or six creative people he is working with. That conversation goes on for the whole of the pre-production and right through the movie and for me it's very important. I've tended to work with the same people maybe because I find it easier to have that conversation with them.[60]

Michael Coulter has worked on all of Forsyth's films as lighting cameraman, including *That Sinking Feeling* and *Gregory's Girl* (which were so low-budget that there weren't many lights available), as operator to Chris Menges on *Local Hero* and *Comfort and Joy*, an experience which was to prove invaluable to Coulter given Menges' own experience and skill as a lighting cameraman, before moving up the ladder to fully-fledged director of photography (with a relatively substantial budget and a sophisticated lighting design) on *Housekeeping*. Coulter explains his relationship with Forsyth in the following manner:

> Bill is a guy who knows what he wants and doesn't make a fuss about it until he's not getting what he wants. Bill and I have quite a good understanding and one idea out of ten gets accepted because I'm happy to suggest things all the time. *Housekeeping* was important to me. That film was very much a team effort. I'm not discounting Bill's leadership, without him nothing would have been done. But it was very much a collaboration.[61]

Mike Radford has enjoyed collaborating with the same people on different productions because it makes things easier: 'You use short-hand in the way you talk about things to one another.'[62] He makes the following remarks regarding his collaboration with cinematographer Roger Deakins and editor Tom Priestley:

> Roger and I have a close creative collaboration because he's such an amazing cameraman. He operates as well as lights and you always have a creative connection with your camera operator. Because he shoots more film than I do he's just got technically better and better. What it means is that, more and more, if I need an angle or something like that, he can actually improve on it . . . . He can also imagine things, like what a louma crane will do for this shot, which I find rather hard to imagine . . . .
>
> I have absolute faith in Tom when he cuts a dramatic scene. I've chosen the takes which I think are best, but I've yet to catch him out: selecting an angle or making a cut which doesn't utilise the best and most subtle of what the actors are giving. And so I leave that to him. I obviously make suggestions, and the final thing is mine, but it's like having two directors: one who is actually manipulating the film and the other is standing back slightly who's got all the rest under him.[63]

Priestley is also very comfortable with the relationship because Radford allows him the flexibility to work with the material and to have a considerable creative input into the process. The necessary trust between director and editor has also been built up over the three films the pair have collaborated on. Radford has also been the beneficiary of Priestley's vast experience. On *Another Time, Another Place*, for example, as Priestley explains:

> I felt that my role was to structure the narrative a bit more. Mike wrote a lot of unnecessary material. The case in point was when the Italians first arrive at the farm. There was a whole scene in which all the farm people were standing around and the Italians arrive, get off the truck, the farm manager makes a speech, you see everybody and it's a general introduction. And it was very slow and almost stodgy and not particularly well set. So in the end we used one shot of the Italians standing and the truck driving off. Then you fade out. It's jsut saying – 'They've arrived at the farm', which is all you need to say.[64]

Tony Lawson has also worked closely with Nicolas Roeg, editing all his films since *Bad Timing*. Like Priestley with Radford, Lawson enjoys considerable flexibility and freedom in his working relationship with Roeg. As Lawson explains:

> I more or less work on my own to begin with and produce a version of the film. I then show it to him. He's very uncommunicative in that he doesn't explain what he wants. He relies on the fact that he knows basically we are sympathetic towards each other and relies entirely upon at least my initial concept of how the film, or a sequence, should go, and then, based on how successful he feels that is, he will make comments. But basically he really doesn't want to know about it until he's finished shooting, that's when he starts to take an interest.[65]

Roeg is noted for the dramatic editing in his films so the contribution of Lawson to Roeg's cinema is considerable. However, Roeg has worked with other editors and his style has remained consistent and as Lawson acknowledges, he does have a good understanding of the power of editing and tends to get highly involved in the more complex sequences which are part of his stylistic trademark. Lawson's remarks support many of Priestley's comments regarding the editor's role. It also demonstrates how, by suggesting what the film should look like, the editor can help the director to direct his creative energies by providing something tangible on which to work.

There are numerous other examples of collaborations which have been sustained over several films. Julien Temple has collaborated with cinematographer Oliver Stapleton on several pop promos and two features: *Absolute Beginners* and *Earth Girls are Easy*, a relationship which goes back to film school. Temple has also worked for a long time with editor Richard Bedford. Stapleton has also collaborated with Stephen Frears on three films: *My Beautiful Laundrette*, *Prick Up Your Ears* and *Sammy and Rosie Get laid*. Editor Mick Audsley has worked on all of Frears' films since *The Hit*, including the three films mentioned above and the more recent *Dangerous Liaisons*.

Most directors look for a cinematographer with whom they can work closely on the visual design of a film. As we have seen in British cinema, there are numerous examples: Radford and Deakins, Forsyth and Coulter, Frears and Stapleton, Peter Greenaway and Sacha Vierny. One notable omission from this group is Neil Jordan. For someone who has demonstrated a strong coherent visual sense in his films it is surprising to find that on his four features to date Jordan has never worked with the same director of photography. As he explains:

> It's difficult when you change cinematographers all the time because you have to have the same conversation again, and it's always a very inarticulate conversation, about lighting and things. But I've worked with the same camera crew. I happen to have worked with the same operator on the last three films.[66]

Given Mike Radford's evaluation of the importance of the director/ operator relationship, perhaps this continuity has proved beneficial to Jordan.

Where Jordan has enjoyed continuity is on the design front, working with production designer Anton Furst on *The Company of Wolves* and *High Spirits*, his two studio-based films:

> I've had a great relationship with Anton Furst. He's the guy who I find is adventurous enough, and he's got enough reference, to push things to their extreme. So I find with Anton I can talk about the whole visual context of the film. I love to do that: talk about the thing as a whole and create something that is new and resonant. All the films I've done have been heavily designed, even *Angel* because even when we were shooting on locations we changed the locations quite radically. In *Angel* I didn't want an emerald green in the film at all. Everywhere there was green we killed it, throwing sand over large stretches of fields. So it was a designed film as well: the whole thing with the fairy lights, the colour of the suits, and all that sort of stuff. I think to me these are the most important aspects of the film.[67]

Creative collaboration can be equally important in examples of lower-budget, more personal film-making. A classic example being Derek Jarman's *The Last of England*: an intensely personal film shot mainly in Super-8 – the gauge of most home movies and therefore relatively inexpensive. Despite the highly autobiographical nature of the film, *The Last of England* is described by Jarman as 'more collaborative than a film done in the normal way'.[68]

The creative contributions of cast and crew are almost as important in this case as the film-maker's overall vision and objectives. The lack of a formal script and the 'open documentary' philosophy of the film meant that the collection of material was often freer than is usually the case on a production tightly controlled by the strictures of schedule and budget. For example, some of the footage was shot in Liverpool by cameraman Chris Hughes under the direction of actor Spencer Leigh. As Jarman explains:

> It doesn't matter who takes the footage. Some of the other footage in the film was things other people were doing in and around the week we were filming in the warehouse. For example, Chris came to me one morning and said he was going to set up a time-lapse shot on the dock.[69]

The absence of a formal script on *The Last of England* placed particular demands on the cast, many of whom were non-professional actors. No one was given a 'part' to play in the conventional sense and directions were, by and large, minimal. As Jarman explains:

> In a way it's quite different for the actors if they are formally trained. They are not going to be given directions beyond the context: 'You are at a wedding. That's it. Go!' They've not even got a rehearsal. It's difficult when an actor just has to be himself.[70]

This stress on improvisation meant that in certain sequences the onus was placed not only on the actors but also the crew to 'seize the moment'. The nature of filming in Super-8, which enabled Jarman to use multi-camera set-ups to record the same action from different angles, was particularly appropriate in this context.

Not all experiences of collaboration are necessarily productive. There can be a clash of ideas between film-maker and chief collaborators which cannot be effectively resolved. This may result when a director who has become accustomed to a particular set of working practices and production methods encounters a different working situation. This was partly Ron Peck's experience with *Empire State* (although ultimately his major collaborative relationships were satisfactory and, in the case of cinematographer Tony Imi extremely fruitful). Peck had previously made his films, such as *Nighthawks*, in a workshop situation involving an approach to film-making which was both more collective and more self-consciously referential. He attempted to bring the same things to *Empire State*, which initially was to have been a lower-budget, more experimental workshop-type of film than it eventually ended up, with less success than he might have wished. Peck had problems in attempting to get certain ideas across by way of references to paintings and other films:

> I asked most of the Art Department to watch 20 minutes of *Written On the Wind*, the Douglas Sirk film, to try to get something across about not cluttering up the decor with detail. And I juxtaposed it with a film called *Number One*, an archetypal sort of British realist film, full of detail and nothing highlighted. And I had quite a struggle. They didn't know what on earth I was talking about, why on earth I was making them watch this old Hollywood movie that none of them had seen or was very interested in.[71]

Peck argues that this tends to be less of a problem in America where directors will often use references to other films when planning a production and crews will understand and appreciate such a strategy. Julien Temple found that American crews from the grips and the sparks upwards were more involved in the idea of making a movie than their British counterparts. Consequently they are much more willing to make suggestions and enter into a dialogue with the director.

Part of Peck's problem was his unfamiliarity with working practices in the commercial, as opposed to workshop, production sector. There were also problems in that he was working closely in conjunction with Mark Ayres, his partner at Team Pictures and credited executive producer on *Empire State*, and Carl Ross who was credited as creative consultant on the film. The crew, however, would only take orders from the director and resented the others, particularly Ross, suggesting to them what they should do. Peck concedes that the intensely collaborative relationship between the three of them should have ended sooner than it did in recognition of the different working practices at this higher level of production.

But in general the process of collaboration is a fruitful and productive experience. Given the nature and scale of even low-budget film production, collaboration is a necessity in both logistical terms and also with regard to the practicalities of day-to-day production. A successful production requires that a range of specialist skills be brought to bear under the guidance and leadership of the director. But directors rely heavily on the contributions of their collaborators. On a purely technical level most technicians have much more experience than a director who has been working for an equivalent time. A cinematographer can perhaps work on two films a year while, on average a director is involved with a single project for a period of between one and two years. Collaboration provides a film-maker with a greater range of expertise upon which to draw as well as providing a source of ideas and a discursive context within which creative energies can be focused more sharply. Communication is vital to this process; collaborators must understand each other's concepts and ideas prior to their realisation. While conflict can be a problem if it engenders hostility, a degree of competitive tension can be productive by encouraging collaborators to greater efforts. Creative collaboration is the basis upon which the film-making process is founded.

# Conclusion
# A Critical Assessment of Current British Cinema

I began this book by considering general theories of creativity as a necessary precursor to examining film-making as a creative process. I suggested that Williams's conception of creativity, with its stress on communication, description and interpretation, constituted a more appropriate model, with regard to current British film-making than Adorno's Modernist perspective, with its emphasis on confrontation, disruption and dissonance. Communication also implies an element of intentionality which, contrary to the arguments of Adorno, represents an important consideration in the creative process. British cinema has never been at the forefront of Modernist experimentation although, like Hollywood, it has appropriated Modernist techniques, particularly those initiated by the French New Wave. These devices are familiar to audiences and no longer have the power to shock. They are merely part of an increasingly eclectic borrowing of visual effects and narrative techniques by film-makers, derived from a variety of contemporary cultural sources including commercials and pop promos.

By and large, film-makers are concerned to establish communication with their audience, irrespective of whether their primary purpose is to entertain, stimulate or inform. This tendency is reinforced by the commercial imperative which underpins practically all film-making. No financier will be keen to invest in a project which by its very nature will have a problem finding an audience. The commercial intentionality of financiers must be reconciled with the artistic or communicative intentionalities of film-makers in this respect. In Britain this general economic constraint is compounded by the fact that film-makers in this country have never enjoyed a stable source of finance, either commercial or state-subsidised. It is also significant that in recent years the BFI production board, which is the last bastion of ostensibly non-commercial film-funding in

Britain, has shifted its emphasis away from experimental avant garde film-making to backing feature projects, often in partnership with Channel 4, which are likely to find an audience. This is not necessarily a regressive step because, given the general scarcity of funds, obscurantism and self-indulgence are unaffordable luxuries.

I proceeded to describe in depth the technological, financial and aesthetic contexts within which current British cinema exists. These interrelated contexts effectively structure the creative process by defining limits, providing resources and imposing constraints. Cinematic creativity is inextricably bound up with questions of technology, time, money, commercial viability and aesthetic modes and techniques of storytelling. By examining these contexts we can begin to understand the process itself. The characteristics of this process also have a crucial bearing on the nature of its products – the films themselves.

As part of this consideration of the film-making process I considered the question of creative collaboration. This question has been largely neglected by critics in favour of auteurism and its variants and, more recently, the examination of the spectator and the process of spectating. It is impossible to dispense with the idea of auteurism altogether. Indeed there are several film-makers working in Britain today who have a readily identifiable style or world view. Their number includes Derek Jarman, Neil Jordan, Peter Greenaway, Terry Gilliam, Bill Forsyth, Mike Leigh, Nicolas Roeg and Ken Russell. Many of them are writer/directors who initiate their own projects and consequently stamp the work with their own thematic and stylistic preoccupations. However, all of these film-makers rely heavily on the contributions of various collaborators. Many have consistently worked with the same individuals on several films, which raises the issue of collective authorship. For example, how much of the impact generated by a Peter Greenaway film is attributable to the lush cinematography of Sacha Vierny or the distinctive musical scores of Michael Nyman?

While I would ultimately reject a collective authorship thesis, it remains the case that no film-maker, regardless of the strength of their own personal vision, would be able to realise that vision without the expertise and creative input of collaborators. The director may be the source of coherence, reconciling the various contributions, but these contributions are an essential part of the creative process. The marks of various collaborators, over and above that of the director, are often identifiable in the finished work. British technicians are renowned for their high standards of technical expertise and resourcefulness, lending weight to the idea of 'quality' as a hallmark of British cinema despite the general lack of funds.

Collaboration also reintroduces the issue of communication as an appropriate understanding of cinematic creativity. In this instance the communication occurs between collaborators as opposed to the film-maker/audience communication derived from Williams. Successful collaboration depends on communication. Collaborators must understand a director's pre-visual concepts and help him or her to transform these concepts into images and sounds. A film crew must also be able to solve technical and aesthetic problems collectively. At the same time, collaboration may also involve a degree of friction which can be productive, forcing a clarification of purpose and providing the impetus for greater effort.

The major thrust of this study has been exploratory and descriptive. By way of a conclusion I wish to move towards a more evaluative stance in considering the current state of British cinema. Since I began this study, there have been significant developments. On the financial side production costs have risen considerably, with the result that companies such as Channel 4 and British Screen have proportionately less to invest in production. In 1989 Channel 4 had a stake in eight features, around half the amount they were able to invest in during the early to mid-eighties. Similarly British Screen were involved with seven projects compared with twelve in 1987.[1] Zenith have tended to concentrate less on feature films and more on television drama, including series such as *The Paradise Club* and *Inspector Morse*, over the past year. The independent film arm of Thames Television, Euston films, withdrew from feature production due to changes in the ITV levy, which may or may not deter other television companies from becoming involved in feature films. To make matters worse, the American interest in British production has declined significantly from 42 per cent in 1988 to 23 per cent in 1989. Several of the 'mini-majors' who helped fund several films by way of North American distribution deals have experienced financial problems and have cut back on investment or have gone out of business altogether. Consequently 1989 saw British film production at its lowest level for nearly a decade with only 38 theatrical features being made, compared to 56 the previous year, representing a fall of 32 per cent.

In light of this general trend it is not surprising that many British directors, including some of the more interesting newcomers from the 'renaissance' period, have recently made films in North America. This group includes Bill Forsyth, Neil Jordan, Roland Joffe, Stephen Frears and Julien Temple. Some have also taken their key collaborators with them. This is the latest manifestation of a familiar career pattern dating back to Alfred Hitchcock who made his first American features in the early forties. The previous generation to make the move west were film-makers like Alan Parker, Ridley and Tony Scott and Adrian Lyne, all of whom had trained in the world of television commercials and graduated to become directors of commercially successful and stylish American genre films. They have been effectively absorbed into the Hollywood mainstream, neutralising any contribution they may or may not have made to British film culture. It remains to be seen if the careers of Forsyth, Jordan and company will develop in the same way, but given the current downward trend in indigenous production there seems little reason for them to stay here. Going 'international' need not be detrimental. The problem is when film-makers are driven abroad by economic considerations, such as a chronic lack of funds, rather than choosing to tackle a subject rooted in a 'foreign' location.

It is interesting to consider how the question of commerciality has affected British cinema. The commercial popularity of British cinema in the eighties was rooted in its sense of comic iconoclasm. The British cinema represented by films such as *My Beautiful Laundrette* and *A Room With a View* displayed a sense of eccentric and eclectic vitality which proved popular with young, largely middle-class audiences, in much the same way as the French New Wave had been twenty-five years previously. But as the money became scarcer, the already-established tendency to 'play safe' by conforming to commercial demands solidified and the stylistic and thematic innovation of the early eighties began to evaporate. The very comic iconoclasm which was the British cinema's commercial strength, also proved to be its aesthetic weakness.

While the British cinema of the eighties was by and large a socially critical progressive cinema, with film-makers rarely indulging in Hollywood style candyfloss or gung-ho action, the heavy reliance on American sources of funding inevitably entailed compromise. One significant difference between television drama and many cinema films is that the former is frequently harder-hitting in terms of its social and political analysis. Television drama does not represent the same commercial risk as cinema and consequently is able to practise less caution in its approach to its subject matter. The progression of

David Leland from television to cinema is an interesting case in point. The four dramas he wrote for Central Television in the early eighties, *Made in Britain*, *Birth of a Nation*, *Flying into the Wind* and *R.H.I.N.O.*, are much bleaker and more hard-hitting than his cinema work which tends to be, in line with general aesthetic trends, softer and rather quirky. Cinematographer Roger Deakins was ultimately unimpressed with *Personal Services*, Leland's second screenplay after *Mona Lisa* which he wrote with Neil Jordan. Deakins was under the impression that the film would be hard-hitting, but it soon degenerated into what he refers to as 'Whitehall farce':

> It upset me because it wasted a fantastic opportunity to actually make a very solid statement about sexuality and politics . . . . That whole hyprocrisy of the establishment in this country.[2]

Similarly the impact of *Wish You Were Here*, the story of a young girl's sexual awakening, is effectively sanitised by its quirky comedic approach. This is revealed forcefully when compared to the approach of French director Catherine Breillat in *Virgin* which is more earthy, astute and challenging. Quirky comedy may enable film-makers to explore difficult issues in an accessible and commercially viable way but it can also serve to dissipate and dilute social criticism.

There is also a tendency in British cinema to enclose the issues it is exploring. Narratives are frequently neatly packaged and audiences are rarely confronted or forced into a critical engagement. A good illustration is provided by the treatment of homosexuality in films like *Maurice* and *Prick Up Your Ears*. The issue of homosexuality is extremely relevant in contemporary society, particularly so in the wake of Clause 28. This makes it a ripe subject for film-makers. Yet both these films subordinate the issue to other aesthetic and commercial concerns. Neither attempts to confront the audience's sensibilities by eroticising homosexuality as Derek Jarman does in *Sebastianne*, or bring it closer to home by focusing on the contemporary experiences of ordinary gay people in the way Ron Peck and Paul Hallam's *Nighthawks* does. *Maurice*, which was Merchant/Ivory's follow-up to the enormously successful *A Room With a View*, is another E. M. Forster adaptation, set comfortably in an aristocratic Edwardian past. It is a worthy film, alluding to Forster's own repressed homosexuality, yet it is too removed from present concerns to contribute to the current debate.

*Prick Up Your Ears* on the other hand, is a classic British biopic. This popular genre in some senses does attempt to critically examine prevailing British social and sexual morality by focusing on individuals who refused to conform and generally paid the price. But such films also pander to a certain 'Sunday colour supplement' type of obsession with social and sexual deviance and the more lurid events of recent British history. These films are rarely able to achieve any significant critical distance from their subjects which would render them less voyeuristic.

There are examples of more challenging approaches both in terms of subject matter and form. *My Beautiful Laundrette* made such an impact precisely because of its tale of the love affair between Omar, a young Asian who inherits a laundrette from his rich uncle, and Johnny, an unemployed former National Front skinhead who comes to work for Omar in his laundrette. Hanif Kureishi's script provocatively examined issues of race and sexuality in contemporary Britain in a manner which broke with the straightforward victim/victimiser structure. The Asian community itself came under close scrutiny as well as the relationship between Asians and the indigenous population.

There are also film-makers who, aesthetically, exist on the margins of British cinema. These are a disparate group of idiosyncratic individuals such as Derek Jarman, Peter Greenaway, Terence Davies and Ken McMullen, who collectively represent the aesthetically innovative and thematically challenging sector of British film-making. Their work ranges from the ultra-low-budget production of Jarman to the lush *tableaux vivants* of Greenaway and is texturally much richer than most British cinema, drawing upon a wide range of aesthetic and cultural influences, including poetry and painting.

These film-makers have a closer affinity to European traditions of cinema than the Hollywood towards which much British cinema tends to aspire. Significantly, all have been backed in recent years by European sources of finance, and in general receive greater critical recognition on the Continent than at home. Each is interested in exploring the possibilities of form and their narratives are less inclined towards the neatly-packaged closure which represents the norm in British cinema. Their cinema is more open, demanding a greater critical engagement on the part of the audience. In terms of communication, they provide much more of a space for two-way dialogue and interpretive response than the British mainstream. It is through the efforts and experiments of such 'marginal' individuals that the medium of cinema itself can expand and develop. They represent an important alternative to the general line, preserving the possibility of a stylistically diverse and innovative British film culture.

# Notes

## Introduction
## Creativity: The Theoretical Context

1.    Raymond Williams, *The Long Revolution* (Harmondsworth: Pelican, 1965).
2.    Williams argues that while Plato and Aristotle shared the conception of art as essentially mimetic they drew different conclusions from it. Plato regarded art as a pale and worthless imitation of reality while Aristotle saw art as reflecting an idealised or higher reality. In *The Creativity Question* (Durham, NC: Duke University Press, 1976), Albert Rothenberg and Carl Hausman identify the differences between Plato and Aristotle's conception of creativity. Plato saw creativity as divine inspiration, the intervention of the Gods, while Aristotle tended to regard creativity as a productive activity following natural laws.
3.    M. H. Abrams, *The Mirror and the Lamp* (London: Oxford University Press, 1953).
4.    Colin Campbell, *The Romantic Ethic and the Spirit of Consumerism* (Oxford: Basil Blackwell, 1987), p. 182.
5.    The phrase is borrowed from the seminal work by Mario Praz, *The Romantic Agony* (Oxford: Oxford University Press, 1933).
6.    Frank Kermode, *Romantic Image* (London: Routledge & Kegan Paul, 1957).
7.    Karl Miller examines numerous literary examples of 'the dynamic metaphor of the second self' in *Doubles: Studies in Literary History* (New York: Oxford University Press, 1985).
8.    Williams, p. 44.
9.    Warren Steinkraus, 'Artistic Creativity and Pain' in M. Mitias (ed.), *Creativity in Art, Religion and Culture* (Amsterdam, 1985), talks about various aspects of pain associated with the creative process including the pain of making a selection from limitless material, the pain of personal exposure; of having one's innermost feelings made transparent through the art-work, and the pain of suppressed emotion.
10.    Coleridge is presented by Laurence Lockridge in *The Ethics of Romanticism* (Cambridge: Cambridge University Press, 1989), as an example of the link between the British Romantic movement and the broader discourse of nineteenth-century European philosophy, including the Idealist tradition of Hegel and Kant.
11.    Theodor Adorno, *Aesthetic Theory* (London: Routledge & Kegan Paul, 1984), p. 245.
12.    Lionel Trilling, 'Freud and Literature' in *The Liberal Imagination* (London: Mercury, 1961).
13.    Trilling 'Art and Neurosis' in *The Liberal Imagination*.

14. Adorno, p. 12.
15. Herbert Marcuse, *One Dimensional Man* (London: Sphere, 1968), p. 69.
16. Williams, p. 42.
17. Ibid., p. 51.
18. Ibid., p. 44.
19. See for example, Peter Dews, 'Adorno, Post-Structuralism and the Critique of Identity', *New Left Review*, No. 157.
20. Adorno, pp. 238–9.
21. Ibid., p. 475.
22. Ibid., p. 243.
23. Roland Barthes, 'The Death of the Author' in *Image/Music/Text* (London: Fontana, 1977).
24. Robert Philip Kolker, *The Altering Eye* (New York: Oxford University Press, 1983).

## 1 Creativity and Cinema

1. Edward Buscombe, 'Ideas of Authorship', *Screen*, Autumn 1973, reproduced in John Caughie (ed.), *Theories of Authorship* (London: Routledge & Kegan Paul/BFI, 1981), p. 22.
2. See Raymond Williams, *The Long Revolution* (Harmondsworth: Pelican, 1965).
3. Andrew Sarris, 'Notes on the Auteur Theory in 1962' in Mast & Cohen (eds), *Film Theory and Criticism*, 2nd Edition (New York: Oxford University Press, 1979).
4. André Bazin, 'La Politique des Auteurs', *Cahiers Du Cinéma*, No. 70, April 1970. Extract in Caughie (ed.).
5. Mast & Cohen (eds), p. 658.
6. Claude Lévi-Strauss, *Structural Anthropology*, Vol. 1 (London: Allen Lane, 1969).
7. Geoffrey Nowell-Smith, extract from *Visconti* in Caughie (ed.), p. 137.
8. Peter Wollen, *Signs and Meaning in the Cinema* (London: Secker and Warburg, 1972).
9. Brian Henderson, 'Critique of Cine Structuralism' in Caughie (ed.).
10. Wollen, p. 146.
11. Nowell-Smith in Caughie (ed.).
12. John Caughie, 'Auteur Structuralism. Introduction' in Caughie (ed.).
13. Will Wright, *Six Guns and Society* (Berkeley, California, 1975).
14. Heath, 'Film and System: Terms of Analysis', *Screen*, Spring 1975 (part I); Summer 1975 (part II).
15. Geoffrey Nowell-Smith, 'Six Authors in Pursuit of *The Searchers*' (extract) in Caughie (ed.), p. 223.
16. Pam Cook, 'The auteur debate', in *The Cinema Book* (London: BFI, 1985).
17. For example, see Roland Barthes, 'The Death of the Author' in *Image/Music/Text* (London: Fontana, 1977, and Stephen Heath, 'Comment on the Idea of Authorship' in Caughie (ed.).

18.  The theory of the enunciating subject is developed by Nowell-Smith in 'A Note on History/Discourse' which refers closely to Metz's article 'History/Discourse' on which it builds. Both essays are included in Caughie (ed.).

19.  Sandy Flitterman, 'Woman, Desire and the Look: Feminism and the Enunciative Apparatus in Cinema' in Caughie (ed.).

20.  Ibid., p. 243.

21.  Nick Browne, 'The Rhetoric of the Specular Text With Reference to *Stagecoach*' in Caughie (ed.).

22.  Derek Jarman, *The Last of England* (London: Constable, 1987), p. 193.

23.  Buscombe in Caughie (ed.), p. 31.

24.  For example, Laura Mulvey, 'Visual Pleasure and Narrative Cinema', *Screen*, Autumn 1975.

25.  Jarman, p. 194.

26.  Frears quoted in James Park, *Learning to Dream* (London: Faber & Faber, 1984), p. 22.

27.  Paul Coates, *The Story of the Lost Reflection* (London: Verso, 1985), p. 80.

28.  Ibid., p. 82.

29.  André Bazin, 'The Ontology of the Photographic Image', 1945, quoted in Pam Cook (ed.), *The Cinema Book* (London: BFI, 1985), p. 224.

30.  Rudolph Arnheim from *Film as Art* in Mast & Cohen, 3rd Edition, 1985.

31.  Bazin, 'Cinematic Realism and the Italian School of the Liberation', quoted in Cook (ed.), p. 225.

32.  Bazin, *Le Journal D'un Curé de Campagne* and the Stylistics of Robert Bresson' in *What is Cinema?*, ed. Hugh Gray (Berkeley: University of California Press, 1967).

33.  Interview with Bill Douglas, Edinburgh, 24/7/88.

34.  Maya Deren, 'Cinematography: The Creative Use of Reality' in Mast & Cohen, 3rd Edition.

35.  Ibid., p. 58.

36.  Ibid., p. 61.

## 2   The Question of Cinema Technology

1.  Robert Allen and Douglas Gomery, *Film History: Theory and Practice* (New York: Kopt, 1985). They refer to several examples of 'The Great Man Theory' from the 'rather simplistic hero worship of Grau' to the 'painstaking descriptions of the invention of early cinematic apparatus in Gordon Hendricks' work'.

2.  Raymond Williams, *Television: Technology and Cultural Form* (London: Fontana, 1974), p. 13.

3.  Stephen Heath, 'The Cinematic Apparatus: Technology as Historical and Cultural Form' in *Questions of Cinema* (London: Macmillan, 1981), p. 225.

4. Raymond Williams, 'British Film History: New Perspectives' in Curran and Porter (eds), *British Cinema History* (London: Weidenfeld & Nicholson, 1983).

5. Barry Salt, 'Film Style and Technology in the Thirties: Sound' in Belton and Weiss (eds), *Film Sound* (New York: Columbia University Press, 1985), p. 37.

6. Barry Salt, *Film Style and Technology: History and Analysis* (London: Starword, 1983), p. 292.

7. Allen and Gomery.

8. Rick Altman, 'The Evolution of Sound Technology' in Belton and Weiss (eds).

9. Peter Wollen, 'Cinema and Technology: a Historical Overview' in *Readings and Writings* (London: Verso, 1982), p. 169.

10. Altman in Belton and Weiss.

11. Williams, *Television*.

12. Gomery and Allen.

13. Ibid., pp. 124–5.

14. Wollen, 'Cinema and Technology'.

15. Paul Virilio, *War and Cinema: The Logistics of Perception* (London: Verso, 1989).

16. Wollen, p. 169.

17. Steve Neale, *Cinema and Technology: Image Sound Colour* (London: Macmillan/BFI, 1985), p. 2.

18. Heath, p. 227.

19. Jean Louis Comolli, 'Machines of the Visible' in Mast and Cohen (eds), *Film Theory and Criticism*, 3rd Edition (New York: Oxford University Press, 1985), pp. 741–2.

20. Gomery and Allen.

21. Robert Carringer, *The Making of Citizen Kane* (London: John Murray, 1985), p. 81.

22. John Ellis, 'Made in Ealing', *Screen*, Spring 1975.

23. Walter Lassally, *Itinerant Cameraman* (London: John Murray, 1987).

24. Interview with Michael Coulter, Glasgow, 11/5/88.

25. Interview with Roger Deakins, London, 18/7/88.

26. Interview with Tom Priestley, London, 11/4/88.

27. Roy Armes, *On Video* (London: Routledge, 1988), p. 1.

28. Stuart Marshall, 'Video: Technology and Practice', *Screen*, Vol. 20, no. 1, Spring 1979.

29. Armes, p. 74.

30. Ibid., p. 74.

31. Antonioni in interview with John Francis Lane, *Sight & Sound*, Winter 1979/80.

32. Lynda Myles, article on *One From the Heart* in *Sight & Sound*, Spring 1982.

33. Julian Petley, review article on *Out of Order* in *Monthly Film Bulletin*, August 1988.

34. Interview with Michael Coulter, Glasgow, 11/5/88.

35. Interview with Roger Deakins, London, 18/7/88.

36. BFI Dossier on *The Boys From the Blackstuff*, edited by Richard Paterson, 1984.
37. Armes, p. 195.
38. Wollen, p. 174. Article was originally written in 1978.
39. Interview with Tony Lawson, London, 4/6/88.
40. Interview with James Mackay, London, 9/4/88.
41. Interview with Alan Fountain, London, 6/6/88.

## 3   The Financing and Production of British Films: Historical Background

1. Interview with Steve Woolley, London, 7/11/88.
2. Michael Chanan, 'The Emergence of an Industry' in Curran and Porter (eds), *British Cinema History* (London: Weidenfeld and Nicholson, 1983), p. 50.
3. This issue is discussed by Annette Kuhn in *Cinema, Censorship and Sexuality 1909–25* (London: Routledge, 1988).
4. A comprehensive breakdown of these categories is provided by James C. Robertson in the appendix to *The British Board of Film Censors: Film Censorship in Britain 1896–1950* (Beckenham: Croom Helm, 1985).
5. The case of *Saturday Night and Sunday Morning* is examined in Jeffrey Richards and Anthony Aldgate, *Best of British: Cinema and Society 1930–1970* (Oxford: Basil Blackwell, 1983).
6. Percentages calculated from figures given in Margaret Dickinson and Sarah Street, *Cinema and State* (London: BFI, 1985), p. 11.
7. Simon Hartog, 'State Protection of a Beleagured Industry' in Curran and Porter (eds).
8. Dickinson and Street, p. 76.
9. George Perry in *The Great British Picture Show* (London: Pavilion, 1985), points out that the exhibition duopoly also constrained film-makers in relation to changing censorship. The introduction of the 'X' category in 1951 was designed to allow more adult treatments of subjects to be shown. However, the ABC circuit decided to show only outstanding 'X'-rated films – usually European art films – while Rank banned all 'X' films on the grounds that they broke up family cinemagoing. This had an obvious effect on British production by promoting self-censorship.
10. Robert Murphy: 'Rank's Attempt on the American Market, 1944–9', in Curran and Porter (eds).
11. Julian Petley, 'Cinema and State' in Charles Barr (ed.), *All Our Yesterdays* (London: BFI/RKP, 1986), pp. 37–8.
12. Dickinson and Street, p. 238.
13. See Matthew Silverstone, 'Finding the Money' in Auty and Roddick (eds), *British Cinema Now* (London: BFI, 1985).
14. Interview with Al Clark, London, 30/5/85.
15. Dickinson and Street, p. 248.
16. Simon Relph: Article on Film Finance in the UK, *Screen International*, May 13–16, 1989.

**4  British Feature Film Production**

1.   Guy Phelps, 'A Degree of Freedom' in *Sight & Sound*, Autumn 1987.
2.   Philipa Bloom, survey of British production in *Screen International*, January 1989.
3.   Simon Perry, 'UK Financing' in *Screen International*, 9–16 May 1987.
4.   Ibid.
5.   Shelly Bancroft (ed.), *Raising Production Finance*, AIP Information Pack, 1986.
6.   Interview with Margaret Matheson, London, 20/7/87.
7.   Interview with Al Clark, London, 17/7/87.
8.   Interview with Gareth Jones, London, 22/7/88.
9.   Relph, 'Producing a New Deal' *Screen International*, 14/5/88.
10.   Interview with Sarah Radclyffe, London, 7/4/88.
11.   Shelly Bancroft (ed.), *Development*, AIP Information Pack, 1986.
12.   A. Harcourt et al., *The Independent Producer: Film and Television* (London: Faber & Faber, 1986), pp. 100–101.
13.   Interview with Steve Woolley, London, 7/11/88.
14.   Interview with Graham Bradstreet, London, 7/4/88.
15.   Interview with Sarah Radclyffe, London, 7/4/88.
16.   Mary Davies, 'Seedy Business' *AIP & Co.*, December 1985.
17.   Alan Stanbrook, article on Budgeting in *Stills*, 1986, MIFED edition.
18.   Interview with Sarah Radclyffe, London, 7/4/88.
19.   Raymond Williams, *Culture* (London: Fontana 1981), pp. 105–6.
20.   Interview with David Rose, London, 22/7/87.
21.   Simon Relph interviewed by Nicolas Kent, *Sight & Sound*, Autumn 1987.
22.   Interview with David Rose, London, 22/7/87.
23.   Ibid.
24.   Georgina Henry, 'Sales of the Unexpected', *Producer*, May 1987.
25.   Interview with David Rose, London, 22/7/87.
26.   Interview with Alan Fountain, London, 6/6/88.
27.   Ibid.
28.   Ibid.
29.   Ibid.
30.   Ibid.
31.   Ibid.
32.   Interview with Charles Gormley, Glasgow, 11/5/88.
33.   Ibid.
34.   Interview with Derek Jarman, Edinburgh, 17/8/87.
35.   Interview with James Mackay, London, 9/4/88.
36.   Information from British Screen handout to producers.
37.   Article in *Producer*, Spring 1988.
38.   Phelps, 'A Degree of Freedom', *Sight & Sound*, Summer 1987.
39.   British Screen, *Information for Producers*, Company Information Handout, 1987.
40.   Phelps, 'A Degree of Freedom'.
41.   Interview with Simon Relph, London, 22/7/87.
42.   Ibid.

43.   Ibid.
44.   Interview with Margaret Matheson, London, 20/7/87.
45.   Ibid.
46.   Ibid.
47.   Ibid.
48.   Ibid.
49.   Graham Wade, *Film, Video and Television: Market Forces, Fragmentation and Technological Advance* (London, 1985), pp. 11–12.
50.   Interview with Margot Gavan Duffy, London, 22/7/88.
51.   Interview with Gareth Jones, London, 22/7/88.
52.   Ibid.
53.   Ibid.
54.   Ibid.
55.   Ibid.
56.   Interview in *Screen International*, 13–20 June, 1987.
57.   Interview with Gareth Jones, London, 22/7/88.
58.   See Sheila Whittaker, 'Declarations of Independence' in Auty & Roddick (eds), *British Cinema Now* (London: BFI/RKP, 1985) for an analysis of the Code of Practice and the Workshop Declaration.
59.   Interview with Colin MacCabe, London, 15/7/87.
60.   Ibid.
61.   Ibid.
62.   Quoted by James Park, 'The Nervous Summer of the British Film Industry', *Sight & Sound*, Winter 1985/6.
63.   Julian Petley, 'All Blast and no Balls', *Producer*, May 1987.
64.   James Park, 'Tarnished Goldcrest', *AIP & Co.*, Summer 1985.
65.   Ibid.
66.   Interview with Al Clark, London, 17/9/87.
67.   Ibid.
68.   Interview with Steve Woolley, 7/11/88.
69.   Ibid.
70.   Interview with Sarah Radclyffe, London, 7/4/88.
71.   Interview with David Rose, London, 22/7/87.
72.   Interview with Tom Priestley, London, 11/4/88.
73.   Interview with Derek Jarman, Edinburgh, 17/8/87.
74.   Ibid.
75.   Interview with Julien Temple, London, 20/7/88.
76.   Interview with Gareth Jones, London, 22/7/88.

## 5   The Film-Making Process: Sales, Distribution and Marketing

1.   See Chapter 4.
2.   Interview with Marc Samuelson, London, 20/7/87.
3.   Richard Kahn, 'Motion Picture Marketing' in J. Squire (ed.), *The Movie Business Book* (London: Columbus, 1986), p. 264.
4.   Raymond Williams, *Culture* (London: Fontana, 1981), p. 53.
5.   Ibid., p. 105.
6.   John Ellis, *Visible Fictions* (London: Routledge & Kegan Paul, 1982).

7. *Sight & Sound*, Winter 1983/4.
8. Interview with Steve Woolley, London, 7/11/88.
9. Ibid.
10. Interview with Gareth Jones, London, 22/7/88.
11. James Park, 'Film Sales Agents: Floggers or Financiers', *AIP & Co.*, November 1985.
12. Interview with Gareth Jones, London, 22/7/88.
13. Interview with Simon Relph in *Sight & Sound*, Autumn 1987.
14. Interview with John Durie, London, 7/4/88.
15. Interview with Steve Woolley, London 7/11/88.
16. Interview with Sarah Radclyffe, London, 7/4/88.
17. Ibid.
18. Interview with John Durie, London, 7/4/88.
19. Ibid.
20. Archie Tait, 'Distributing the Product' in Auty and Roddick (eds), *British Cinema Now* (London: BFI, 1985).
21. Interview with Patrick Cassavetti, London, 21/7/87.
22. B. J. Franklin in Pirie (ed.), *Anatomy of the Movies* (London: Windward, 1981).
23. Interview with Al Clark, London, 17/7/87.
24. Interview with Margaret Matheson, London, 20/7/87.
25. Kahn in Squire (ed.), p. 265.
26. Paul Webster: 'Pictures of Pictures', *Producer*, May 1987.
27. Interview with Steve Woolley, London, 7/11/88.
28. Interview with Ron Peck, London, 8/4/88.
29. Ibid.
30. Ellis, *Visible Fictions*.
31. Kahn in Squire (ed.), p. 271.
32. Ibid.
33. Interview with John Durie, London, 7/4/88.
34. Figure quoted by Kahn in Squire (ed.).
35. Shelly Bancroft, 'Hard Hype, Hard Sell, Hard Cash', *AIP & Co.*, Summer 1985.
36. Interview with John Durie, London, 7/4/88.
37. Interview with Steve Woolley, London, 7/11/88.
38. Franklin in Pirie (ed.).
39. Interview with Ron Peck, London, 8/4/88.
40. Interview with Steve Woolley, London, 7/11/88.
41. Information from Julian Senior, Vice-President, European Advertising and Publicity, Warner Brothers, lecturing at an AIP Seminar: 'Marketing the Movie' at BAFTA, Piccadilly, London on 28/5/85.
42. Information from Paul Webster, lecturing at the above seminar.
43. Interview with Neil Jordan, Shepperton, 2/6/88.
44. Interview with Steve Woolley, London, 7/11/88.

**6 Genre, Aesthetics and Criticism**

1. Raymond Williams, *The Long Revolution* (Harmondsworth: Pelican, 1965), Chapter 1: 'The Creative Mind'.

2.   Christine Gledhill, 'History of Genre Criticism' in Pam Cook (ed.), *The Cinema Book* (London: BFI, 1985), p. 58.

3.   The first critical study to use the term *film noir* was Raymond Borde and Etienne Chaumerton's *Panorame du Film Noir Americain* (Paris) 1955.

4.   Leo Braudy, 'Genre. The Conventions of Connection' in Gerald Mast and Marshall Cohen (eds), *Film Theory and Criticism*, 3rd Edition (New York: Oxford University Press, 1984), p. 415.

5.   Edward Buscombe, 'The Idea of Genre in American Cinema', in Barry K. Grant (ed.) *Film Genre: Theory and Criticism*, (Metuchen, NJ: Scarecrow Press, 1977), p. 34.

6.   Tom Ryall, *Alfred Hitchcock and the British Cinema* (London: Croom Helm, 1986), p. 73.

7.   See John Hill, *Sex, Class and Realism* (London: BFI, 1986).

8.   Andy Medhurst, 'Music Hall and British Cinema' in Charles Barr (ed.), *All Our Yesterdays*, (London: BFI, 1986).

9.   Andrew Higson, 'Britain's Outstanding Contribution to the Film' in Barr (ed.), *All Our Yesterdays*.

10.  See Charles Barr, *Ealing Studios* (London: Cameron & Tayleur, 1977).

11.  John Ellis, 'Art, Culture and Quality: Terms for a Cinema in the Forties and Seventies', *Screen*, Autumn 1978.

12.  Ian Christie, 'The Scandal of *Peeping Tom*' in *Powell, Pressburger and Others* (London: BFI, 1978).

13.  Alexander Walker, *Hollywood England* (London: Harrap, 1986).

14.  Andrew Higson, 'Britain's Outstanding Contribution to the Film', in *All Our Yesterdays*, p. 95.

15.  Alexander Walker, *Hollywood England*, p. 60.

16.  Raymond Williams, 'A Lecture on Realism', *Screen*, Spring 1977, p. 67.

17.  Martyn Auty, 'But is it Cinema?' in Auty and Nick Roddick (eds), *British Cinema Now* (London: BFI, 1985).

18.  Interview with Tony Lawson, London, 4/6/88.

19.  John Ellis, 'Made in Ealing', *Screen*, Summer 1975.

20.  Roy Armes, *A Critical History of British Cinema* (London: Secker & Warburg, 1978), p. 333.

21.  John Hill, *Sex, Class and Realism*, p. 57.

22.  Ibid., p. 59.

23.  Raymond Williams, 'A Lecture on Realism'.

24.  Robert Philip Kolker, *The Altering Eye* (New York: Oxford University Press, 1983), p. 6.

25.  Christine Gledhill, 'The Melodramatic Field: An Investigation' in Gledhill (ed.), *Home Is Where the Heart Is: Studies in Melodrama and the Woman's Film* (London: BFI, 1987).

26.  Interview with Christopher Hobbs, London, 7/4/88.

27.  James Park, *Learning to Dream: The New British Cinema* (London: Faber & Faber, 1984).

28.  Important texts include Sue Aspinall and Robert Murphy (eds), *Gainsborough Melodrama* (London: BFI Dossier, 1983); several of

the essays in Barr (ed.), *All Our Yesterdays*, particularly Charles Barr: 'Schizophrenia and Amnesia' and Julien Petley: 'The Lost Continent'; Ian Christie, *Powell, Pressburger and Others* (London: BFI, 1978); David Pirie: *A Heritage of Horror* (London: Gordon Fraser, 1973).

29. Interview with Patrick Cassavetti, London 21/7/87.
30. Interview with Marc Samuelson, London 20/7/88.
31. Interview with Christopher Hobbs, London, 7/4/88.
32. George Orwell, 'Charles Dickens' in *Collected Essays* (London: Secker & Warburg, 1961), p. 75.
33. Ibid., p. 86.
34. Andy Medhurst, Presentation on British Comedy, BFI Summer School, Stirling Unviersity 26/7/89.
35. Ken Annakin, article in *Film* 15, Jan–Feb. 1958.
36. Interview with Charles Gormley, Glasgow, 11/5/88.
37. Interview with Tom Priestley, London, 11/4/88.
38. Interview with Derek Jarman, Edinburgh, 12/8/87.
39. Interview with Charles Gormley, Glasgow, 11/5/88.
40. Interview with Tony Lawson, London 4/6/88.
41. Julian Petley, 'The Lost Continent' in Barr (ed.), *All Our Yesterdays*, p. 102.
42. Brian McFarlane, 'A Literary Cinema' in Barr (ed.), *All Our Yesterdays*.
43. Ibid., p. 120.
44. Interview with Roger Deakins, London, 18/7/88.
45. Armes, *A Critical History of British Cinema*.
46. Norman Marshall, 'Reflections on the English Film', *The Bookman*, October 1931, p. 71.
47. Julian Petley, 'The Lost Continent' in Barr (ed.), p. 102.
48. See Geoff Brown, '"Sister of the Stage": British Film and British Theatre' in Barr (ed.), *All Our Yesterdays*.
49. John Ellis, *Visible Fictions* (London: Routledge & Kegan Paul, 1982), p. 24.
50. Charles Barr, 'A Conundrum for England', *Monthly Film Bulletin*, August 1984.
51. Interview with Sarah Radclyffe, London, 7/4/88.
52. Interview with Michael Coulter, Glasgow, 11/5/88.
53. Interview with Ron Peck, London, 8/4/88.
54. Ibid.
55. Interview with Julien Temple, London, 20/7/88.
56. Interview with Bill Forsyth, London, 21/7/87.
57. Interview with James Mackay, London, 9/4/88.

## 7 Creative Collaboration and the Production Process

1. Paul Coates, *The Story of the Lost Reflection* (London: Verso, 1985), Chapter 2.
2. Interview with Steve Woolley, London, 7/11/88.
3. Alexander Walker, *Hollywood England* (London: Harrap, 1986), p. 215.

4.  Interview with Bill Forsyth, London, 21/7/87.
5.  Interview with Mike Radford, London, 21/7/87.
6.  Interview with Ron Peck, London, 8/4/88.
7.  Interview with Bill Forsyth, London, 21/7/87.
8.  Interview with Tom Priestley, London, 11/4/88.
9.  Interview with Colin MacCabe, London, 15/7/87.
10. James Brabazon, 'Writer's Block' in *AIP & Co.*, June 1986.
11. Hanif Kureishi, 'The Diary. "Some Time With Stephen" ' in *Sammy and Rosie Get Laid* (London: Faber & Faber, 1988), p. 62.
12. Ibid., p. 95.
13. Interview with Neil Jordan, Shepperton, 2/6/88.
14. Ibid.
15. Interview with Mike Radford, London, 21/7/87.
16. James Park, *Learning to Dream: The New British Cinema* (London: Faber & Faber, 1984), p. 118.
17. Interview with Patrick Cassavetti, London, 21/7/87.
18. Alexander Walker, *National Heroes* (London: Harrap, 1985).
19. Park, *Learning to Dream*.
20. Interview with Sarah Radclyffe, London, 7/4/88.
21. Interview with Steve Woolley, London, 7/11/88.
22. Interview with James Mackay, London, 9/4/88.
23. Interview with Steve Woolley, London, 7/11/88.
24. Interview with Marc Samuelson, London, 20/7/87.
25. Interview with Mike Radford, London, 21/7/87.
26. Interview with Steve Woolley, London, 7/11/88.
27. Interview with Al Clark, London, 17/7/87.
28. Ibid.
29. John Caughie: 'Television and Cinema: Converging Histories', in Barr (ed.), *All Our Yesterdays* (London: BFI, 1986).
30. Ibid. p. 200.
31. Interview with Mark Shivas, London, 16/7/87.
32. Interview with Derek Jarman, Edinburgh, 17/8/87.
33. Interview with Bill Forsyth, London, 21/7/87.
34. Interview with Julien Temple, London, 20/7/88.
35. Interview with Ron Peck, London, 8/4/88.
36. Interview with Derek Jarman, Edinburgh, 17/8/87.
37. Interview with Ron Peck, London, 8/4/88.
38. Nestor Almendros: 'Some Thoughts On My Profession' in Mast and Cohen (eds), *Film Theory and Criticism*, Third Edition (New York: Oxford University Press, 1985).
39. Dennis Schaeffer and Larry Salvato, *Masters of Light: Conversations with Contemporary Cinematographers* (London: University of California Press, 1984), p. 1.
40. Interview with Michael Coulter, Glasgow, 11/5/88.
41. Ibid.
42. Interview with Roger Deakins, London, 18/7/88.
43. Ibid.
44. Ibid.
45. Interview with Rita McGurn, Glasgow, 20/6/88.

46.   Interview with Christopher Hobbs, London, 7/4/88.
47.   Ibid.
48.   Interview with Christopher Hobbs, London, 4/6/88.
49.   Interview with Tom Priestley, London, 11/4/88.
50.   Ibid.
51.   Ibid.
52.   Interview with Nestor Alemendros in Schaeffer and Salvato, *Masters of Light*.
53.   Interview with Tony Lawson, London, 4/6/88.
54.   Interview with Tom Priestley, London, 11/4/88.
55.   Ibid.
56.   John Ellis, *Visible Fictions* (London: Routledge & Kegan Paul, 1982), p. 91.
57.   Interview with Bill Douglas, Edinburgh, 24/7/88.
58.   Interview with Bill Forsyth, London, 21/7/87.
59.   Interview with Bill Douglas, Edinburgh, 24/7/88.
60.   Interview with Bill Forsyth, London, 21/7/87.
61.   Interview with Michael Coulter, Glasgow, 11/5/88.
62.   Interview with Mike Radford, London, 21/7/87.
63.   Ibid.
64.   Interview with Tom Priestley, London, 11/4/88.
65.   Interview with Tony Lawson, London, 4/6/88.
66.   Interview with Neil Jordan, Shepperton, 2/6/88.
67.   Ibid.
68.   Interview with Derek Jarman, Edinburgh, 17/8/87.
69.   Ibid.
70.   Ibid.
71.   Interview with Ron Peck, London, 8/4/88.

**Conclusion**
**Critical Assessment of Current British Cinema**

1.   Figures from a survey by Philipa Bloom in *Screen International*, 6–12 January 1990.
2.   Interview with Roger Deakins, London, 18/7/88.

# Appendix 1
# List of Films
# Mentioned in the Text

The following list comprises only feature films mentioned in the text. (It does not include television dramas, films made for TV, documentaries or short films.) They are listed alphabetically by title, followed by director and year of release.

*Absolute Beginners*, Julien Temple, 1986
*Acceptable Levels*, John Davies, 1983
*Accident*, Joseph Losey, 1967
*The Adventures of Baron Munchhausen*, Terry Gilliam, 1989
*Angel*, Neil Jordan, 1982
*The Alf Garnett Saga*, Bob Kellet, 1972
*Alfie*, Lewis Gilbert, 1966
*Alien*, Ridley Scott, 1979
*Another Time, Another Place*, Mike Radford, 1983
*Aria*, Various, 1987
*Ascendancy*, Edward Bennett, 1983
*The Assam Garden*, Mary McMurray, 1985

*The Bad Sister*, Peter Wollen/Laura Mulvey, 1983
*Bad Timing*, Nicolas Roeg, 1980
*Barry Lyndon*, Stanley Kubrick, 1975
*Batman*, Tim Burton, 1989
*The Battle of Britain*, Guy Hamilton, 1969
*The Bed Sitting Room*, Richard Lester, 1969
*Bellman and True*, Richard Loncraine, 1987
*Belly of an Architect*, Peter Greenaway, 1987
*The Big Man*, David Leland, 1990
*The Bill Douglas Trilogy*, Bill Douglas, 1972–79
*Billy the Kid and the Green Baize Vampire*, Alan Clarke, 1986
*Black Narcissus*, Michael Powell/Emeric Pressburger, 1947
*Blade Runner*, Ridley Scott, 1982
*Blazing Saddles*, Mel Brooks, 1974
*Blood Red Roses*, John McGrath, 1986
*Blood Simple*, Joel and Ethan Coen, 1983
*Bonnie and Clyde*, Arthur Penn, 1967
*Boy Soldier*, Karl Francis, 1987
*Brazil*, Terry Gilliam, 1985

*Bridge On the River Kwai*, David Lean, 1957
*Bronco Bullfrog*, Barney Platts-Mills, 1970
*Bullshot*, Dick Clement, 1983
*Burning an Illusion*, Menelik Shabazz, 1981
*Business as Usual*, Lezli-An Barrett, 1987
*Buster*, David Green, 1988

*Can't Stop the Music*, Nancy Walker, 1980
*Captive*, Paul Mayersberg, 1986
*Caravaggio*, Derek Jarman, 1986
*Carry on Sergeant*, Gerald Thomas, 1958
*Castaway*, Nicolas Roeg, 1987
*Chariots of Fire*, Hugh Hudson, 1981
*Charlie Bubbles*, Albert Finney, 1966
*Chinese Boxes*, Chris Petit, 1985
*Citizen Kane*, Orson Welles, 1941
*Comfort and Joy*, Bill Forsyth, 1984
*Company of Wolves*, Neil Jordan, 1984
*Comrades*, Bill Douglas, 1987
*Consuming Passions*, Giles Foster, 1988
*The Courier*, Joe Lee/Frank Deasey, 1988
*Crocodile Dundee*, Peter Faiman, 1986
*Cry Freedom*, Richard Attenborough, 1987
*The Curse of Frankenstein*, Terence Fisher, 1957

*Dance With a Stranger*, Mike Newell, 1985
*Dancing Thru the Dark*, Mike Ockrent, 1990
*Dangerous Liaisons*, Stephen Frears, 1989
*Danny the Champion of the World*, Gavin Millar, 1989
*Dark Passage*, Delmer Daves, 1947
*The Dead*, John Huston, 1987
*Dealers*, Colin Bucksey, 1989
*The Deer Hunter*, Michael Cimino, 1978
*Defence of the Realm*, David Drury, 1985
*Diamond Skulls*, Nick Broomfield, 1990
*Distant Voices, Still Lives*, Terence Davies, 1988
*Diva*, Jean Jaques Beineix, 1982
*Doctor Zhivago*, David Lean, 1965
*The Draughtsman's Contract*, Peter Greenaway, 1982
*Dreamchild*, Gavin Millar, 1986
*The Dream Demon*, Harley Cokliss, 1988
*The Dresser*, Peter Yates, 1984
*The Dressmaker*, Jim O'Brien, 1988
*Drowning by Numbers*, Peter Greenaway, 1988.

*E.T.*, Steven Speilberg, 1982
*Earth Girls are Easy*, Julien Temple, 1990
*Easy Rider*, Dennis Hopper, 1969
*Eat the Rich*, Peter Richardson, 1987

*Educating Rita*, Lewis Gilbert, 1984
*Electric Dreams*, Steve Barron, 1984
*Empire State*, Ron Peck, 1987
*The Endless Game*, Bryan Forbes, 1990
*Eureka*, Nicolas Roeg, 1983
*The Evil Dead*, Sam Raimi, 1982

*Fellow Traveller*, Philip Saville, 1990
*Fires Were Started*, Humphrey Jennings, 1942
*A Fish Called Wanda*, Charles Chrichton, 1988
*Five Corners*, Tony Bill, 1988
*For Queen and Country*, Martin Stellman, 1989
*Friday the Thirteenth*, Sean S. Cunningham, 1980
*The Fruit Machine*, Philip Saville, 1988

*Gandhi*, Richard Attenborough, 1982
*The Garden*, Derek Jarman, 1990
*Ghostbusters*, Ivan Reitman, 1984
*Ghost Dance*, Ken McMullen, 1984
*Giro City*, Karl Francis, 1982
*The Go-Between*, Joseph Losey, 1970
*The Gold Diggers*, Sally Potter, 1984
*The Good Father*, Mike Newell, 1986
*Gothic*, Ken Russell, 1987
*The Graduate*, Mike Nichols, 1967
*Gregory's Girl*, Bill Forsyth, 1980
*Gremlins*, George Millar, 1984
*Guns in the Afternoon*, Sam Peckinpah, 1962

*Halloween*, John Carpenter, 1978
*A Handful of Dust*, Charles Sturridge, 1988
*A Hard Day's Night*, Richard Lester, 1964
*Heat and Dust*, James Ivory, 1983
*Heavenly Pursuits*, Charles Gormley, 1987
*Hellraiser*, Clive Barker, 1987
*Help!*, Richard Lester, 1965
*Hidden City*, Steven Poliakoff, 1988
*High Anxiety*, Mel Brooks, 1977
*High Hopes*, Mike Leigh, 1989
*Highlander*, Russell Mulcahy, 1986
*High Season*, Clare Peploe, 1987
*High Spirits*, Neil Jordan, 1988
*The Hit*, Stephen Frears, 1984
*The Holcroft Covenant*, John Frankenheimer, 1985
*Honky Tonk Freeway*, John Schlesinger, 1981
*Hope and Glory*, John Boorman, 1987
*Hotel du Paradis*, Jana Bokova, 1989
*Housekeeping*, Bill Forsyth, 1988
*How I Won the War*, Richard Lester, 1967

*Indiana Jones and the Last Crusade*, Steven Speilberg, 1989
*The Innocent*, John Mackenzie, 1985
*Insignificance*, Nicolas Roeg, 1985
*It Always Rains on Sunday*, Robert Hamer, 1947
*It Couldn't Happen Here*, Jack Bond, 1988

*Jabberwocky*, Terry Gilliam, 1977
*The Jazz Singer*, Richard Fleischer, 1980
*Joyriders*, Aisling Walsh, 1989
*Jubilee*, Derek Jarman, 1977

*Kes*, Ken Loach, 1969
*Killing Dad*, Michael Austin, 1989
*The Killing Fields*, Roland Joffe, 1984
*Kind Hearts and Coronets*, Robert Hamer, 1949
*A Kind of Loving*, John Schlesinger, 1962
*The Kitchen Toto*, Harry Hook, 1987
*The Knack*, Richard Lester, 1965
*Kramer versus Kramer*, Robert Benton, 1979
*The Krays*, Peter Medak, 1990

*The Ladykillers*, Alexander Mackendrick, 1955
*The Lair of the White Worm*, Ken Russell, 1989
*The Last Emperor*, Bernardo Bertolucci, 1987
*The Last of England*, Derek Jarman, 1987
*Lawrence of Arabia*, David Lean, 1962
*A Letter to Brezhnev*, Chris Bernard, 1985
*The Life and Death of Colonel Blimp*, Powell/Pressburger, 1943
*Little Dorrit*, Christine Edzard, 1987
*Local Hero*, Bill Forsyth, 1983
*The Lonely Passion of Judith Hearne*, Jack Clayton, 1988
*The Loneliness of the Long Distance Runner*, Tony Richardson, 1962
*The Long Good Friday*, John Mackenzie, 1980
*Look Back in Anger*, Tony Richardson, 1959
*Looks and Smiles*, Ken Loach, 1983
*Loose Connections*, Richard Eyre, 1984
*Loser Takes All*, James Scott, 1990
*The Love Child*, Robert Smith, 1987

*The Magic Toyshop*, David Wheatley, 1987
*The Man Who Fell to Earth*, Nicolas Roeg, 1976
*Marnie*, Alfred Hitchcock, 1964
*A Matter of Life and Death*, Powell/Pressburger, 1946
*Maurice*, James Ivory, 1987
*Melancholia*, Andi Engel, 1989
*Merry Christmas, Mr Lawrence*, Nagisa Oshima, 1983
*The Mission*, Roland Joffe, 1986
*The Missionary*, Richard Loncraine, 1983
*Mona Lisa*, Neil Jordan, 1986

*A Month in the Country*, Pat O'Connor, 1987
*Monty Python and the Holy Grail*, Terry Gilliam/Terry Jones, 1975
*Monty Python's Life of Brian*, Terry Jones, 1979
*Moonlighting*, Jerzy Skolimowski, 1982
*Morons from Outer Space*, Mike Hodges, 1985
*My Beautiful Laundrette*, Stephen Frears, 1985

*The Name of the Rose*, Jean Jaques Annaud, 1986
*Nanou*, Connie Templeman, 1986
*Nineteen Eighty Four*, Mike Radford, 1984
*Nighthawks*, Ron Peck/Paul Hallam, 1979
*A Nightmare on Elm Street*, Wes Craven, 1985
*No Surrender*, Peter Smith, 1986
*Number One*, Les Blair, 1985

*The Oberwald Mystery*, Michelangelo Antonioni, 1980
*Odd Man Out*, Carol Reed, 1946
*On the Buses*, Harry Booth, 1971
*One From the Heart*, Francis Coppola, 1981
*Out of Order*, Jonnie Turpie, 1988

*Paperhouse*, Bernard Rose, 1989
*Paris by Night*, David Hare, 1989
*Parker*, Jim Goddard, 1985
*Pascali's Island*, James Dearden, 1989
*A Passage to India*, David Lean, 1985
*Passport to Pimlico*, Henry Cornelius, 1949
*Patty Hearst*, Paul Schrader, 1989
*Peeping Tom*, Michael Powell, 1960
*Personal Services*, Terry Jones, 1987
*Ping Pong*, Po Chih Leong, 1986
*The Ploughman's Lunch*, Richard Eyre, 1983
*Police Academy*, Hugh Wilson, 1984
*The Pow Wow Highway*, Jonathan Wacks, 1990
*Prick Up Your Ears*, Stephen Frears, 1987
*A Private Function*, Malcolm Mowbray, 1984
*The Private Life of Henry VIII*, Alexander Korda, 1933
*Privates on Parade*, Michael Blakemore, 1983
*Private Road*, Barney Platts Mills, 1971
*A Prayer for the Dying*, Mike Hodges, 1988

*Radio On*, Chris Petit, 1980
*The Raggedy Rawney*, Bob Hoskins, 1989
*The Rainbow*, Ken Russell, 1989
*Raise the Titanic*, Jerry Jameson, 1980
*The Red Desert*, Michelangelo Antonioni, 1964
*The Red Shoes*, Michael Powell/Emeric Pressburger, 1948
*Restless Natives*, Michael Hoffman, 1985
*The Return of the Soldier*, Alan Bridges, 1982

*Revolution*, Hugh Hudson, 1986
*Rita, Sue and Bob Too*, Alan Clarke, 1987
*The Robe*, Henry Koster, 1953
*Rocky*, John G. Avildsen, 1976
*A Room With a View*, James Ivory, 1986

*Sammy and Rosie Get Laid*, Stephen Frears, 1988
*Saturday Night and Sunday Morning*, Karel Reisz, 1960.
*Scandal*, Michael Caton Jones, 1989
*Sebastianne*, Derek Jarman, 1975
*Secret Places*, Zelda Barron, 1984
*The Servant*, Joseph Losey, 1963
*Shadey*, Philip Saville, 1986
*Shag*, Zelda Barron, 1988
*Shanghai Surprise*, Jim Goddard, 1986
*The Shooting Party*, Alan Bridges, 1985
*Sid and Nancy*, Alex Cox, 1986
*Siesta*, Mary Lambert, 1988
*The Simon Wiesenthal Story*, Brian Gibson, 1990
*Slam Dance*, Wayne Wang, 1987
*Slayground*, Terry Bedford, 1984
*Sour Sweet*, Mike Newell, 1989
*Stagecoach*, John Ford, 1939
*Star Wars*, George Lucas, 1987
*Steptoe and Son*, Cliff Owen, 1972
*Stormy Monday*, Mike Figgis, 1989
*Strapless*, David Hare, 1990
*The Supergrass*, Tony Richardson, 1985
*Sweeney*, David Wickes, 1976

*The Tall Guy*, Mel Smith, 1989
*A Taste of Honey*, Tony Richardson, 1961
*The Tempest*, Derek Jarman, 1980
*The Terence Davies Trilogy*, Terence Davies, 1976–83
*That Sinking Feeling*, Bill Forsyth, 1981
*The Third Man*, Carol Reed, 1949
*This Sporting Life*, Lindsay Anderson, 1963
*Time Bandits*, Terry Gilliam, 1981
*Tom Jones*, Peter Richardson, 1963
*Touch of Evil*, Orson Welles, 1958
*Track 29*, Nicolas Roeg, 1988
*Tree of Hands*, Giles Foster, 1989

*The War Game*, Peter Watkins, 1965
*War Requiem*, Derek Jarman, 1989
*Water*, Dick Clement, 1985
*Wetherby*, David Hare, 1985
*Whiskey Galore*, Alexander Mackendrick, 1949
*White Mischief*, Mike Radford, 1988

*Wild Geese II*, Peter Hunt, 1985
*Wish You Were Here*, David Leland, 1987
*The Witches*, Nicolas Roeg, 1990
*Withnail and I*, Bruce Robinson, 1988
*The Wolves of Willoughby Chase*, Stuart Orme, 1989
*A World Apart*, Chris Menges, 1988
*Written on the Wind*, Douglas Sirk, 1956

*Young Frankenstein*, Mel Brooks, 1974

*A Zed and Two Noughts*, Peter Greenaway, 1985
*Zina*, Ken McMullen, 1986

# Appendix 2
## Interviews

The following interviews were conducted during the course of my research and these are extensively referenced in the main text.

| | *Where interviewed* | *Date* |
|---|---|---|
| Graham Bradstreet | London | 07/04/88 |
| Patrick Cassavetti | London | 21/07/87 |
| Al Clark | London | 17/07/87 |
| Michael Coulter | Glasgow | 11/05/88 |
| Roger Deakins | London | 18/07/88 |
| Bill Douglas | Edinburgh | 24/07/88 |
| John Durie | London | 07/04/88 |
| Bill Forsyth | London | 21/07/87 |
| Alan Fountain | London | 06/06/88 |
| Margot Gavan-Duffy | London | 22/07/88 |
| Charles Gormley | Glasgow | 11/05/88 |
| Christopher Hobbs | London | 07/04/88 |
| Derek Jarman | Edinburgh | 17/08/87 |
| Gareth Jones | London | 22/07/88 |
| Neil Jordan | Shepperton | 02/06/88 |
| Tony Lawson | London | 04/06/88 |
| Margaret Matheson | London | 20/07/87 |
| Colin MacCabe | London | 15/07/87 |
| Rita McGurn | Glasgow | 20/06/88 |
| James Mackay | London | 09/04/88 |
| Ron Peck | London | 08/04/88 |
| Tom Priestley | London | 11/04/88 |
| Sarah Radclyffe | London | 07/04/88 |
| Mike Radford | London | 21/07/87 |
| Simon Relph | London | 22/07/87 |
| Mary Jane Reyner | Glasgow | 20/06/88 |
| David Rose | London | 22/07/87 |
| Mark Samuelson | London | 20/07/87 |
| Mark Shivas | London | 16/07/87 |
| Julien Temple | London | 20/07/88 |
| Steve Woolley | London | 07/11/88 |
| Colin Young | Edinburgh | 17/08/88 |

# Bibliography

ABRAMS, M. H., *The Mirror and the Lamp* (London: Oxford University Press, 1953).

ADAIR, GILDERT and NICK RODDICK, *A Night and the Pictures: Ten Decades of British Cinema* (London: Columbus, 1985).

ADORNO, THEODOR W., *Aesthetic Theory* (London: Routledge & Kegan Paul, 1984).

ALLEN, ROBERT and DOUGLAS GOMERY, *Film History: Theory and Practice* (New York: Kopt, 1985).

ALMENDROS, NESTOR, 'Some Thoughts on my Profession' in Mast and Cohen (eds), *Film Theory and Criticism*, 3rd Edition (New York: Oxford University Press, 1985).

ALTMAN, RICK, 'The Evolution of Sound Technology' in Belton and Weiss (eds), *Film Sound* (New York: Columbia University Press, 1985).

ALVARADO, MANUEL and JOHN STEWART, *Made for Television: Euston Films* (London: British Film Institute, 1985).

ARMES, ROY, *A Critical History of British Cinema* (London: Secker & Warburg, 1978).

ARMES, ROY, *On Video* (London: Routledge, 1988).

ARNHEIM, RUDOLPH (extract) from *Film as Art* in Mast and Cohen (eds), *Film Theory and Criticism*, 3rd Edition (New York: Oxford University Press, 1985).

ASPINALL, SUE and ROBERT MURPHY (eds), *Gainsborough Melodrama*, BFI Dossier (London: British Film Institute, 1983).

AUTY, MARTYN and NICK RODDICK (eds), *British Cinema Now* (London: British Film Institute, 1985).

AUTY, MARTIN, 'But is it Cinema?' in Auty and Roddick (eds), *British Cinema Now* (London: British Film Institute, 1985).

BANCROFT, SHELLEY (ed.), *Raising Production Finance: AIP Information Pack* (London: Association of Independent Producers, 1986).

BANCROFT, SHELLEY (ed.), *Development: AIP Information Pack* (London: Association of Independent Producers, 1986).

BANCROFT, SHELLEY, 'Hard Hype, Hard Sell, Hard Cash', *A.I.P. & Co.*, Summer 1985.

BARR, CHARLES, 'A Conundrum For England', *Monthly Film Bulletin*, August 1984.

BARR, CHARLES (ed.), *All Our Yesterdays* (London: British Film Institute/Routledge & Kegan Paul, 1986).

BARR, CHARLES, *Ealing Studios* (London: Cameron & Tayleur, 1977).

BARR, CHARLES, 'Schizophrenia and Amnesia', in *All Our Yesterdays* (London: British Film Institute/Routledge & Kegan Paul, 1986).

BARTHES, ROLAND, *Image/Music/Text*, edited by Stephen Heath (London: Fontana, 1977).

BAZIN, ANDRÉ, 'The Evolution of Film Language', in Mast and Cohen (eds), *Film Theory and Criticism*, 3rd Edition (New York: Oxford University Press, 1985).

BAZIN, ANDRÉ, *What Is Cinema?*, Vol. I, ed. Hugh Gray (Berkeley: University of California Press, 1967–71).

BELTON, E. and J. WEISS, *Film Sound* (New York: Columbia University Press, 1985).

BORDE, RAYMOND and CHAUMERTON, ETIENNE, *Panorame du Film Noir Americain* (Paris, 1955).

BRABAZON, JAMES, 'Writer's Block', *A.I.P. & Co.*, June 1986.

BRAUDY, LEO, 'Genre: The Conventions of Connection', in Mast and Cohen (eds), *Film Theory and Criticism*, 3rd Edition (New York: Oxford University Press, 1985).

BROWN, GEOFF, 'Sister of the Stage: British Film and British Theatre', in Barr (ed.), *All Our Yesterdays* (London: British Film Institute/Routledge & Kegan Paul, 1986).

BROWNE, NICK, 'The Rhetoric of the Specular Text with Reference to *Stagecoach*', in Caughie (ed.), *Theories of Authorship* (London: Routledge & Kegan Paul/British Film Institute, 1981).

BUSCOMBE, EDWARD, 'Ideas of Authorship' in Caughie (ed.), *Theories of Authorship* (London: Routledge & Kegan Paul/British Film Institute, 1981).

BUSCOMBE, EDWARD, 'The Idea of Genre in the American Cinema', in Grant (ed.), *Film Genre: Theory and Practice* (Metuchen, NJ: The Scarecrow Press, 1977).

CAMPBELL, COLIN, *The Romantic Ethic and the Spirit of Consumerism* (Oxford: Basil Blackwell, 1987).

CARRINGER, ROBERT, *The Making of Citizen Kane* (London: John Murray, 1985).

CAUGHIE, JOHN, 'Television and Cinema: Converging Histories', in Barr (ed.), *All Our Yesterdays* (London: British Film Institute/Routledge & Kegan Paul, 1986).

CAUGHIE, JOHN (ed.), *Theories of Authorship* (London: Routledge & Kegan Paul/British Film Institute, 1981).

CHANAN, MICHAEL, 'The Emergence of an Industry', in Curran and Porter (eds), *British Cinema History* (London: Weidenfeld & Nicholson, 1983).

CHRISTIE, IAN, *Powell, Pressburger and Others* (London: British Film Institute, 1978).

COATES, PAUL, *The Story of the Lost Reflection* (London: Verso, 1985).

COMOLLI, JEAN LOUIS, 'Machines of the Visible', in Mast and Cohen (eds), *Film Theory and Criticism*, 3rd Edition (New York: Oxford University Press, 1985).

COOK, PAM (ed.), *The Cinema Book* (London: British Film Institute, 1985).

CURRAN, JAMES and VINCENT PORTER (eds), *British Cinema History* (London: Weidenfeld & Nicholson, 1983).

DAVIES, MARY, 'Seedy Business', *A.I.P. & Co.*, December 1985.

DAVY, CHARLES (ed.), *Footnotes to the Film* (London: Lavat Dickson, 1938).

DEREN, MAYA, 'Cinematography: The Creative use of Reality', in Mast and Cohen (eds), *Film Theory and Criticism,* 3rd Edition (New York: Oxford University Press, 1985).

DEWS, PETER, 'Adorno, Post-Structuralism and the Critique of Identity', *New Left Review,* no. 157.

DICKINSON, MARGARET and SARAH STREET, *Cinema and State* (London: British Film Institute, 1985).

DICKINSON, MARGARET, 'The State and the Consolidation of Monopoly' in Curran and Porter (eds), *British Cinema History* (London: Weidenfeld & Nicholson, 1983).

DUTTON, D. and M. KRAUSZ (eds), *The Concept of Creativity in Science and Art* (The Hague: Nijhoff, 1981).

ELLIS, JOHN, 'Art Culture and Quality: Terms for a Cinema in the Forties and Seventies', *Screen,* Autumn 1978.

ELLIS, JOHN, 'Made in Ealing', *Screen,* Summer 1975.

ELLIS, JOHN, *Visible Fictions* (London: Routledge & Kegan Paul, 1982).

FLITTERMAN, SANDY, 'Woman, Desire and the Look: Feminism and the Enunciative Apparatus in Cinema', in Caughie (ed.), *Theories of Authorship* (London: Routledge & Kegan Paul/British Film Institute, 1981).

FREUD, SIGMUND, Pelican Freud Library, Vol. 14: *Art and Literature* (Harmondsworth: Pelican, 1985).

GLEDHILL, CHRISTINE, 'The Melodramatic Field' in Gledhill (ed.), *Home Is Where the Heart Is: Studies in Melodrama and the Woman's Film* (London: British Film Institute, 1987).

GRANT, BARRY K., *Film Genre: Theory and Practice* (Metuchen, NJ: Scarecrow Press, 1977).

HARCOURT, AMANDA et al., *The Independent Producer* (London: Faber & Faber, 1986).

HARTOG, SIMON, 'State Protection of a Beleagured Industry', in Curran and Porter (eds.), *British Cinema History* (London: Weidenfeld & Nicholson, 1983).

HEATH, STEPHEN, *Questions of Cinema* (London: Macmillan, 1981).

HEATH, STEPHEN, 'Comment on the Idea of Authorship', in Caughie (ed.), *Theories of Authorship* (London: Routledge & Kegan Paul/British Film Institute, 1981).

HEATH, STEPHEN, 'Film and System: Terms of Analysis' (Part I) *Screen,* Spring 1975; (Part II) *Screen,* Summer 1975.

HELD, DAVID, *An Introduction to Critical Theory* (London: Hutchinson, 1980).

HENDERSON, BRIAN, 'Critique of Cine-Structuralism', in Caughie (ed.), *Theories of Authorship* (London: Routledge & Kegan Paul/British Film Institute, 1981).

HENRY, GEORGINA, 'Sales of the Unexpected', *Producer,* May 1987.

HIGSON, ANDREW, 'Britain's Outstanding Contribution to the Film', in Barr (ed.), *All Our Yesterdays* (London: British Film Institute/Routledge & Kegan Paul, 1986).

HILL, JOHN, *Sex, Class and Realism* (London: British Film Institute, 1986).

HILLIER, JIM (ed.), *Cahiers du Cinéma, Vol. I: The 1950s* (London: Routledge & Kegan Paul/British Film Institute, 1985).

JAY, MARTIN, *The Dialectical Imagination* (London: Heinemann, 1973).

JARMAN, DEREK, *The Last of England* (London: Constable, 1987).

KAHN, RICHARD, 'Motion Picture Marketing', in Squire (ed.), *The Movie Business Book* (London: Columbus, 1986).

KERMODE, FRANK, *Romantic Image* (London: Routledge & Kegan Paul, 1957).

KOLKER, ROBERT PHILIP, *The Altering Eye* (New York: Oxford University Press, 1983).

KUHN, ANNETTE, *Cinema Censorship and Sexuality, 1909–25* (London: Routledge, 1988).

KUREISHI, HANIF, *Sammy and Rosie Get Laid* (London: Faber & Faber, 1988).

LASSALLY, WALTER, *Itinerant Cameraman* (London: John Murray, 1987).

LÉVI-STRAUSS, CLAUDE, *Structural Anthropology, Vol. I* (London: Allen Lane, 1969).

LOCKRIDGE, LAURENCE, *The Ethics of Romanticism* (Cambridge University Press, 1989).

LYOTARD, JEAN FRANÇOIS, *The Postmodern Condition* (Manchester University Press, 1986).

MARCUSE, HERBERT, *One Dimensional Man* (London: Sphere, 1968).

MARSHALL, NORMAN, 'Reflections on the English Film, *The Bookman*, October 1931.

MARSHALL, STUART, 'Video – Technology and Practice', *Screen*, Spring 1979.

MARX, KARL, *Selected Writings*, edited by David McLellan (Oxford: Oxford University Press, 1977).

MAST, GERALD and MARSHALL COHEN (eds), *Film Theory and Criticism* (New York: Oxford University Press, 2nd Edition 1979, 3rd Edition 1985).

McFARLANE, BRIAN, 'A Literary Cinema', in Barr (ed.), *All Our Yesterdays* (London: British Film Institute/Routledge & Kegan Paul, 1986).

MEDHURST, ANDY, 'Music Hall and British Cinema', in Barr (ed.), *All Our Yesterdays* (London: British Film Institute/Routledge & Kegan Paul, 1986).

METZ, CHRISTIAN, *Film Language: A Semiotics of the Cinema* (New York: Oxford University Press, 1974).

METZ, CHRISTIAN, *Language and Cinema* (The Hague: Mouton, 1974).

METZ, CHRISTIAN, *The Imaginary Signifier* (London: Macmillan, 1982).

MILLER, KARL, *Doubles: Studies in Literary History* (New York: Oxford University Press, 1985).

MITIAS, MICHAEL (ed.), *Creativity in Art, Religion and Culture* (Amsterdam: Wurzburg Konigshausen & Neuman; distributed in the USA by the Humanities Press, 1985).

MONACO, JAMES, *How to Read a Film*, Revised Edition (New York:

Oxford University Press, 1981).

MULVEY, LAURA, 'Visual Pleasure and Narrative Cinema', *Screen*, Autumn 1975.

MURPHY, ROBERT, 'Rank's Attempt on the American Market', in Curran and Porter (eds), *British Cinema History* (London: Weidenfeld & Nicholson, 1983).

NEALE, STEVE, *Cinema and Technology: Image, Sound, Colour* (London: Macmillan/British Film Institute, 1985).

NICHOLS, BILL (ed.), *Movies and Methods* (Berkeley: University of California Press, Vol. I, 1976; Vol. II, 1985).

NOWELL-SMITH, GEOFFREY, extract from *Visconti*; 'A Note on History/Discourse'; 'Six Authors in Pursuit of *The Searchers*', all in Caughie (ed.), *Theories of Authorship* (London: Routledge & Kegan Paul/British Film Institute, 1981).

ORWELL, GEORGE, *Collected Essays* (London: Secker & Warburg, 1961).

PARK, JAMES, 'Film Sales Agents: Floggers or Financiers' *A.I.P. & Co.*, November 1985.

PARK, JAMES, *Learning to Dream: The New British Cinema* (London: Faber & Faber, 1985).

PARK, JAMES, 'The Nervous Summer of the British Film Industry', *Sight & Sound*, Winter 1985/86.

PARK, JAMES, 'Tarnished Goldcrest', *A.I.P. & Co.*, Summer 1985.

PATERSON, RICHARD (ed.), *Boys From the Blackstuff*, BFI Dossier (London: British Film Institute, 1984).

PERRY, GEORGE, *The Great British Picture Show*, 2nd Edition (London: Pavilion, 1985).

PETLEY, JULIAN, 'All Blast and No Balls', *Producer*, May 1987.

PETLEY, JULIAN, 'The Lost Continent', in Barr (ed.), *All Our Yesterdays* (London: British Film Institute/Routledge & Kegan Paul 1986).

PIRIE, DAVID, *Anatomy of the Movies* (London: Windward, 1981).

PIRIE, DAVID, *A Heritage of Horror* (London: Gordon Fraser, 1973).

PORTER, VINCENT, *On Cinema* (London: Pluto Press, 1985).

PRAZ, MARIO, *The Romantic Agony* (Oxford University Press, 1933).

RICHARDS, JEFFREY and ANTHONY ALDGATE, *Best of British: Cinema and Society, 1930–1970* (Oxford: Basil Blackwell, 1983).

ROBERTSON, JAMES C., *The British Board of Film Censors: Film Censorship in Britain, 1896–1950* (Beckenham: Croom Helm, 1985).

ROSE, GILLIAN, *The Melancholy Science: An Introduction to the Thought of Theodor W. Adorno* (London: Macmillan, 1978).

ROTHENBERG, ALBERT and CARL HAUSMAN (eds), *The Creativity Question* (Durham, NC: Duke University Press, 1976).

RYALL, TOM, *Alfred Hitchcock and the British Cinema* (London: Croom Helm, 1986).

SALT, BARRY, *Film Style and Technology: History and Analysis* (London: Starword, 1983).

SALT, BARRY, 'Film Style and Technology in the Thirties: Sound' in Belton and Weiss (eds), *Film Sound* (New York: Columbia University Press, 1985).

SAMUELSON, DAVID, *Motion Picture Camera and Lighting Equipment*, 2nd Edition, Media Manuals (London: Focal Press, 1986).

SARRIS, ANDREW, 'Notes on the Auteur Theory in 1962', in Mast and Cohen (eds), *Film Theory and Criticism*, 2nd Edition (New York: Oxford University Press, 1979).

SCHAEFFER, DENNIS AND SALVATO, LARRY, *Masters of Light: Conversations with Contemporary Cinematographers* (Berkeley: University of California Press, 1984).

SILVERSTONE, MATTHEW, 'Finding the Money' in Auty and Roddick (eds), *British Cinema Now* (London: British Film Institute, 1985).

SQUIRE, J., *The Movie Business Book* (London: Columbus, 1986).

STENKRAUS, WARREN, 'Artistic Creativity and Pain' in Mitias (ed.), *Creativity in Art, Religion and Culture* (Amsterdam: Wurzburg Konigshausen & Neuman, distributed in the USA by the Humanities Press, 1985).

STONE, NORMAN, 'Through a Glass Darkly', *The Sunday Times*, 10 January 1988.

TAIT, ARCHIE, 'Distributing the Product', in Auty and Roddick (eds), *British Cinema Now* (London: British Film Institute, 1985).

TRILLING, LIONEL, *The Liberal Imagination* (London: Mercury, 1961).

VIRILIO, PAUL, *War and Cinema: The Logistics of Perception* (London: Verso, 1989).

WADE, GRAHAM, *Film, Video and Television: Market Forces, Fragmentation and Technological Advance* (London: Comedia, 1985).

WALKER, ALEXANDER, *Hollywood England* (London: Harrap, 1986).

WALKER, ALEXANDER, *National Heroes* (London: Harrap, 1985).

WEBSTER, PAUL, 'Pictures of Pictures', *Producer*, May 1987.

WHITAKER, SHEILA, 'Declarations of Independence', in Auty and Roddick (eds), *British Cinema Now* (London: British Film Institute, 1985).

WILLIAMS, CHRISTOPHER (ed.), *Realism and the Cinema* (London: British Film Institute/Routledge & Kegan Paul, 1980).

WILLIAMS, RAYMOND, 'British Film History: New Perspectives', in Curran and Porter (eds), *British Cinema History* (London: Weidenfeld & Nicholson, 1983).

WILLIAMS, RAYMOND, *Culture* (London: Fontana, 1981).

WILLIAMS, RAYMOND, 'A Lecture on Realism', *Screen*, Spring 1977.

WILLIAMS, RAYMOND, *The Long Revolution* (Harmondsworth: Pelican, 1965).

WILLIAMS, RAYMOND, *Television: Technology and Cultural Form* (London: Fontana, 1974).

WRIGHT, WILL, *Six-Guns and Society* (Berkeley: University of California Press, 1975).

WOLLEN, PETER, *Readings and Writings* (London: Verso, 1982).

WOLLEN, PETER, *Signs and Meaning in the Cinema*, Revised Edition (London: Secker & Warburg, 1972).

WOOD, LINDA (ed.), *British Film Industry* (London: British Film Institute Library Service, 1980).

**Periodicals Consulted**

*A.I.P. & Co.*
*Producer*
*Screen International*
*Sight & Sound*
*Stills*
*Televisual*

# Index